The Rockwool Foundation Research Unit

Immigration to Denmark

An Overview of the Research Carried Out from 1999 to 2006 by the Rockwool Foundation Research Unit

Poul Chr. Matthiessen

University Press of Southern Denmark
Odense 2009

Immigration to Denmark
An Overview of the Research Carried Out from 1999 to 2006
by the Rockwool Foundation Research Unit

Published by:
© The Rockwool Foundation Research Unit and
University Press of Southern Denmark

Copying from this book is permitted only within
Institutions that have agreements with CopyDan,
and only in accordance with the limitations laid
down in the agreement

Linguistic adviser: Tim Caudery

Address:
The Rockwool Foundation Research Unit
Sejroegade 11
DK-2100 Copenhagen Oe

Telephone: +45 39 17 38 32

Fax: +45 39 20 52 19

E-mail: forskningsenheden@rff.dk

Home page: www.rff.dk

ISBN 978 87 7674 413 7
October 2009
Cover Photo: Süddeutsche Zeitung Photo
Print run: 800
Printed by Special-Trykkeriet Viborg a-s

Price: 235.00 DKK, including 25% VAT

Foreword

The Rockwool Foundation aims to provide new knowledge of society to inform Denmark's decision-makers and the public debate. Since 1997, the Rockwool Foundation has given high priority to the study of conditions of life for non-Western immigrants in Denmark among the research topics that it supports. A whole range of research reports in this field have been published from 1999 onwards, mainly in Danish, together with some more readily accessible presentations intended to provide a wider public with access to the main results of the research. At one hand there had been a very involved public debate during the 1990s and even before this, and on the other hand the issue had only scarcely been empirically considered in Denmark at the time of the unit's first publication in 1999.

Initially, the research focused especially on issues concerned with the integration of non-Western immigrants into the Danish labour market, supplemented by a number of analyses of other important factors concerning conditions of life in Denmark for immigrants, and of demographic factors.

Later, the work was extended to include analyses of other related topics. In addition, a comparative study was conducted in collaboration with Professor Klaus F. Zimmermann of the Institut zur Zukunft der Arbeit (IZA – Institute for the Study of Labor) in Bonn. The study was based on data of an almost identical nature concerning the integration of non-Western immigrants into the labour markets of Denmark and Germany as well as other aspects of their conditions of life and their situation in relation to the welfare state.

In 2007, with a view to providing the international research community with access to this very comprehensive body of material through an overview presentation in English, I approached Poul Chr. Matthiessen, former professor of demography at the University of Copenhagen, and invited him to write a summary of the central results in a readily accessible form. Professor Matthiessen was in an excellent position to undertake the task of disseminating information in this area, since he had also played a central role in the Rockwool Foundation's work on immigration from the outset. This book is the outcome of his work. At the same time as summarising previous work, Professor Matthiessen has aimed to update the factual information involved as far as possible, so that the book now presents not only the research that has been carried out but also a great deal of information about the most recent immigration to Denmark and about immigrants' integration into Danish society.

In the writing of this book, the author and the Rockwool Foundation Research Unit have benefited from comments on the text from various experts in the areas covered by the different analyses. The former Head of Research at the Research Unit, Gunnar Viby Mogensen, who was responsible for starting the programme of research on this topic under the auspices of the Rockwool Foundation, and who has himself published various books in the field, has read and commented on the entire manuscript, as has Bent Jensen of the Research Unit.

Several researchers currently or previously employed at the Research Unit, namely Jens Bonke, Claus Larsen, Niels-Kenneth Nielsen and Marie Louise Schultz-Nielsen, have also contributed to the work by reading through and commenting on the chapters concerned with their particular research projects in the field. Similarly, Professor Eskil Wadensjö from the University of Stockholm and Hans Jørgen Nielsen, former Associate Professor at the Department of Political Science, University of Copenhagen, have commented on the sections where their research is presented.

I would like to mention in particular the very helpful cooperation we have received from Statistics Denmark, which is under the direction of Jan Plovsing. Statistics Denmark not only works closely with the Rockwool Foundation Research Unit but also hosts our offices within their premises.

I would like to express my thanks to a number of people working within the Research Unit. Mai-britt Sejberg, the Research Unit secretary, has corrected the proofs, prepared the manuscript for printing and carried out other practical tasks in connection with the production of the book. Johannes K. Clausen and Peer Skov, both students of Political Science, have provided skilled research assistance, while Bent Jensen, in addition to providing academic commentary on the manuscript, has been responsible for liaison with our ever-patient and highly professional publisher, the University Press of Southern Denmark.

As always with the Research Unit's projects, the work on this book has been carried out in complete academic independence and free from the influence of any party, including the Rockwool Foundation itself, who have generously provided the necessary resources. Poul Chr. Matthiessen and I would like to extend our warmest thanks to the staff of the Foundation, including the President, Elin Schmidt, and the Board, chaired by Tom Kähler, for their unfailing support and cooperation.

Copenhagen, October 2009 *Torben Tranæs*

Contents

1.	Immigration to Denmark since the 1960s	9
1.1.	Introduction	9
1.2.	Numbers of immigrants and second generation immigrants	10
1.3.	Naturalisation	15
1.4.	Remigration	18
1.5.	Gender and age distributions	18
1.6.	Fertility	19
1.7.	Immigration of labour, family reunification and refugees	20
	1.7.1. Permits for work and study	20
	1.7.2. Family reunification	21
	1.7.3. Refugees	22
	1.7.4. Annual asylum statistics and longitudinal analyses	23
1.8.	Summary	24
2.	The various stages of the research and the datasets used	29
2.1.	Introduction	29
2.2.	The 1999 study	30
	2.2.1. Introduction	30
	2.2.2. The questionnaire survey	31
	2.2.3. The omnibus surveys	35
	2.2.4. Register information	35
	2.2.5. The Law Model	36
2.3.	The 2001 study	36
2.4.	The German dataset	39
2.5.	Summary	42
3.	Education and Danish language proficiency	45
3.1.	The 1999 study	45
	3.1.1. Introduction	45
	3.1.2. Education from countries of origin	46
	3.1.3. The overall picture of the education level of non-Western immigrants	47
	3.1.4. Significant factors for the level of education of non-Western immigrants	50
	3.1.5. Danish language proficiency skills among non-Western immigrants and second generation immigrants	52
3.2.	The 2001 study	56
3.3.	The 2004 study	58
3.4.	Summary	59
4.	Crime among immigrants	63
4.1.	Introduction	63
4.2.	Convictions 1993-1998	64
4.3.	Summary	68

5.	Labour market conditions	71
5.1.	Introduction	71
5.2.	Trends in employment 1985-2007	71
5.3.	The link between year of immigration and participation in the labour market	77
5.4.	Distribution of employment categories among immigrants from non-Western countries	80
5.5.	Discrimination	81
5.6.	Incentives to work	83
5.7.	Comparative analyses for employed and unemployed immigrants	85
5.8.	Summary	88
6.	Immigrants and the Danish Welfare System	93
6.1.	Introduction	93
6.2.	Welfare payments	93
	6.2.1. Long-term benefits	93
	6.2.2. Short-term benefits	94
	6.2.3. Entitlements	95
6.3.	Transfer payments to immigrants	96
	6.3.1. Long-term benefits	96
	6.3.2. Short-term benefits	100
6.4.	Duration of benefit payments	103
6.5.	The average level of public support	106
6.6.	Likelihood of receiving welfare benefits	108
6.7.	Summary	110
7.	Immigrants and the public exchequer	113
7.1.	Introduction	113
7.2.	Changes over the period 1991-2001	114
7.3.	Factors affecting the amount of net transfers to or from individuals	117
7.4.	A cohort analysis: The long-term effects of one year's immigration	119
7.5.	Studies in other countries	120
7.6.	Summary	121
8.	The geographical distribution of non-Western immigrants in Denmark	125
8.1.	The residential pattern of non-Western immigrants, 1985-2004	125
	8.1.1. Introduction	125
	8.1.2. The Dissimilation Index	126
	8.1.3. The Isolation Index	127
	8.1.4. Delimitation of residential districts	128
	8.1.5. Trends in the two indices, 1985-2004	129
8.2.	Where do non-Western immigrants live?	133
8.3.	The effects of living in a municipality with many other refugees on refugees' employment prospects and salary	134

8.4.	Summary	139
9.	The integration of non-Western immigrants in Denmark and Germany	143
9.1.	Introduction	143
9.2.	Educational attainment and training	144
9.3.	Employment trends	146
9.4.	Employment incentives	146
9.5.	Earnings dispersion	147
9.6.	Immigrant self-employment	149
9.7.	Welfare take-up	150
9.8.	Crime	151
9.9.	The public exchequer	152
9.10.	Socio-economic consequences	153
9.11.	Summary	154
10.	The attitudes of the Danish population to the admission of refugees to Denmark	159
10.1.	Introduction	159
10.2.	Danes' opinions on the admission of refugees	160
10.3.	The opinions of Danes and the populations of neighbouring countries on the admission of refugees	162
10.4.	Immigrants' opinions on admission of refugees	165
10.5.	Summary	166
11.	Are Danes hostile towards immigrants? Foreign media images of Denmark	169
11.1.	Introduction	169
11.2.	Scanning the press	171
11.3.	The image of the Danes as xenophobic	173
11.4.	Selectivity in the description	176
11.5.	The attitudes of the Danish people, according to the foreign media	179
11.6.	Generalisations	181
11.7.	Norms for what may be written and for how it is written	182
11.8.	Are the Danes more "xenophobic" than anyone else?	184
11.9.	Is the Danish debate more "xenophobic" than that in other countries?	186
11.10.	A reality created by opinions?	189
11.11.	Summary	191
12.	Foreigners in the Danish newspaper debate	195
12.1.	Introduction	195
12.2.	The migration of labour	195
	12.2.1. The immigration of Swedish labour	195
	12.2.2. The Polish workers in Denmark	197
	12.2.3. Immigrant labour, 1963-1980	198

12.3.	Refugees and asylum seekers	200
	12.3.1. Russian Jews and revolutionary refugees, 1905-1920	200
	12.3.2. Prisoners of war, revolutionary agents and White Russian refugees, 1915-1920	202
	12.3.3. Refugees from Hitler's Germany, 1933-1940	203
	12.3.4. German refugees in Denmark, 1945-1949	203
	12.3.5. The Hungarian refugees, 1956 and 1957	204
	12.3.6. Asylum seekers, 1983-1995	205
12.4.	Summary	207
13.	Summary	211
13.1.	Aims, background and sources	211
13.2.	Education, Danish language proficiency and crime	214
13.3.	The labour market, the social security system and the public sector	216
13.4.	Distribution of housing	220
13.5.	The Danish-German project	222
13.6.	The media and opinions of immigration	224
13.7.	Main points	227

Publications in English from the Rockwool Foundation Research Unit 229

The Rockwool Foundation Research Unit on the Internet 232

1. Immigration to Denmark since the 1960s

1.1. Introduction

Ever since the sixteenth century, Europeans have been emigrating to North and South America, Australia and New Zealand in the hope of creating better lives for themselves. There has also been a smaller flow of emigrants to African countries such as South Africa, Kenya and Algeria. Until the middle of the twentieth century, the flow of emigrants out of Europe was greater than the number of immigrants; however, during the second half of the century the situation altered, and Europe saw net immigration. The picture in Denmark has reflected these trends.

Figure 1.1. Number of immigrants and emigrants to and from Denmark, 1946-2007.

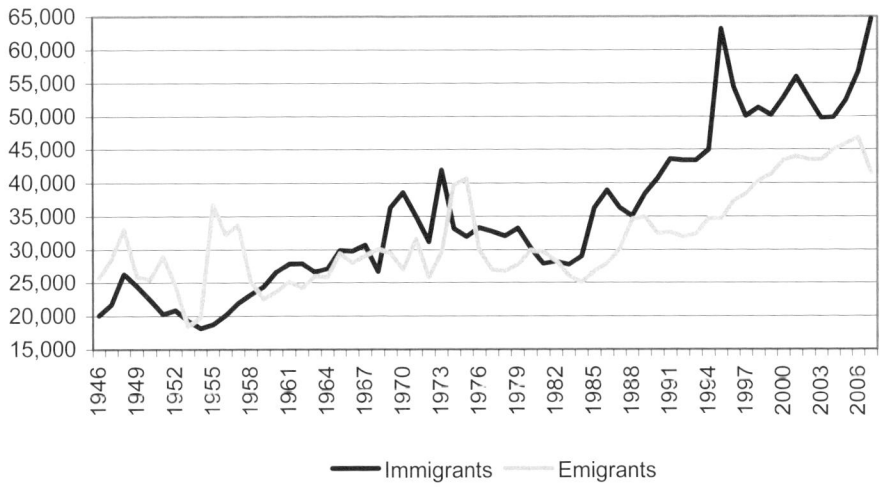

Note: The statistics include both Danish and foreign nationals.
Source: Statistikbanken (StatBank Denmark[1]), Table HISB3.

Figure 1.1 shows the annual flows of migrants in and out of Denmark since the end of World War II, and covers both Danish and foreign nationals. Up until 1960 there was net emigration in most years; after that date, however, Denmark generally saw net immigration, with the body of immigrants changing not only in size but also in composition.

---

[1] StatBank Denmark contains detailed statistical information on Danish society.

Until the mid-1960s, immigrants to Denmark came principally from Norway, Sweden, the United Kingdom, Germany and the USA – the same countries as those to which emigrants mainly chose to go. The immigrants were in many cases Danish citizens returning home after a period abroad, while many emigrants were similarly returning to their respective home countries after a period of residence in Denmark. Since the 1960s, Denmark has experienced immigration from non-Western countries. Western and non-Western countries are here defined as follows:

Western countries: EU member states, Iceland, Norway, Switzerland, USA, Canada, Australia and New Zealand.

Non-Western countries: All countries other than those listed above.

A large number of countries have joined the EU since the 1970s (see Table 1.1), so that the categories of Western and non-Western countries have not included the same countries at all times. Poland, for example, is counted among the Western countries from the start of 2005 onwards, following its accession to the EU in 2004.

Up until the suspension of immigration in 1973, which was introduced in the wake of the huge oil price increases and the subsequent fear of unemployment, immigration from non-Western countries was principally comprised of "guest workers" from Turkey, Pakistan and Yugoslavia, who came to work in the Danish industrial sector. A long period of economic growth and low levels of unemployment had created a demand for labour which could not be fully met by the local workforce, even though the size of the workforce had been swollen by the "baby boomer" generation born during and immediately after the war and by the increasing number of women active on the labour market. As a result, Denmark – like many other Western European countries – welcomed labour immigrating from the countries mentioned above. After the suspension of immigration, the composition of immigration from non-Western countries changed once more, now consisting largely of members of the families of the original guest workers or their children, of refugees, and of people joining those refugees through family reunification (Pedersen 1999 and 2000; Larsen and Matthiessen 2002; Bauer, Larsen and Matthiessen 2004a).

1.2. Numbers of immigrants and second generation immigrants

Immigration after the mid-1960s has led to a significant increase in the number of foreign nationals from non-Western countries residing in Denmark. According to Pedersen (1999), the numbers of citizens of Yugoslavia and Turkey resident in Denmark were below 500 for each of the two countries in 1965 – the first year in which separate counts were made of nationals from these countries – and that remained the situation until 1967. 1971 is the first year for which information is available regarding the number of Pakistani nationals in Denmark; there were over 2,000. The figures for the years since 1974 – which is the first year for which precise and complete figures are available for the numbers of resident foreign nationals – are shown in Table 1.1. It should be noted that 1974 was the year following the suspension of immigration mentioned above.

The numbers of residents from the three original source countries for guest workers all increased after 1974. The number of citizens of Yugoslavia increased by two thirds between 1974 and 1995, at which time the civil war in that country created an extraordinary situation. As a result, a large number of refugees who had temporary residence permits were granted permanent resident status within a very short space of time, so that by the turn of the century the total number of residents from the former Yugoslavia – as the area had now become known as – was five times what it was in 1974. The number of Turkish citizens quadrupled during the same period, while the figure for Pakistani nationals doubled. The total number of foreign nationals from other non-Western countries increased five-fold. Since the turn of the millennium, the number of citizens from the three original guest-worker countries resident in Denmark has fallen. In contrast, the number of citizens from the EU and North America resident in Denmark has increased significantly since the expansion of the EU in 2004.

A definition purely on the basis of citizenship of the section of the population which has a foreign background is, however, too narrow to be useful for purposes such as the consideration of integration policy. It is not in fact the case that all immigrants who adopt Danish nationality become fully integrated into Danish society. Since there are some national groups who have a greater tendency than others to become naturalised, grouping foreign nationals according to their countries of origin creates a misleading picture of the numerical relationships between the various nationalities.

With a view to creating a more realistic and relevant division of the resident population of Denmark for purposes of scientific analysis or formation of integration policies, the legal definitions in terms of citizenship used in official statistics were supplemented in 1991 with the concepts *immigrants*, *second generation immigrants* and *others* (i.e. Danes), based on origin – first and foremost on the basis of the parents' place of birth and citizenship. In place of *others* (the description *people of Danish origin* is used in the official Danish statistics today), we shall use the more idiomatic term *Danes* in this book to describe the 90-95% of the population who are neither immigrants nor second generation immigrants.

Table 1.1. Numbers of resident foreign citizens shown according to nationality, 1974-2008.

	Nordic countries	EU member states and North America	(Former) Yugoslavia	Turkey	Pakistan	Non-Western countries Other countries	Total	Total
1974	21,774	28,895	6,779	8,138	3,733	20,536	39,186	89,855
1975	21,945	30,683	6,892	8,129	4,982	21,300	41,303	93,931
1976	21,096	29,450	6,396	7,857	5,178	20,877	40,308	90,854
1977	21,419	29,211	6,434	8,628	5,400	20,563	41,025	91,655
1978	21,886	29,605	6,674	10,299	5,557	20,394	42,924	94,415
1979	22,432	30,177	6,955	11,985	5,912	20,154	45,006	97,615
1980	22,608	29,308	7,126	14,086	6,400	20,268	47,880	99,796
1981	22,390	29,379	7,317	15,838	6,598	20,078	49,831	101,600
1982	22,147	28,418	7,402	16,705	6,822	20,420	51,349	101,914
1983	22,201	28,296	7,344	17,240	6,750	21,221	52,555	103,052
1984	22,334	28,424	7,397	17,827	6,659	21,421	53,304	104,062
1985	22,600	29,299	7,617	18,806	6,692	22,712	55,827	107,726
1986	23,021	30,783	7,943	20,408	6,619	28,175	63,145	116,949
1987	23,377	31,924	8,348	22,313	6,590	35,701	72,952	128,253
1988	23,130	32,097	8,799	24,423	6,500	41,228	80,950	136,177
1989	22,977	31,658	9,149	26,072	6,454	45,706	87,381	142,016
1990	23,064	31,829	9,535	27,929	6,285	52,002	95,751	150,644
1991	23,242	33,265	10,039	29,680	6,231	58,184	104,134	160,641
1992	23,512	33,766	10,719	32,018	6,081	63,429	112,247	169,525
1993	23,745	35,196	11,306	33,653	6,259	69,944	121,162	180,103
1994	24,192	37,058	11,618	34,658	6,368	75,120	127,764	189,014
1995	25,378	39,593	11,324	34,967	6,401	79,042	131,734	196,705
1996	27,052	41,511	28,081	35,739	6,552	83,811	154,183	222,746
1997	28,660	43,638	32,184	36,835	6,736	89,642	165,397	237,695
1998	29,927	45,403	33,931	37,519	6,934	95,914	174,298	249,628
1999	30,646	47,052	34,456	38,055	7,135	98,930	178,576	256,274
2000	31,313	47,451	35,062	36,569	7,115	101,847	180,593	259,357
2001	31,763	47,905	34,954	35,232	7,071	101,704	178,961	258,629
2002	32,080	48,831	35,354	33,383	7,160	109,921	185,818	266,729
2003	32,842	49,367	33,127	31,898	6,917	111,273	183,215	265,424
2004	33,735	50,335	32,700	30,273	7,022	117,146	187,141	271,211
2005	34,362	62,260	28,981	29,956	6,859	105,186	170,982	267,604
2006	34,828	65,967	27,705	29,491	6,671	105,389	169,256	270,051
2007	35,865	75,023	26,872	28,752	6,587	104,921	167,208	278,096
2008	37,054	83,777	26,762	28,843	6,724	107,330	169,659	290,490

Note: Greece is counted as an EU member state from 1 Jan 1981, Portugal and Spain from 1 Jan 1986, the former East Germany (DDR) from 1 Jan 1991, Austria from 1 Jan 1995, the ten new Eastern and Southern European members from 1 Jan 2005, and Bulgaria and Romania from 1 Jan 2007. Iceland, Sweden and Finland are included in the figures for the Nordic countries. Sources: 1974-1978: Matthiessen (2007); 1979-2006: Statistikbanken, Table Bef:2A, 2007-2008: Statistikbanken, Table KRBEF: 2A.

The three categories of the population are defined as follows:

Immigrants: People born abroad whose parents were both (or in cases where only one parent is known, that parent) foreign nationals or born abroad. If no information is available about either parent, and the person was born abroad, the person is also classified as an immigrant (Danmarks Statistik (Statistics Denmark) 2005). The concept covers equally those who have immigrated in order to work, in connection with family reunification, or as refugees.

Second generation immigrants: People born in Denmark of parents neither of whom (or in cases where only one parent is known, that parent) is a Danish citizen born in Denmark. If no information is available about either of the parents, and the person in question is a foreign citizen, the person is also classified as a second generation immigrant (Danmarks Statistik 2005).

Danes: People born to parents of whom at least one is a Danish citizen born in Denmark, regardless of the country of birth of the person in question or his/her citizenship. If no information is available about either of the parents, the person is classified as a Dane if he/she is a Danish citizen born in Denmark (Tænketanken (Think Tank on Integration in Denmark) 2002).

This division based on parents' countries of birth and citizenship has been applied retroactively as far back as 1980. Categorisation according to this method naturally places a larger proportion of the Danish population in the group of people with a foreign background than does categorisation based on citizenship, since Danish nationals may also be included in the group with foreign origins. This is illustrated in Table 1.2, which shows the figures for all years since 1980 for the people with foreign backgrounds calculated in terms of numbers of foreign nationals and in terms of numbers of immigrants and second generation immigrants. Percentages of the population are also shown. The proportion of the Danish population with foreign citizenship increased from 1.9% in 1980 to 5.5% in 2008, while the proportion of immigrants and second generation immigrants increased from 3.0% to 9.1% over the same period. The proportion of second generation immigrants among the total immigrant population doubled from 12% to 24% between 1980 and 2008.

As is the case for foreign nationals, there are more immigrants and second generation immigrants today from non-Western countries than from Western countries. In 2008, immigrants and second generation immigrants from non-Western countries made up around 70% of the immigrant population, as compared to just 34% in 1980. Changes in the numbers of immigrants and second generation immigrants from Western and non-Western countries since 1980 are shown in Figure 1.2.

Table 1.2. Foreign nationals, immigrants and second generation immigrants, 1980-2008.

	Foreign nationals	Immigrants	2nd generation	Immigrants and 2nd gen. in total	Foreign nationals as a percentage of the entire Danish population	Immigrants and 2nd gen. as a percentage of the entire Danish population
1980	99,796	134,705	18,253	152,958	1.9	3.0
1981	101,600	136,229	19,423	155,652	2.0	3.0
1982	101,914	136,411	20,554	156,965	2.0	3.1
1983	103,052	136,976	21,552	158,528	2.0	3.1
1984	104,062	137,541	22,278	159,819	2.0	3.1
1985	107,726	140,566	23,360	163,926	2.1	3.2
1986	116,949	149,476	24,439	173,915	2.3	3.4
1987	128,253	160,358	26,203	186,561	2.5	3.6
1988	136,177	167,837	28,369	196,206	2.7	3.8
1989	142,016	173,576	30,527	204,103	2.8	4.0
1990	150,644	181,109	33,462	214,571	2.9	4.2
1991	160,641	189,649	36,553	226,202	3.1	4.4
1992	169,525	198,898	40,343	239,241	3.3	4.6
1993	180,103	208,865	44,507	253,372	3.5	4.9
1994	189,014	217,154	48,915	266,069	3.6	5.1
1995	196,705	224,995	53,464	278,459	3.8	5.3
1996	222,746	249,885	58,838	308,723	4.2	5.9
1997	237,695	265,794	64,498	330,292	4.5	6.3
1998	249,628	276,781	70,252	347,033	4.7	6.6
1999	256,276	287,681	75,741	363,422	4.8	6.8
2000	259,361	296,924	81,238	378,162	4.9	7.1
2001	258,630	308,674	87,273	395,947	4.8	7.4
2002	266,729	321,794	93,537	415,331	5.0	7.7
2003	265,424	331,506	99,183	430,689	4.9	8.0
2004	271,211	337,802	104,234	442,036	5.0	8.2
2005	267,604	343,367	108,728	452,095	4.9	8.4
2006	270,051	350,436	112,799	463,235	5.0	8.5
2007	278,096	360,902	116,798	477,700	5.1	8.8
2008	298,490	378,665	119,297	497,962	5.5	9.1

Sources: For foreign nationals, immigrants and second generation immigrants: Statistikbanken, Table BEF3. For calculating the totals as percentages of the entire population: Statistikbanken, Table BEF1A. For 2007-2008: KRBEF3 and BEF1A07.

The distribution by geographical origin of the immigrant population from non-Western countries has changed significantly in the space of less than thirty years. In 1980, the ten largest groups (in descending order) had their origins in the following countries: Turkey, Pakistan, Yugoslavia, Poland, the Soviet Union, Morocco, India, Vietnam, Chile and the Philippines. In 2008, the ten leading countries of origin were: Turkey, former Yugoslavia, Iraq, Lebanon, Pakistan, Somalia, Iran, Vietnam, Afghanistan and Sri Lanka (Danmarks Statistik 2008).

As mentioned previously, Poland was included in the group of Western countries as from 1 January 2005.

Figure 1.2. Number of immigrants and second generation immigrants from Western and non-Western countries, 1980-2008.

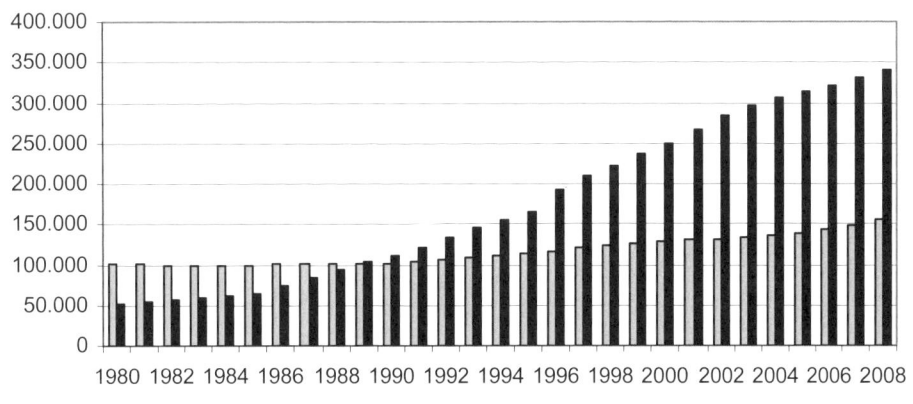

Notes: All the present 27 EU member states are counted as Western countries.
Source: Statistikbanken, BEF 3 and KRBEF 3.

1.3. Naturalisation

As can be seen in Table 1.1, there was a fall in the number of Turkish nationals in 2000. This fall occurred after a steady increase in numbers over the previous decades, while in contrast the number of Pakistani nationals has varied little over the past thirty years. As mentioned previously, however, such changes cannot necessarily be seen as indications of the true size of these national groups, but may equally well be a reflection of a difference in the propensity of various national groups to become naturalised Danish citizens.

Until 1 July 2002, the main requirements for adopting Danish citizenship were as follows:

Nationals of the Nordic countries were required to have been legally resident in Denmark for an unbroken period of at least two years. Citizens of other countries had to have had at least seven years of residence, though this was reduced to six years in the case of refugees and stateless persons.

Since July 2002, however, significantly more stringent requirements have been applied for obtaining Danish citizenship. For example, foreigners are now required to have been resident in Denmark for at least nine years, or eight years in the case of refugees. This period is reduced, however, for the spouses of Danish citizens. A criminal record or outstanding debts to the public purse can prevent or delay naturalisation. Finally, it is a condition for naturalisation that the applicant can participate with ease in a general conversation in Danish.

Foreign nationals who have lived in Denmark as children and who fulfil certain requirements with respect to length of residence can obtain Danish citizenship by a simple declaration. All that is required of the person concerned is that after reaching the age of 18, but before the age of 23, he or she should make a declaration to the local authorities of a wish to become a Danish citizen. However, since mid-2004 this rule has only applied in the case of citizens of Nordic countries and of former Danish citizens.

With effect from 2006, the requirements for obtaining Danish citizenship have been tightened up even further. The requirements concerning proficiency in the Danish language have been increased, and applicants must also pass a test in Danish history, culture and society. Finally, the applicant must have been self-supporting in four out of the previous five years.

It should be noted that naturalisation, in addition to changing the distribution of foreign nationals by country, may also affect the categorisation of a person as immigrant, second generation immigrant or Dane in the classification of the population. For example, if a second generation immigrant is naturalised, the status of any children that person may have will change from being second generation immigrants to being Danes – that is, if they are not already Danes by virtue of their other parent being a Danish national born in Denmark.

There were around 3,000 to 4,000 naturalisations per year in the period from 1980 to 1990, and this increased to around 5,000 to 6,000 annually during the years 1991 to 1997. The numbers then increased in each of the following three years, the annual total reaching a peak of just under 19,000 in 2000 before falling back to around 12,000 in 2001. In 2007 fewer than 4,000 people were naturalised. The general increase in the number of people changing their nationality from a foreign citizenship to Danish is associated with an increase in the size and a change in the composition of the immigrant population. In the 1980s, a larger number of refugees came to Denmark than previously, and they had a greater propensity to seek Danish nationality than the foreign nationals who were already in the country. The increased numbers of naturalisations after the mid-1990s were from among nationals of Turkey, Iran, Iraq, and Somalia, and from among Lebanese and the stateless. Western citizens have a limited propensity to seek Danish nationality.

Pedersen (2000) studied the proportions of naturalised Danes in a given year in comparison with the number of citizens entitled to acquire Danish nationality in 1991 and 1997. These naturalisation percentages, with equivalent calculations for 1999 and 2000, are shown for selected countries in Figure 1.3 (Larsen and Matthiessen 2002).

Figure 1.3. Percentages of naturalised nationals from selected countries for the years 1991, 1997, 1999 and 2000.

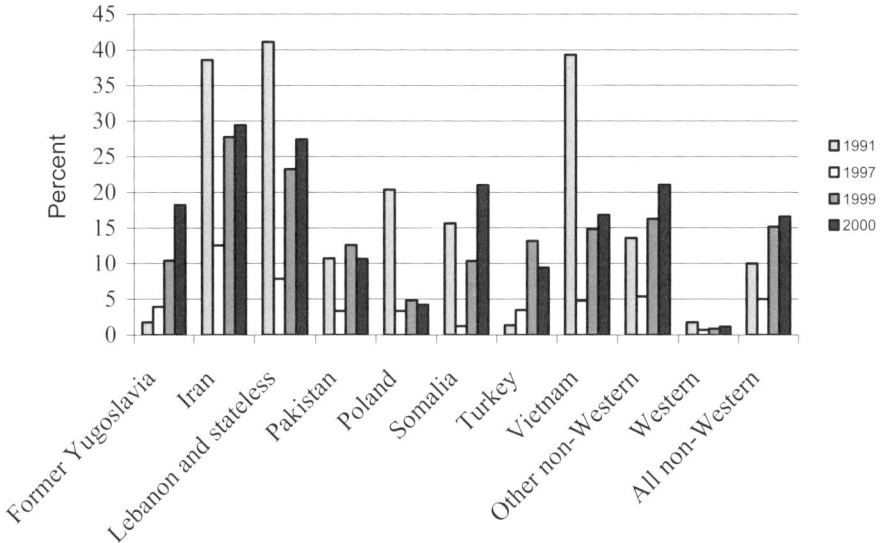

Source: Pedersen (2000) and Larsen and Matthiessen (2002).

As can be seen from Figure 1.3, the percentages of those naturalised were greater in 1991 than in 1997 for most groups, but there was an increase in 1999 and 2000. In 1991 the proportions were especially high for immigrants from Iran, Lebanon (including the stateless), Vietnam and – to a lesser degree – from Poland. The people involved were often refugees who came to Denmark during the 1980s and who applied for citizenship relatively soon after they became entitled to do so. In 1997 the proportion was highest for foreign nationals from Iran and Lebanon (including the stateless), and these categories were also the largest in 1999 and 2000. In comparison, the naturalisation percentages among nationals from the original "guest worker" source countries – Turkey, the former Yugoslavia and Pakistan – are much smaller. In 1991 a greater proportion of Pakistani nationals were naturalised than Turkish nationals, but this relationship had changed by the end of the 1990s. This change can explain the fall in the number of residents with Turkish citizenship; see Table 1.1.

Changes in the propensity to remigrate out of Denmark may also be a factor, as the next section explains.

1.4. Remigration

The effects of immigration on the size and composition of the population of Denmark are partly dependent on the number of immigrants who remigrate. If one considers only those who retain their foreign nationality, then there is a significant level of remigration among people from Western countries (Pedersen 1999). Of immigrants from the Nordic countries, the EC/EU and North America who came to Denmark in 1977 and 1990, between two thirds and nine-tenths had remigrated after five years. This ties in well with the low propensity of people in this group to seek Danish nationality.

Remigration is much less frequent among immigrants with Turkish nationality; of those who immigrated to Denmark in 1977, only 14% remigrated within the next five years. For Yugoslav and Pakistani nationals the corresponding figures were 24% and 26% respectively. Remigration was even less frequent among those who immigrated in 1990, and this situation does not appear to have changed in the course of the 1990s.

The relatively large increase in the number of Turkish nationals in comparison with citizens of other countries during the period from 1974 to 2000 can be explained in part by the lower propensity to remigrate, while the fall after 2000 can be attributed to the greater number of naturalisations.

1.5. Gender and age distributions

The immigrant population is in general younger than the population as a whole. As of 1 January 2008, there was a greater percentage of the male immigrant population in each 5-year age band for groups up until the age of 50 than was the case for the whole male population of Denmark, and the same was true up to the age of 45 for females. This overall picture, however, conceals the fact that among Western immigrants and second generation immigrants there are relatively fewer people of ages up to twenty than is the case for non-Western immigrants and Danes. In the age range 20-59, the proportion of male Western immigrants and second generation immigrants is greater in each age band than for the population as a whole, and, with a couple of minor exceptions, the same is true for the proportions of Western women right up to the age of 85. For non-Western immigrants and second generation immigrants, the proportions are below the average from age 45 upwards.

While a little over half the entire population is female (50.5%), the proportion is only 50% for the non-Western immigrant and second generation immigrant population. In contrast, 51.4% of Western immigrants and second generation immigrants are women.

With respect to patterns of place of residence, there are differences between the non-Western immigrant community on the one hand and the Western immigrants and Danes on the other. The largest percentage of non-Western immigrants and second generation immigrants live in the larger urban areas and the smallest percentage in country districts, while Western immigrants and second generation immigrants are more evenly spread over the country, and a majority of Danes live in small provincial towns and in rural districts.

1.6. Fertility

There are marked differences in fertility between Danes and immigrants from Western and non-Western countries. In the period 2002-2006 the fertility rate for Danish women was 1.75 children each, while the figures for Western and non-Western immigrant women were 1.53 and 2.34 respectively. Women from Somalia gave birth to an average of 4.43 children, while the fertility rates for women from Pakistan, Turkey and the former Yugoslavia were 3.10, 2.20 and 2.17 children respectively. The fertility rates for nationals of Pakistan and Turkey were 4.44 and 3.50 children per women in 1990, significantly higher than in 2002-2006. There was thus some convergence with the fertility rates for Danish women, which increased slightly over the same period.

Pedersen (2000) analysed fertility among immigrant women by country of origin and age at the time of immigration for the period 1994-1998, using data from the Danish National Board of Health on births, combined with information about the women from Statistics Denmark. This analysis showed that age at the time of immigration had great significance for the number of children born by non-Western women. Pedersen distinguishes between women who immigrated when they were between 18 and 49 years old and those who were under 18 years of age. Those women who came to the country as adults had a markedly higher level of fertility than women who had lived in Denmark for all or most of their childhood. For all non-Western women the figures were 3.2 and 2.4 children for the two age groups respectively. For Turkish women the figures were 4.9 and 2.5, and for Pakistani women 5.6 and 2.7. Thus this study again shows a convergence towards the fertility rates of the receiving country.

The overall fertility rate for the total population of Denmark in 2007 was 1.85 children per woman and was thus not at a level that would sustain the size of the population in the long term without further immigration. The level that is required to sustain the population is today just under 2.1 children per woman (Matthiessen 2007).

1.7. Immigration of labour, family reunification and refugees

The structure of immigration has changed since the first guest workers came to Denmark in the 1960s. This change is evident from Figure 1.4, which shows the number of residence permits granted during the period 1988-2007 grouped by basis for the granting of the permit (1988 is the first year for which there are statistics available for residence permits granted on the basis of family reunification). The three categories for granting a residence permit are work and study, family reunification and asylum.

Figure 1.4. Number of asylum cases, family reunifications and work or study permits in relation to the total number of residence permits granted, 1988-2007.

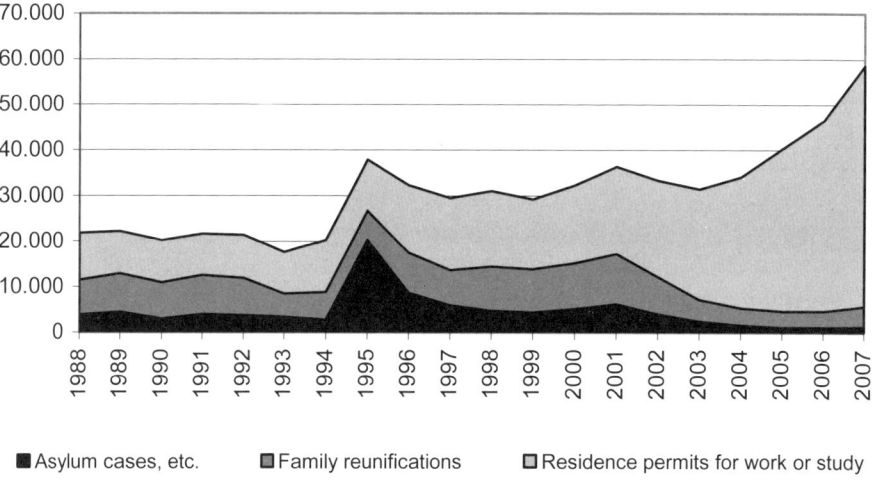

Note: From May 2000 onward it has been a requirement that children of foreigners with residence permits, including children born in Denmark, must have their own separate residence permits; these children's permits are not included in the figures. Around 2,550 and 2,237 such children's permits were issued for the years 2000 and 2001 respectively (Udlændingestyrelsen 2002b).
Sources: For 1988-1995: Befolkningens bevægelser 1996, p.155; for 1995-2004: Statistiske Efterretninger: Befolkning og Valg "Asylansøgninger og opholdstilladelser 2004" 2005/12, pp. 2 and 9; for 2005: Statistiske Efterretninger: Befolkning og Valg "Asylansøgninger og opholdstilladelser 2005" 2006/10, pp. 2 and 9; for 2006-2007: Statistikbanken VAN6.

1.7.1. Permits for work and study

Until 1983, access to Denmark for foreign nationals was regulated on the basis of the Aliens Act of 1952. The Act originally allowed foreigners relatively free entry to the country to apply for work and residence permits. A halt to immigration was introduced as a result of the oil crisis in 1973. However, this did not apply to citizens of the Nordic countries, who were covered by a joint Nordic agreement of 1954 allowing free movement of labour; nor did it apply to citizens of European Community member states, Denmark having become an EC member in 1973.

The restrictions on the immigration of labour were retained in the Aliens Act of 1983. The 10,400 work and study permits granted in 1988 were divided fairly equally between residence granted on the basis of a European Community nationality, permits in connection with employment, and residence permits in connection with study or work as an au-pair. After remaining at a fairly constant level, the number of these permits increased after the mid-1990s to reach 53,000 in 2007, a five-fold increase, accounting for 90% of the residence permits granted.

1.7.2. Family reunification

An Act of Parliament of 1983 introduced a legal right to family reunification with children, spouses and parents. The number of family reunification permits granted in 1988, the first year for which separate records were kept, was just under 8,000. Apart from dips in 1993 and 1997, the number steadily increased up until 2001, when just under 11,000 such permits were granted. Except in the year 1995, the number of family reunifications accounted for between a quarter and a third of the total number of residence permits granted.

An important factor to note in connection with the number of family reunifications is that in 1998 around 90% of all married or cohabiting immigrants from the former Yugoslavia, Pakistan, Somalia, Turkey and Vietnam had compatriots as their partners. The figure for non-Western immigrants as a group was 75%, compared with just 13% for Western immigrants and second generation immigrants. Family reunification with spouses might either have been related to reuniting couples who were married before one spouse came to Denmark, or be a matter of the creation of new families as a result of an immigrant or second generation immigrant living in Denmark finding a spouse in his or her home country. Among young immigrants and second generation immigrants without Danish citizenship aged 18 to 25 with at least ten years of residence in Denmark, around 70% of both men and women from the former Yugoslavia and Pakistan, and 90% of men and 80% of women from Turkey, had found spouses in their home countries. For young non-Western males of all nationalities taken together the figure was 80%, and for women it was 70%.

It is possible to get an impression of the number of spousal family reunifications that are related to the reuniting of long-time spouses and how many involved the formation of new families by looking at the date of the marriage. If the limit for the cases which can be considered as creating new families is set to marriages taking place less than a year before, or less than six months after the time of immigration, then almost 30% of married non-Western men and nearly 50% of women who arrived in Denmark can be defined as coming to the country in connection with the establishment of new families.

After 2001 the number of family reunifications fell dramatically, with the result that the figure in 2007 was a little over 4,500, accounting for barely 8% of the total number of residence permits issued. This development was primarily due to a revision of the Aliens Act in 2002 which made it more difficult to obtain permits for family reunification (Bauer, Larsen and Matthiessen, 2004b). The requirements under the existing rules were tightened up, both with respect to demonstrating that one could provide for a spouse financially and with regard to the groups of people covered by the regulations. In practice, the rules were not previously applied to Danish citizens, nationals of other Nordic countries, and refugees; but they are now. Previously, immigrants who were not Danish citizens or refugees were required to have had a permanent residence permit for at least three years before they could bring a spouse of partner to join them in the country. Now it is a requirement that the person should have been legally resident for a period of seven years before a permanent residence permit can be granted. In addition, it is no longer permitted for parents of adult children living in Denmark to come to the country under the family reunification system. The right to family reunification with spouses has been scrapped for people under the age of 24, with the stated aim of preventing pro forma and forced marriages. Finally, the total connection to Denmark of the two spouses taken together must be stronger than their connection to any other country.

1.7.3. Refugees

The total number of spontaneous asylum *applications* has shown great variation for the years since 1980, although it rose steadily up until the turn of the millennium. Spontaneous asylum *applications* are defined as those actually handled in Denmark. The fluctuations in the figures reflect both alterations to the law and changes in the size of the flow of refugees caused by wars. Having remained in the low hundreds for each year from 1980 to 1983, the total figure rose after the changes in the law in 1983 to over 9,000 in 1986, when the legislation was revised once more in the light of the large influx. These changes placed additional limitations on the right to enter and reside in Denmark while the application for asylum was processed: in part because of the introduction of an administrative rejection procedure on the grounds of an application being "clearly groundless" (a procedure which cannot be appealed if the Danish Refugee Council supports the decision of the Danish Immigration Service); and in part because of the possibility of sending refugees back if they had come to Denmark via another EU country or other secure country (Bauer, Larsen and Matthiessen, 2004b). The number of spontaneous asylum seekers fell to under 3,000 in 1987 before rising again to around 5,000 annually in the period 1988 to 1991. The civil war in the former Yugoslavia was partly responsible for a sharp increase in asylum seekers to 14,000 in both 1992 and 1993. In the period 1994 to 1999 the annual total of asylum seekers was between 5,000 and 6,000. It then rose to 8,000-10,000 in the years 2000 and 2001 before dropping dramatically, bringing the numbers right down to a little over 1,000 in 2007 (Statistikbanken VAN5). The present low number of asylum seekers can be explained in part by the general fall in the numbers coming to Europe from refugee-producing countries.

There is naturally a close connection between the number of *applications* for asylum made in Denmark and the number of *residence permits* granted in asylum cases. The large number of residence permits granted in asylum cases in 1995 was due first and foremost to the large number of people from the former Yugoslavia who were awarded permanent resident status. The reduction in the number of asylum seekers since 2002 has also been accompanied by a fall in the number of permits issued, with the result that the total of permits in 2007 only reached just over 1,000 (Statistikbanken VAN6). Another contributory cause of the fall was the abolition of the concept of "*de facto*" refugees in 2002, that is to say refugees who, unlike "Convention" refugees, did not meet the conditions laid down in the UN Convention on Refugees.

1.7.4. Annual asylum statistics and longitudinal analyses

It is not possible to state very accurately the proportion of asylum applications processed in a given country that actually result in the award of a residence permit, let alone to begin to make comparisons between countries, simply on the basis of the asylum statistics for a given year or years. Nevertheless, the UN High Commission for Refugees has attempted to do this using statistics for the calendar years 1998 and 1999. The Commission's figures place Denmark ahead of comparable countries such as Norway, Sweden, Germany and the Netherlands, both in terms of the proportion of completed cases that end with the award of residence status, with rates of 54.5% and 51.8% for the two years in question, and in terms of the award of Convention Refugee status (UNHCR 1999 and 2000). In the case of Denmark, there must be added the many more people with *de facto* refugee status who have also achieved an approximately similar final result. An analysis in which all asylum seekers from 1998 are traced individually until the resolution of their cases shows that 70% of those whose cases were actually processed in Denmark were granted the right of residence in the country (Udlændingestyrelsen 2002b).

The Danish Immigration Service and the corresponding German institution have provided access to unpublished figures in order to allow a comparison for three selected nationalities of asylum seekers – Afghans, Iraqis and Sri Lankans. The situation as of 31 December 2000, when 21% to 31% of the German cases as opposed to 1% of those in Denmark were still unresolved, suggested that unless all the pending cases in Germany ended with the granting of residence permits, the percentage of refugees in Denmark who were granted permits was relatively high.

1.8. Summary

Up until the year 1960, the flow of emigrants from Denmark exceeded the number of immigrants to the country. In the course of the 1960s the situation changed to one of net immigration, and Denmark began to receive immigrants from non-Western countries. Until the suspension of immigration in 1973 these were primarily guest workers from Turkey, Yugoslavia and Pakistan, and subsequently most immigration came as the result of family reunification and, later, of the arrival of refugees.

On 1 January 2008 the total of immigrants and second generation immigrants residing in Denmark was 498,000, or 9.1% of the population. Of these, 290,000 were foreign nationals, corresponding to 5.5% of the population. In 1980 the corresponding figures were 3.0% and 1.9% respectively. While in 1980 a slight majority of immigrants and second generation immigrants were from Western countries, only 30% of the immigrant population fall into this category today.

The five largest nationalities in the immigrant population from non-Western countries in 2008 are Turks, people from the former Yugoslavia, Iraqis, Lebanese and Pakistanis.

The fact that the number of people with a foreign background – immigrants and second generation immigrants – exceeds the number of foreign nationals is due to naturalisation. It is primarily people from non-Western countries who have become naturalised Danes. In line with the fact that relatively few immigrants from Western countries seek naturalisation, the majority of people in this category eventually emigrate again.

In general, the immigrant population is younger than the population as a whole, whereas the distribution between the genders is essentially the same for all groups. The greatest proportion of non-Western immigrants and second generation immigrants live in large towns and the smallest proportion in rural areas, while Western immigrants and second generation immigrants live more evenly spread across the country.

During the period 2002 to 2006 the fertility rate for Danish women was an average of 1.8 children per woman. For women from Western and non-Western countries living in Denmark the rates were 1.5 and 2.3 children respectively, though with considerable differences between countries of origin in the latter group. More detailed analyses suggest a gradual trend in the direction of convergence with the fertility rate of the host country.

The total number of spontaneous asylum seekers has shown great variation from year to year for the period since 1980, but with an overall rising trend up until the turn of the millennium. An increase to 8,000-10,000 in 2000 and 2001 was followed by a sharp decline, which has brought the figure down to a little over 1,000 in 2007. In parallel with these changes, the number of residence permits issued to asylum seekers in 2007 also totalled just over 1,000.

The number of family reunifications showed a rising trend from 1988 – the first year for which figures were recorded – to 2001, when almost 11,000 permits were granted. After this there was a sharp fall in the numbers, so that the total in 2007 was a little over 4,500. This reduction was due primarily to the introduction of more stringent regulations for obtaining permission for family reunification, as well as a reduced number of refugees.

After 1988, the number of work and study permits issued increased from just over 10,000 to more than 53,000 in 2007, accounting in that year for 90% of the total residence permits issued.

An analysis in which all asylum seekers from 1998 are traced individually until the resolution of their cases shows that 70% of those whose cases were actually processed in Denmark also received the right of residence in the country.

References

Bauer, Thomas, Claus Larsen and Poul Chr. Matthiessen. 2004a. "Immigration Policy and Danish and German Immigration", in Torben Tranæs and Klaus F. Zimmermann (eds), *Migrants, Work, and the Welfare State.* Odense: University Press of Southern Denmark.

Bauer, Thomas, Claus Larsen and Poul Chr. Matthiessen. 2004b. "Indvandringspolitik og indvandringen til Danmark og Tyskland". *Nyt fra Rockwool Fondens Forskningsenhed,* October 2004. Copenhagen: Rockwool Foundation Research Unit.

Danmarks Statistik. *Befolkningens Bevægelser 1996.* Copenhagen.

Danmarks Statistik. 2005. *Befolkningens Bevægelser 2004.* Copenhagen.

Danmarks Statistik. 2005. "Asylansøgninger og opholdstilladelser 2004". *Statistiske Efterretninger: Befolkning og Valg.* Copenhagen.

Danmarks Statistik. 2006. "Asylansøgninger og opholdstilladelser 2005". *Statistiske Efterretninger: Befolkning og Valg.* Copenhagen.

Danmarks Statistik. 2008. "Udenlandske statsborgere, personer født i udlandet samt indvandrere og efterkommere 1. januar 2008". *Statistiske Efterretninger, Befolkning og Valg* 2008/4. Copenhagen.

Larsen, Claus and Poul Chr. Matthiessen. 2002. "Indvandrerbefolkningens sammensætning og udvikling i Danmark", in Gunnar Viby Mogensen and Poul Chr. Matthiessen (eds), *Indvandrerne og arbejdsmarkedet.* Copenhagen: Spektrum, 25-79.

Matthiessen, Poul Chr. 2007. *Befolkning og Samfund.* Copenhagen.

Pedersen, Søren. 1999. "Vandringen til og fra Danmark i perioden 1960-1997", in David Coleman and Eskil Wadensjö with contributions by Bent Jensen and Søren Pedersen, *Indvandringen til Danmark.* Copenhagen: Spektrum, 233-284.

Pedersen, Søren. 2000. "Indvandrernes demografiske forhold", in Gunnar Viby Mogensen and Poul Chr. Matthiessen (eds), *Integration i Danmark omkring årtusindeskiftet.* Aarhus: Aarhus University Press, 27-47.

Tænketanken om udfordringer for integrationsindsatsen i Danmark. 2002. *Befolkningsudviklingen 2000-2001 – mulige udviklingsforløb.* Copenhagen.

Udlændingestyrelsen. 2002a. "Nøgletal på udlændingeområdet 2001". Copenhagen.

Udlændingestyrelsen. 2002b. "Ny type statistik på asylområdet: Forløbsanalyser i spontane asylsager". *U S Statistik serie nr. 1*. Copenhagen.

UNHCR (United Nations High Commissioner for Refugees). 1999. *Refugees and Others of Concern to UNHCR. 1998 Statistical Overview*. Geneva.

UNHCR (United Nations High Commissioner for Refugees). 2000. *Refugees and Others of Concern to UNHCR. 1999 Statistical Overview*. Geneva.

2. The various stages of the research and the datasets used

2.1. Introduction

The previous chapter showed the development in and nature of immigration to Denmark since the 1960s, the time when immigration to Denmark began to exceed emigration from the country, and showed how immigration altered both in extent and nature. It was against the background of these changes that, in 1997, the Rockwool Foundation decided to give high priority to "Immigrants and their conditions of life" as one of the topics which they sought to investigate through research projects, in order to provide a solid and detailed basis of knowledge to be used for political decision-makers.

Key questions to be addressed by this research concerned the interface between immigrants and second generation immigrants on the one hand and Danish society on the other, as well as the influence this relationship had on the conditions of life for immigrants and second generation immigrants. The process of integration into the Danish labour market was a significant factor in this context. The previous experience from the research at the Rockwool Foundation Research Unit and the abundant statistical data available in this area provided a good basis for this research.

A pilot project was conducted in 1998-99 with the participation of international experts. It was intended that this project should give a broader background picture of the nature of immigration in the form of, for example, analyses of the global demographic situation. The results from this study were published in 1999 in a book by David Coleman and Eskil Wadensjö, which appeared in Danish as *Indvandringen til Danmark. Internationale og nationale perspektiver* (Spektrum) and in English as *Immigration to Denmark. International and national perspectives* (Aarhus University Press).

In the first three chapters of the book Dr Coleman, of the University of Oxford, described immigration to Denmark in an international perspective. Chapter 1 described and analysed the contemporary global and European demographic processes, and how these affected Denmark. In Chapter 2 there were analyses of the structure of and trends in recent migration, with particular emphasis on the situation in Europe. Finally, Chapter 3 presented the policies introduced by various European countries to regulate migration and to find solutions to the new problems created by the arrival of large numbers of immigrants who came primarily from non-European countries.

Professor Eskil Wadensjö of the University of Stockholm contributed a special chapter on the socioeconomic consequences of immigration. The analyses were based primarily on the Danish "Law Model", which is described further in section 2.2.5.

In Chapter 4, Søren Pedersen (MSc) presented a statistical overview of the extent and composition of immigration to Denmark and of the integration of immigrants into the labour market. Finally Bent Jensen (MA) devoted two chapters to describing how major Danish newspapers had treated the topic of immigration over the previous decade.

2.2. The 1999 study

2.2.1. Introduction

The 1999 study, published in Danish as Gunnar Viby Mogensen and Poul Chr. Matthiessen (eds) (2000), *Indvandringen til Danmark omkring årtusindeskiftet* (Immigration to Denmark around the turn of the millennium) (Aarhus University Press), aimed to discover new information about immigrants and their conditions of life, with special emphasis on the process of integration into the Danish labour market. "Integration into the labour market" was understood as relating to the extent to which immigrants were not only part of the labour force, but actually had jobs.

Among the conditions of life that formed part of the study, emphasis was placed first of all on three factors of clear relevance for employment, namely knowledge of the Danish language, education, and health. Secondly, the relationship of immigrants to the social welfare system was also taken into account. This was an area of particular interest, in that the Danish welfare system supported a number of unemployed people through social security payments (as opposed to unemployment benefits), and these were people who might later have a formal relationship to the labour market. A third area studied was one which has a very real, if less clear cut, relationship to employment status: crime.

Furthermore, attempts were made in the data collection process to cover a number of aspects of social relevance which were slightly more difficult to measure. Among these aspects were perceptions and experiences of relationships between different population groups, including discrimination towards immigrants in Denmark and opinions concerning how open the country should be to continued immigration.

Finally, the study had the aim of determining the economic consequences of immigration for Denmark, including the effects on the Danish welfare system of redistribution of wealth through public finances.

2.2.2. The questionnaire survey

The first source of new knowledge about immigrants and second generation immigrants was a questionnaire survey – referred to below as the main survey – which was based on 3,615 interviews conducted between November 1998 and July 1999 among non-Western immigrants and second generation immigrants of eight different nationalities (Nielsen and Pedersen, 2000). Respondents were selected from among immigrants and second generation immigrants between the ages of 16 and 70 who had been resident in Denmark for at least two years. The eight national groups – people from the former Yugoslavia, Iran, Lebanon, Pakistan, Poland, Somalia, Turkey and Vietnam – were the largest groups of non-Western immigrants in the Danish population at that time. People from these countries accounted for 66% of the non-Western immigrants and second generation immigrants living in Denmark. As mentioned previously, Poles have been categorised as Western immigrants since 1 January 2005 as a result of the accession of Poland to the EU in 2004.

The interviews were conducted by bilingual interviewers, so that respondents had the choice of being interviewed either in Danish, or in the language of their national group (or English). The use of bilingual interviewers meant that it was possible to assess the respondents' Danish language proficiency.

Interviewers were recruited through advertisements at various educational institutions in the Copenhagen area, advertisements on the Internet, contact with schools of interpreting, and contacts with interviewers already permanently employed at Statistics Denmark. Approximately 75 applicants for the posts were interviewed, and 28 of these were selected, providing at least two interviewers per national group. The interviewers were then involved in the process of translating the questionnaire into the relevant languages. Some of the translations were actually made by the interviewers themselves, and the remainder by external consultants. The translated versions of the questionnaire were then given to all the interviewers for their comments, and the forms revised in the light of these.

The respondents were all sent a letter in advance that explained about the survey and informed them that they would be contacted for a telephone interview in the near future. At the outset, an attempt was made to obtain telephone interviews with all the selected respondents. However, this proved to be impossible, as it was often difficult to obtain the necessary telephone numbers. It was therefore necessary to supplement the telephone interviews with visits in person in order to obtain a sufficiently high response rate for each of the eight nationality groups. For example, it was possible to obtain telephone numbers for only 62% of the Somalis in the sample.

Where it was possible to carry out telephone interviews, the CATI method (Computer Assisted Telephone Interviewing) was used; interviewers read out the questions from their computer screens and entered the responses as they were given.

Table 2.1. Respondents in the main survey distributed by interview language and national origin. Percent.

	Former Yugoslavia	Iran	Lebanon	Pakistan	Poland	Somalia	Turkey	Vietnam	All
Own language[1][2]	75.3	58.0	82.4	42.1	58.9	96.3	78.0	48.2	65.5
Danish	24.7	42.0	17.6	57.9	41.1	3.7	22.0	51.8	34.5
Total	100.0	100.0	100.0	100.0	100.0	100.0	100.0	100.0	100.0
Number of respondents	489	410	421	430	438	410	565	452	3,615

[1] Respondents' own language was defined as: for the former Yugoslavia: Serbo-Croat; for Iran: Persian (Farsi); for Lebanon: Arabic; for Pakistan: Urdu/Punjabi; for Poland: Polish; for Somalia: Somali; for Turkey: Turkish; and for Vietnam: Vietnamese.
[2] Two people, one from the former Yugoslavia and one from Pakistan, were interviewed in English.
Source: Rockwool Foundation Research Unit interview surveys of 1999 conducted among immigrants and second generation immigrants in Denmark.

In the case of interviews conducted at the place of residence, interviewers brought a laptop computer and similarly read the questions direct from the screen. This meant that the interview format remained consistent whatever language was used. The telephone interviews took an average of around 25 minutes each, but for technical reasons it was not possible for Statistics Denmark to record interview times for interviews conducted in person.

As can be seen from Table 2.1, the majority of the interviews were conducted in the respondents' own languages. However, the proportions of interviews conducted in Danish varied significantly from one national group to another. The largest proportion to be interviewed in Danish was among Pakistani respondents. The lowest proportion was among the Somalis: only 3.7% were interviewed in Danish.

Using the Danish Civil Registration Number system, information about the respondents in the sample from a number of different official registers containing data on, for example, gender, age, education, income, employment, social security payments, criminal record and use of the health services was linked to the interview responses. The whole survey was, however, conducted on the basis of anonymised data, so that no individual could be identified.

The Danish Civil Register was introduced in 1968 and contains information on all residents of Denmark, including name, address, gender and marital status. Each person in the register is allocated a 10-digit identification number. The Register is constantly kept up to date through the entry of live births, deaths, immigration and emigration, marriages and divorces. This means that there is a precise census of the Danish population available in electronic form at any time. In addition, there are a number of registers, covering various aspects of life such as education, work, income, unemployment, crime, and use of the social services, which use the Civil Registration Numbers of the individuals entered in the register. By using the Civil Registration Numbers, then, it is possible to combine information about a given individual from a variety of registers.

The main results of the survey are presented in statistical format in Table 2.2, displayed by country of origin. As can be seen from the table, the response rate varied considerably from country to country, from 46.4% for Somalia to 63.6% for Vietnam. The overall response rate for the survey was 57.8%, meaning that interviews were not obtained for 42.2% of the selected random sample. In comparison with other equivalent surveys conducted by means of interviews with immigrant groups, a response rate of 57.8% seems to be the norm (Togeby, 1999; Gulløy et al., 1997).

Given the fairly considerable non-completion rate, it is difficult to estimate the extent to which non-completion influenced the degree to which the respondents could be said to be a representative sample of the non-Western immigrant and second generation immigrant populations from the eight selected countries. In principle, we would wish to determine whether the responses to any given question (the dependent variables) were distributed in a manner equivalent to the distribution that would have been obtained if the whole population of immigrants and second generation immigrants from the eight countries had been asked the question. Since this is in the nature of things an impossibility, a check was instead made of how the respondents in the sample were distributed according to the main background variables (the independent variables) such as gender, age, geographical distribution and personal income. If these independent variables were distributed for the people who completed interviews consistently with the distribution of the same variables for the whole of the population in question, there would be reason to assume that the respondents in the sample did not differ substantially in their responses from those the entire population would have given.

A comparison of the sample and of the whole population of immigrants and second generation immigrants from the eight countries showed approximately the same distribution with regard to gender, age, marital status, labour market status and income. Deviations were found in certain variables, for example an under-representation of single people and people from the Copenhagen area in the sample, and a slight over-representation of wage earners.

Table 2.2. Response rates etc. of the main survey.

	Total random sample size	Interviews conducted			Not completed			Completion rate	Refusal rate[1]
		Telephone	Visit	Total	Refused[1]	Other	Total		
		Number of persons						percentage	
Former Yugoslavia	837	463	26	489	87	261	348	58.4	14.1
Iran	712	328	82	410	48	254	302	57.7	11.8
Lebanon	711	340	81	421	40	250	290	59.2	9.7
Pakistan	709	333	97	430	32	247	279	60.6	8.0
Poland	710	425	13	438	61	211	272	61.7	11.8
Somalia	884	363	47	410	54	420	474	46.4	11.5
Turkey	983	456	109	565	75	343	418	57.5	12.8
Vietnam	711	420	32	452	31	228	259	63.6	5.9
Total	6,257	3,128	487	3,615	428	2,214	2,642	57.8	10.9

[1] Based on telephone interviews only.
Source: Rockwool Foundation Research Unit interview surveys of 1999 conducted among immigrants and second generation immigrants in Denmark.

In the group of 428 people categorised as having refused to be interviewed, only just over 50% actually refused, while the rest of the group could not be interviewed because of changes of address or language problems.

Table 2.2 above shows how many interviews were completed, and how large the sample was for each of the eight immigrant groups. The relative sizes of the samples were determined primarily on the basis of expectations – in part based on the experience from a survey in Norway (Gulløy et al., 1997) – of how large a completion rate could be expected for each group. This meant that the sizes of the samples were not proportionate to the sizes of the eight populations within the immigrant population as a whole. We are thus dealing with a stratified sample with eight strata. When results are reported for the whole sample in the following, the sample from each country is therefore weighted with its proportion in the entire population.

In many of the tables in the book, a special weighting is used with respect to gender and age for each of the immigrant groups. In order to be better able to compare the analyses for the immigrant groups with corresponding analyses for Danes, the immigrant groups were weighted by gender and age so that the distributions of these variables were made equivalent to those of the Danish population.

2.2.3. The omnibus surveys

In order to make comparisons of the responses of the survey sample of immigrants and second generation immigrants from the eight countries with corresponding data for the entire population of Denmark, selected questions from the main survey were included in a national "omnibus" survey. These national telephone interview surveys are carried out every month by the permanent body of interviewers employed by Statistics Denmark, and they cover different subjects on different occasions. The omnibus survey that was used in connection with this study was conducted in February 1999, and interviews were completed with 961 people. The original random sample selected for the survey consisted of 1,499 people drawn from the entire population of Denmark (i.e. including immigrants and second generation immigrants), and the completion rate was thus 64.1%.

Just as the sample of immigrants and second generation immigrants from the eight countries formed a reasonably representative sample of that population, the same is generally true with respect to the sample for the omnibus survey.

2.2.4. Register information

The data used for the study also included three datasets taken from the Danish Civil Registration System, which – as mentioned earlier – contains information about all persons legally resident in Denmark (the *de jure* population of the country).

As described in Chapter 1, the population of Denmark is divided into three groups for certain statistical purposes, these groups consisting of non-Western immigrants and second generation immigrants, Western immigrants and second generation immigrants, and Danes. The primary register population for the study was made up of all non-Western immigrants and second generation immigrants who were legally resident in Denmark on 1 January in any year between 1984 and 1998, or on 1 July 1998, and who were between the ages of 16 and 70 inclusive on at least one of those dates. This part of the data material covered 209,499 people.

Second, a sample was drawn consisting of 25% of all Western immigrants and second generation immigrants who were legally resident in Denmark on 1 January in any year between 1984 and 1998, or on 1 July 1998, and who were between the ages of 16 and 70 inclusive on at least one of those dates. This sample contained 41,615 people.

In order to be able to compare the data for Western and non-Western immigrants and second generation immigrants with results for the entire Danish population, a 2% random sample was drawn from the whole population of Denmark (including immigrants and second generation immigrants). The basis for this sample was exactly the same as for the other data material, i.e. the sample consisted of 2% of all persons who were legally resident in Denmark on 1 January in any year between 1984 and 1998, or on 1 July 1998, and who were between the ages of 16 and 70 inclusive on at least one of those dates. This sample contained 93,673 people.

As the first data set covered the whole target population, the question of representativeness does not arise in this context. As far as the two other samples are concerned, the very large size and randomness of the samples drawn ensured that they were representative of the entire populations to a high degree.

2.2.5. The Law Model

Chapter 7 of this book presents an analysis of the economic consequences of immigration for which a special model known as the Law Model was used.

This model was developed at the end of the 1970s and was originally based on a random sample of 3.3% of the entire Danish population. Later this was expanded with a possibility of using up to 33% of the population. A large amount of personal data, taken largely from the registers kept by Statistics Denmark, was linked to this sample (Danmarks Statistik 1998). A new sample is drawn each year, which means that the Law Model does not allow for the same individuals to be tracked over time. The Model has built into it sets of regulations related to different parts of Danish legislation, together with current rates for various relevant areas such as taxation and pensions.

The Law Model is used primarily to estimate the effects of legislative proposals, for example to calculate the effects on individuals of a major income tax reform. Similarly, the Law Model can calculate the consequences of a tax reform for public funds. The high level of detail which can be obtained in calculations using the Law Model with respect to income transfers from the public purse to individuals and to the amount individuals pay in taxes makes it also very suitable for analysing the socioeconomic effects of immigration.

2.3. The 2001 study

As the 1999 study, the 2001 study was based on both interview data and register data (Nielsen 2002). The results were published as Gunnar Viby Mogensen and Poul Chr. Matthiessen (eds) (2002), *Indvandrerne og arbejdsmarkedet* (Immigrants and the labour market) (Spektrum). The interview survey was based on a re-interviewing of the respondents from the 1999 study. As explained above, that survey was based on a random sample taken from among the eight largest ethnic groups in Denmark at that time. In total, interviews were completed with 3,262 people from a sample of 6,257.

Interviewees in the 1999 survey were asked if they would be willing to be re-interviewed at a later date. 3,307 said that they would, and these people formed the basis for the 2001 survey. However, some of these people had died or remigrated by 2001, so the total sample for these re-interviewees consisted of 3,161 people. Interviews were completed with 2,348 people out of this sample, corresponding to an interview completion rate of 74.2%. In order to compensate for the unavoidable loss of some respondents who had been interviewed in 1999, the sample was supplemented with new respondents who had not been interviewed previously. There were, as already mentioned, two special criteria for inclusion in the sample used for the 1999 questionnaire survey, namely that those in the sample should have been resident for at least two years in Denmark, and that they should have been aged between 16 and 70 inclusive. This meant that re-interviewees in 2001 had been resident in Denmark for at least four years, and were in the age range 18-72. The sample was therefore supplemented with people aged 18-70 with a minimum of four years' residence, with people aged 16 or 17, and with people aged 18-70 with two or three years' residence. Figure 2.1 shows how the interviewees were distributed across the two interview rounds.

A study of the representativeness of the sample showed that there was an over-representation of people who were members of the labour force. Since this was a key variable that could have a significant effect on the results, a weighting system was used which would compensate for the skewness of the sample with respect to the labour market status in addition to factors such as country of origin and age.

In order to provide a basis for comparison with the whole population of Denmark, a number of questions from the main survey had been given to Danes in three of the earlier omnibus surveys described above. These were conducted in February, March and July of 2001, with a total sample size from the three surveys of 4,440 people. Of these, interviews were completed with a total of 2,712 people, giving a completion rate of 61.1%.

As in the 1999 study, an important element of the data used comprised three sets of register data drawn from registers at Statistics Denmark. These three datasets contained information on the following groups:

- The entire population of non-Western immigrants and second generation immigrants who were legally resident in Denmark on 1 January in any

38 *The various stages of the research and the datasets used*

Figure 2.1. Overview of the composition of the interview panels in 1999 and 2001.

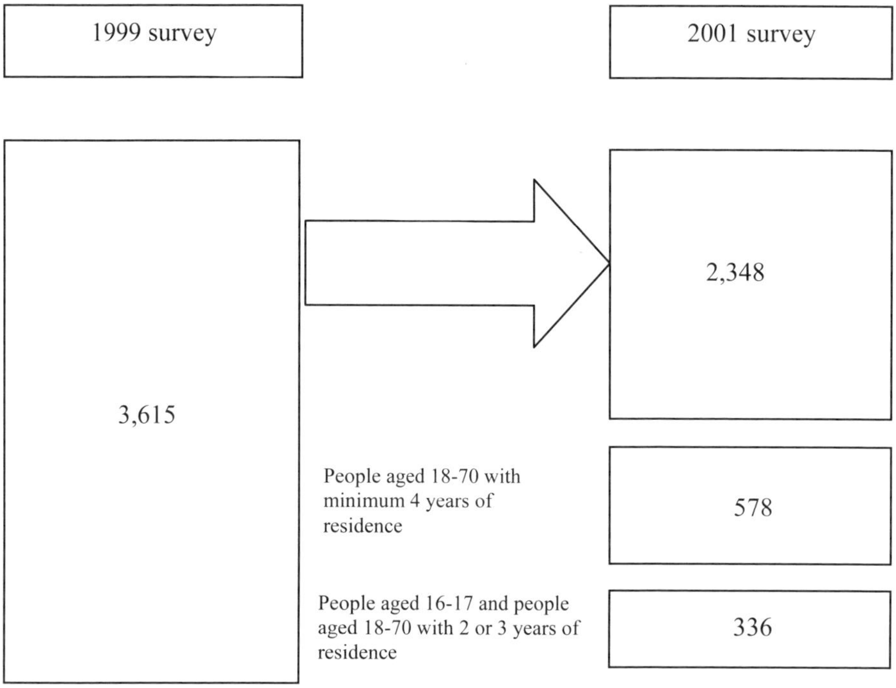

```
┌─────────────────────┐              ┌─────────────────────┐
│    1999 survey      │              │    2001 survey      │
└─────────────────────┘              └─────────────────────┘


┌─────────────────────┐              ┌─────────────────────┐
│                     │              │                     │
│                     │     ═══▶     │       2,348         │
│                     │              │                     │
│                     │              └─────────────────────┘
│       3,615         │
│                     │    People aged 18-70 with    ┌──────────┐
│                     │    minimum 4 years of        │   578    │
│                     │    residence                 └──────────┘
│                     │
│                     │    People aged 16-17 and people
│                     │    aged 18-70 with 2 or 3 years of   ┌──────────┐
│                     │    residence                         │   336    │
└─────────────────────┘                                      └──────────┘
```

Notes: The figures show the numbers of people with whom interviews were completed.
Source: Rockwool Foundation Research Unit interview surveys of 2001 conducted among immigrants and second generation immigrants in Denmark.

year between 1984 and 2001, or on 1 July 2000, and who were between the ages of 16 and 70 inclusive on at least one of these dates. This sample consisted of 253,529 people.

- 25% of the population of Western immigrants and second generation immigrants who were legally resident in Denmark on 1 January in any year between 1984 and 2001, or on 1 July 2000, and who were between the ages of 16 and 70 inclusive on at least one of these dates. This produced a sample size of 47,475 people.

In order to be able to compare the data for Western and non-Western immigrants and second generation immigrants with results for the entire Danish population, a 2% random sample was once again drawn from the whole population (including immigrants and second generation immigrants). This sample was drawn consistently with the two other samples, that is to say, it consisted of 2% of all people who were resident in Denmark on one of the dates listed above for the immigrant population samples and who were aged between 16 and 70 on one of the dates in question; this produced a sample of 98,918 people.

As with the 1999 study, these three register samples were linked to data from registers held by Statistics Denmark, including background information (gender, age, marital status, etc.), information about education, information about employment, income, and many other variables.

2.4. The German dataset

The results of the 2001 study were also used in a joint Danish-German research project concerning integration of immigrants in the two countries. This study was conducted as a collaborative project between the Rockwool Foundation Research Unit and Professor Klaus Zimmermann and his associates at the Institut zur Zukunft der Arbeit (IZA) in Bonn. The results of this study were published in Torben Tranæs and Klaus F. Zimmermann (eds) (2004), *Migrants, Work, and the Welfare State* (University Press of Southern Denmark). A brief description of the German dataset follows below.

The dataset comprised responses from 5,669 interviews with foreign nationals from Turkey, the former Yugoslavia, Poland, Iran and Lebanon who were legally resident in Germany. Residents from these countries comprise two thirds of all foreign residents from non-Western countries. In contrast to the Danish dataset from the 2001 survey, the German dataset did not include immigrants from Pakistan, Somalia or Vietnam (Bauer and Nielsen, 2004).

The questionnaire used for the 2001 Danish survey formed the basis for the questionnaire used in Germany. This procedure produced an ideal data set for a comparative study. The Danish questionnaire was translated into German in cooperation with Infratest Sozialforschung. Some adaptation was necessary to the situation in Germany, however, with respect to a number of questions connected with education and the labour market. While a large part of the information needed for the Danish interviewees could be extracted from administrative registers, this was not possible to the same extent for the German survey, both because the German registration system is not as highly developed as that of Denmark and because access to the data is more restricted. This made it necessary to include some extra questions in the German survey, for example about respondents' income.

The German dataset was collected between April and August 2002 by means of face-to-face interviews using the CAPI method (Computer Assisted Personal Interviews). This contrasted with the Danish survey, where the principal data collection method involved telephone interviews. In Germany, an attempt was always made to conduct the interview in German, thus enabling the interviewer to make an assessment of the respondent's proficiency in the language. If the interviewee had difficulty in understanding German, the interviewer could make use of a printed copy of the questions in the respondent's own language – and if necessary, also a printed list of the possible answers. In addition, the interviewer had the possibility of using an interpreter to resolve any problems of communication.

Unlike Denmark, Germany has no *central* civil registration system from which a sample can be drawn. A different selection method therefore had to be used. The method applied was based on local *Einwohnermeldeamt* (population registers), in which every legal resident in Germany must enrol. First, Infratest Sozialforschung went to the local population registers in the 100 largest towns in the former West Germany and the three largest towns in the former East Germany to obtain information about the number of immigrants and their nationalities in each of these areas. On the basis of this information, it was decided that 500 sampling points would be used. These points would be randomly distributed among the 103 towns that formed the basis for the sample selection, though this did not necessarily mean that all 103 towns would be represented in the survey. It was planned that around 5,500 interviews would be conducted on the basis of these sampling points, with 1,100 interviews for each nationality and 11 interviews per sampling point. This procedure for selecting the sample meant that the sample population was composed mainly of immigrants who lived in urban areas.

In contrast to the Danish 2001 survey sample, the German dataset was composed entirely of people with foreign nationality. It is not possible to distinguish naturalised Germans in the population registers. In these respects, then, the Danish and German samples were not completely comparable. The problem was somewhat reduced, however, by the fact that the rules for naturalisation were much tougher in Germany at that time than in Denmark, so that the proportion of immigrants who became naturalised Germans was significantly smaller in Germany than in Denmark.

The 5,669 completed and usable interviews in the German survey represent a response rate of 43.5%. Response rates varied between nationalities from 37.3% for nationals of the former Yugoslavia to 51.0% for Lebanese nationals. The overall response rate was on a par with that in other similar surveys in Germany. Difficulty in contacting the selected respondents at the addresses given was the primary reason for non-completion of interviews, accounting for 22.9% of the selected sample. In addition, 16% of the selected sample population refused to participate in the survey.

Among the completed interviews, there were a significant number of people who refused to answer some specific questions, in particular those concerning income. Respondents were asked to specify the types of income received in the month prior to the interview. In the case of households consisting of more than one person, 34% of respondents failed to answer the question on the gross income of the household. Unfortunately, there is little information available that would give an indication of the degree to which these missing responses may have biased the estimates obtained in the regressions made on the basis of income.

As with the Danish survey, a check was made on the representativeness of the German sample by comparing the distributions of background variables such as gender, age, region and nationality in the sample with those of the entire population in Germany of people from Turkey, the former Yugoslavia, Poland, Iran and Lebanon. Data for this total population were obtained from the *Ausländerzentralregister* (AZR), which is an administrative register of all foreigners legally resident in Germany. The check on representativeness covered only people aged 15 and over. The register, however, is not completely reliable, since a number of foreigners – especially Poles, who are often in Germany on a short-term basis – fail to sign off from the register when they leave the country.

The comparisons made reveal a certain bias with respect to the background variables examined. The conclusion is therefore that the German sample was less representative than the corresponding Danish sample.

As mentioned previously, the procedure for selecting the sample was designed to ensure that the number of people interviewed was approximately equal for each of the five nationalities, in order to make it possible to carry out separate analyses for each nationality. Table 2.3 shows that the distribution of nationalities in the sample was indeed approximately equal, even though, for example, the proportion of people from Turkey was larger than the proportion of people from Lebanon (26% of the sample as opposed to 17%).

This procedure meant that the sample did not reflect the distribution of nationalities in the population as a whole. As can be seen from the table, Turks and people from the former Yugoslavia together accounted for 85% of the total population in Germany from the five countries at that time, but they comprised only 44% of the sample. To make the sample representative of the whole population with respect to the distribution of nationalities it was necessary to weight the results so that respondents from Turkey and the former Yugoslavia were weighted more heavily and people from Poland, Iran and Lebanon less heavily. Calculations showed that the weighting procedure improved the overall representativeness of the sample with regard to geography, gender and length of residence.

Table 2.3. Distribution of nationalities in the German dataset and in the whole population of immigrants from the five countries. Ages 15 and over. Percent.

	German sample	Register of resident foreigners (AZR)
Turkey	26.0	54.0
Former Yugoslavia	17.9	31.1
Poland	21.5	10.6
Iran	17.8	3.1
Lebanon	16.8	1.2
Total	100.0	100.0
Number of observations	5,669	2,713,299

Sources: RFMS-G (Rockwool Foundation Migratory Survey-Germany), *Ausländerzentralregister* (AZR) (the German central register for foreign nationals), and own calculations.

2.5. Summary

The first source of new knowledge about immigrants and second generation immigrants was comprised by the two questionnaire surveys (the main surveys) conducted among the eight largest groups of non-Western immigrants and second generation immigrants in Denmark at that time, these being people from the former Yugoslavia, Iran, Lebanon, Pakistan, Poland, Somalia, Turkey and Vietnam. In the first of these questionnaire surveys (the 1999 survey), 3,615 interviews were completed during the period from November 1998 to July 1999, while in the second survey (the 2001 survey) 3,262 interviews were completed during the first half of 2001. A total of 2,348 of the people interviewed in the 2001 survey were re-interviewees from the first survey. The response rate for each of the surveys was close to 60%. A comparison of the samples and of the entire population of immigrants from the eight countries showed approximately the same distributions with respect to gender, age, marital status, labour market status and income.

In order to be able to compare immigrants and second generation immigrants from the eight countries with the entire population of Denmark, a selection of questions from the two main surveys were also asked in the "omnibus surveys" of the entire Danish population conducted by Statistics Denmark.

The data used for the study also included three datasets extracted from the Danish Civil Registration System, which contains information about all persons legally resident in Denmark (the *de jure* population of the country). The three datasets consisted of information about non-Western immigrants and second generation immigrants, Western immigrants and second generation immigrants, and Danes. In the case of the first group, the entire population aged between 16 and 70 was used. Analyses of the other two groups were based on random samples of 25% and 2% respectively of the full populations.

In Chapter 7 of this book an account is given of the economic consequences of immigration based on a special model, known as the Law Model. This model was developed at the end of the 1970s, and at that time was based on a sample of 3.3% of the Danish population. A large amount of personal information about the people in that sample, taken primarily from the registers held by Statistics Denmark, was linked to the sample. The high level of detail which can be obtained in calculations using the Law Model with respect to income transfers from the public purse to individuals and to the amount individuals pay in taxes makes it very suitable for analysing the socioeconomic effects of immigration.

The results of the 2001 survey were also used in a joint Danish-German project to study the integration of immigrants in the two countries. Based on the Danish questionnaire, the same set of information was acquired in the two countries thus providing an ideal basis for a comparative study. The German dataset comprised responses from 5,669 interviews with foreign nationals from Turkey, the former Yugoslavia, Poland, Iran and Lebanon who were legally resident in Germany. In contrast to the Danish 2001 data, the German dataset did not cover immigrants from Pakistan, Somalia and Vietnam.

References

Bauer, Thomas and Niels-Kenneth Nielsen. 2004. "Data Description", in Torben Tranæs and Klaus Zimmermann (eds) 2004, *Migrants, Work, and the Welfare State*. Odense: University Press of Southern Denmark, 405-427.

Coleman, David and Eskil Wadensjö. 1999. *Indvandringen til Danmark. Internationale og nationale perspektiver*. Copenhagen: Spektrum.

Coleman, David and Eskild Wadensjö. 1999. *Immigration to Denmark. International and national perspectives*. Aarhus: Aarhus University Press.

Danmarks Statistik. *Nyheder og Information fra Danmarks Statistik 1998:1*. Copenhagen.

Gulløy, Elisabeth, Svein Blom and Agnes Aall Ritland. 1997. *Levevilkår blant innvandrere 1996. Dokumentasjonsrapport med tabeller*. Oslo: Statistisk Sentralbyro.

Møller, Birgit and Lise Togeby. 1999. *Oplevet diskrimination. En undersøgelse blandt etniske minoriteter*. Copenhagen: Nævnet for Etnisk Ligestilling.

Nielsen, Niels-Kenneth and Søren Pedersen. 2000. "Databeskrivelse", in Gunnar Viby Mogensen and Poul Chr. Matthiessen (eds), 2000. *Integration i Danmark omkring årtusindeskiftet*. Aarhus: Aarhus University Press, 379-406.

Nielsen, Niels-Kenneth. 2002. "Databeskrivelse", in Gunnar Viby Mogensen and Poul Chr. Matthiessen (eds), 2002. *Indvandrerne og arbejdsmarkedet*. Copenhagen: Spektrum, 327-348.

Tranæs, Torben and Klaus Zimmermann (eds.). 2004. *Migrants, Work, and the Welfare State*. Odense: University Press of Southern Denmark.

3. Education and Danish language proficiency

3.1. The 1999 study

3.1.1. Introduction

This chapter focuses on two variables, education and Danish language proficiency, which must be considered crucial for the opportunities which immigrants and second generation immigrants have for participating in Danish society. Such participation includes integrating into the labour market, which is the main theme of this study. However, prior to this study, these factors and their significance in Denmark had scarcely been studied at all.

Official statistics had previously only registered courses of education taken in Denmark. Courses of education taken abroad – including courses which immigrants might have taken in their home countries or elsewhere before coming to Denmark – were not recorded. In the summer of 1999, Statistics Denmark launched a project aimed at improving their statistics on education by registering any courses which immigrants who had not taken vocational training or higher education in Denmark might have taken abroad. The results of that project, however, were not available soon enough to be used in connection with the 1999 study; and no comprehensive studies at all had been carried out with regard to immigrants' Danish language proficiency.

The interviews with immigrants and second generation immigrants of the eight nationalities in the survey included questions about education and employment before arrival in Denmark, including enquiries about father's education and employment. Knowledge of Danish and courses taken in Danish language proficiency were also covered.

This chapter presents the results of the analyses, which combined these interview data with register data concerning courses of education taken in Denmark (Larsen 2002). A distinction is made between immigrants who came to Denmark aged 12 or under, and who had thus been in the Danish education system for at least part of their obligatory schooling, and those who had come to the country as children aged 13 or over, or as adults. As far as the first group was concerned, information about education would normally be available through the registers held by Statistics Denmark. It may also be assumed that these children would have had better opportunities for learning Danish through their association with Danish children of the same age in and outside school than would have been the case for older immigrants. Moreover, it was primarily the older immigrant group for whom information about education was missing in the statistics.

With respect to formal education, then, the study primarily focussed on those immigrants who had come to Denmark as teenagers or adults in other words, the group for whom information was lacking prior to 1999.

Information about proficiency in Danish was collected solely through the interview survey, and this covered both age groups.

3.1.2. Education from countries of origin

This section presents the answers that were provided to the new questions about education in the country of origin (or elsewhere) before arrival in Denmark.

Table 3.1 shows how many people from each country had completed a course of education, had attended school without completing a course of education, or had not attended school at all. In the totals for all countries shown at the bottom of the table and in subsequent tables, the responses have been weighted in accordance with the proportions of the various nationalities in the population as a whole. The table shows that it was only among immigrants from the former Yugoslavia, Iran and Poland that around half or more had completed a course of education before coming to Denmark. The lowest proportions were among immigrants from Pakistan, Somalia and Turkey, and it was these groups that also had the largest proportions – around 15% – with no formal education at all. In total, the entire group of respondents, including those with no formal education, had an average of nine years of education per person. Immigrants from Iran and Poland had the most years of education, while those from Turkey had by far the lowest average number of years of education. The table also shows, however, that immigrants from Turkey were those who immigrated at the lowest average age (23 years), while immigrants from Iran and Poland were close to or over the average age of immigration, which was 27 years.

If the immigrants with schooling are further divided up according to the level of education completed, then people from Poland, Iran and the former Yugoslavia stand out as those possessing the most vocational training and academic qualifications above high school level on arrival in Denmark. Of course, the amount of education may depend to some extent on age at the time of immigration. The three countries listed above were also those with the lowest proportions of immigrants who were under the age of 20 on arrival. However, this seems only to constitute a small part of the explanation, since the same tendency is also evident if one only takes into account those immigrants who were in their twenties or older on arrival.

Table 3.1. Immigrants who were at least 13 years old on arrival in Denmark, distributed according to country of origin and level of education at the time of immigration. Ages 16-70. Percent.

	Completed obligatory schooling or higher level of education	Attended school without completing	No schooling	Total	Schooling and higher education, average	Average age on arrival	Number of individuals
	---------- Percent ----------				Number of years	Age	
Former Yugoslavia	54	43	3	100	10	33	426
Iran	46	49	6	100	12	27	235
Lebanon	23	68	9	100	9	26	333
Pakistan	12	71	17	100	9	24	237
Poland	87	10	2	100	13	28	342
Somalia	19	67	15	100	9	27	379
Turkey	17	68	15	100	6	23	344
Vietnam	20	72	8	100	8	27	337
The eight countries in total [1]	37	54	9	100	9	27	2,633

[1] Weighted in accordance with the proportion of the Danish population of the national group.
Source: Rockwool Foundation Research Unit interview survey conducted in 1999 among immigrants and second generation immigrants in Denmark.

3.1.3. The overall picture of the education level of non-Western immigrants

By combining interview responses on education in immigrants' countries of origin with register information on courses of education taken in Denmark, an overall picture can be formed of immigrants' education. The information provided on level of education in countries of origin may sometimes have been exaggerated, consciously or unconsciously, by the respondents. It should also be noted that it can be difficult to make direct comparisons between courses of education in different countries.

The overall measures of educational level shown in Table 3.2, which are also used in other chapters in this book, can be said to be the result of a principle of cautious interpretation. The measures were constructed so that if information existed about Danish education, whether from register data or from interview data, then the Danish educational level was that used, regardless of any information given about education in the country of origin. Data about education in the country of origin were only used if there was no information available about education in Denmark; Danish education was thus given priority over education in the country of origin. This approach was inspired by that taken by the Norwegian Central Bureau of Statistics as their "minimum estimate" (see Blom and Ritland 1997: 172 and Blom 1998: 15-17). The Bureau used this minimum estimate approach because of the difficulty in evaluating education from abroad and because of the risk of a certain degree of exaggeration in the answers.

The figures given in Table 3.2 for all immigrants counted jointly are calculated as if the group had the same gender and age distributions as the Danish population with which they are compared; the differences apparent between the groups must therefore be due to other causes. Differences between the various immigrant groups may, in contrast, be partly or wholly due to differences in the gender and age distributions.

The table shows that there were relatively more immigrants than Danes who only had education at the level of compulsory schooling, while the opposite was the case for vocational and higher education. However, figures for immigrants from Iran and Poland were somewhat higher than the average for the Danish population as a whole with respect to high school and higher education, while those for immigrants from the former Yugoslavia were at about the average level for the Danish population with respect to vocational training. Immigrants from the "old" immigrant source countries Turkey and Pakistan were particularly notable for their lack of vocational and higher education.

At the bottom of the table, the figures for men and women have been separated; this shows that the general level of education for immigrant women was lower than that for immigrant men. In particular, there were many women who had not attended school at all. However, this measurement of immigrant women as a single group conceals significant differences between countries of origin.

If the material in Table 3.2 is presented on the basis of the highest level of education recorded in either the register information about education in Denmark or the interview information about Danish or foreign education (a maximal as opposed to a minimal measure), the average level of education for the immigrant groups taken as a whole is increased by a couple of percentage points for both vocational training and higher education. This approach has the greatest significance for immigrants from Poland and Iran, who were measured as having a high level of education in any event, and also in part for immigrants from Somalia. The explanation for this is that some immigrants began studies in the Danish education system at a lower level than they had previously reached in their countries of origin.

Table 3.2. Immigrants who were at least 13 years old on arrival in Denmark, distributed according to country of origin and overall minimum level of completed Danish and foreign education taken together,[1] compared with Danes. Ages 16-70. Percent.

	No schooling	Compulsory schooling	High school	Vocational training	Higher education	Total	Number of individuals
Former Yugoslavia	2	51	5	33	10	100	426
Iran	3	31	14	20	32	100	235
Lebanon	8	66	5	15	6	100	333
Pakistan	9	73	8	4	6	100	237
Poland	1	26	12	31	31	100	342
Somalia	11	65	6	6	12	100	379
Turkey	9	77	3	4	7	100	344
Vietnam	6	59	7	19	9	100	337
The eight countries taken together[3]	7	58	6	17	12	100	2,633
Danes	2[2]	36	8	35	19	100	66,650
Women							
The eight countries taken together	10	57	6	16	11	100	1,350
Danes	2	38	9	31	20	100	33,116
Men							
The eight countries taken together	3	59	6	19	13	100	1,283
Danes	2	33	7	39	19	100	33,534

[1] Where register or interview information was available about education in Denmark, this was the information used. Information from the interview survey on foreign education was only used if there was no information available about Danish education.
[2] This figure shows the proportion of Danes for whom no information was available about education level; the figure is thus not necessarily an indication of people with no schooling at all.
[3] Weighted according to the actual size of the various immigrant groups as a proportion of the Danish population, and standardised so that the figures are calculated as if the immigrant group had the same gender and age distribution as the Danish population with which they are compared.
Sources: Rockwool Foundation Research Unit interview survey conducted in 1999 among immigrants and second generation immigrants in Denmark, plus calculations made by the Rockwool Foundation Research Unit on the basis of register information from Statistics Denmark.

3.1.4. Significant factors for the level of education of non-Western immigrants

To conclude this discussion on the overall level of education, the following section uses logistic regressions to elucidate the factors which are significantly associated with whether immigrants who had arrived in Denmark aged 13 or over had taken Danish and/or foreign courses of education. The analysis is based on the minimum measurement approach described earlier, and compares those who had education at high school, vocational or higher education levels with those who had education at no more than the level of obligatory schooling, including those with no education at all. The age range for the analysis is 20-70 years. Explanations are sought in the circumstances of immigrants before and in connection with their immigration to Denmark, at a time when many had either completed their education or had already laid the foundations on which their future choice of courses was based. It was noted above that women had a lower level of education than men. Consequently, separate regression analyses were made for men and women, as is also the case in the other chapters in this book. An overview of the results is presented in Table 3.3.

Table 3.3. Significant factors for level of education[1] for immigrants aged at least 13 on arrival in Denmark. Ages 16-70.

	Men	Women
Age	***	Not significant
Degree of urbanisation of place of residence	Not significant	Not significant
Country of origin	***	***
Father's education	***	Not significant
Father's occupation	**	*
Basis for granting of residence permit	***	***
Primary occupation in country of origin	Not significant	***
Religion	**	**
Length of residence	*	Not significant

Note: Significant at *** = the 1% level, ** = the 5% level, * = the 10% level.
[1] Where register or interview information was available about education in Denmark, this was the information used. Information from the interview survey on foreign education was only used if there was no information available about Danish education.
Sources: Rockwool Foundation Research Unit interview survey conducted in 1999 among immigrants and second generation immigrants in Denmark, plus calculations made by the Rockwool Foundation Research Unit on the basis of register information from Statistics Denmark.

The table shows how the level of education depended on various other factors. It indicates the degree of certainty that there were links between the various factors and the level of education; significance at the 1% level indicates that it is statistically virtually certain that there was a connection; significance at the 5% level indicates a fair degree of certainty, while significance at the 10% level indicates that there is a connection, but that it is relatively weak.

Age had significance for the probability that men had education above the level of obligatory schooling, but it was not significant for women. In the case of men, the probability increased with age up until a certain level.

Residence in Denmark in large or small towns or in rural areas had no significance, either for men or for women. This variable was included in the analysis in order to see whether residence in an area with few or many educational institutions had any bearing on decisions to supplement education in Denmark.

In the case of men, the probability of having an educational level above that of obligatory schooling was greatest among those coming from Poland, Iran, the former Yugoslavia or Somalia. There was a significant difference in this respect between immigrants from these four countries and those coming from Vietnam, but this was not the case for immigrants from Lebanon, Pakistan or Turkey. In the case of women, having Poland or the former Yugoslavia as the country of origin had a strong, positive effect on the probability of having a level of education above that of obligatory schooling; women immigrating from Iran and Lebanon were also more likely to have a higher level of education.

The education level and the employment history of parents are known to be of significance for their children's educational opportunities and choices. This effect, measured in this study by taking into account the father's work and level of education, is also observable among immigrants; in this model, however, the effect was only evident in the case of men, which may indicate that different traditions regarding the education of women were more important than their home background. The effect of this variable was that the more years of education the father had, the greater the probability that the interviewee had an education himself or herself. With respect to work background, it made a significant difference for men to come from a family where the father was employed as a white-collar worker or a craftsman, or if the father was self-employed in a sector other than in farming or fishing. For women, there was a significant difference in the case of those who came from families where the father was a white-collar worker, though the link was weaker than for men.

The basis on which a residence permit had been granted was relevant for both sexes, though the correlation was especially clear for men: those who had immigrated as refugees were more likely to have an education than other groups.

It made no significant difference in the case of men whether they had been employed in their country of origin, but for women there was a strong negative effect on the probability of having an education if they had been housewives or worked at home in their country of origin.

Religion played a certain role for both sexes, in that strong associations with religious groups had a negative effect on the probability of having an education above the level of obligatory schooling.

The length of the period of residence in Denmark had a weak significant effect for men, in that the probability of having a higher level of education was greater for those who had been in the country for 11-15 years. This may be an indication of a tendency to take courses of education in Denmark. There was no corresponding significant effect for women.

Overall, a picture emerges of a very heterogeneous group in which country of origin and varying traditions regarding women's education and work appear to have a strong impact.

3.1.5. Danish language proficiency skills among non-Western immigrants and second generation immigrants

As mentioned previously, the survey included a number of questions on Danish language courses taken, and on respondents' own evaluations of their level of language proficiency both in general and in specific situations. Since all the immigrants in the survey had been legally resident in Denmark for at least two years, they had all had the opportunity to acquire at least some knowledge of Danish.

Table 3.4 presents a very general picture of the respondents' evaluations of their own Danish language proficiency.

All respondents, both immigrants and second generation immigrants, were asked the question: "Do you consider your knowledge of Danish to be very good, good, average, poor or very poor?" If for the sake of simplicity we reduce the five categories to four, i.e. fluent, good, average and poor (poor and very poor), we can conclude that around one third of all Poles and Pakistanis estimated their Danish level as fluent. On the other hand, a fifth of Pakistanis said that their Danish was poor or very poor, as opposed to only six percent of Poles. The weakest Danish skills, according to respondents' own evaluations, were to be found among Somalis, of whom only one tenth believed they spoke the language fluently, while a third assessed their skills as poor or very poor.

Around one fifth of immigrants from the former Yugoslavia, Lebanon and Pakistan considered themselves to be in the poor or very poor category. For those from Iran and Poland the figure was less than ten percent, and for immigrants from Somalia and Vietnam it was around thirty percent. If we ignore immigrants from Pakistan, Poland and Somalia, then we find that around one fifth of respondents assessed themselves in the highest category. Fifty to sixty percent of all respondents, or a little more, assessed themselves as having good or average knowledge of Danish.

Table 3.4. In your view, is your level of Danish language proficiency ....? Immigrants and second generation immigrants, distributed by country of origin. Ages 16-70. Percent.

	Former Yugoslavia	Iran	Lebanon	Pakistan	Poland	Somalia	Turkey	Vietnam	All respondents[1]
Very good (fluent)	22	24	25	31	35	11	20	18	23
Good	23	45	24	21	34	27	31	17	28
Average	35	23	30	29	24	32	34	38	32
Poor	14	6	15	16	5	20	11	20	13
Very poor	6	2	6	5	1	11	4	8	5
Total	100	100	100	100	100	100	100	100	100
Number of respondents	476	404	402	424	430	401	548	441	3,526

[1] Weighted in accordance with the proportion of the Danish population of the national group.
Source: Rockwool Foundation Research Unit interview survey conducted in 1999 among immigrants and second generation immigrants in Denmark.

This project had a new feature, in that regardless of the language used for the interview, the conversation was *always* started in Danish. The interviewer thus had the opportunity to evaluate the respondent's Danish skills on a scale. A comparison of the two evaluations suggested – as previous research in the area also indicated – that there was a certain tendency for respondents to overestimate their knowledge. In 60% of the interviews there was agreement between the responses shown in Table 3.4 and the interviewers' assessments. In 24% of the interviews the respondent assessed his or her Danish proficiency one category higher than did the interviewer, and in 4% of cases, two or more categories higher. Some respondents placed their Danish skills in a lower category than did the interviewer: in 11% of cases, one category lower, and in 2% of cases, two or more categories lower. Using the respondents' evaluations as the basis for analysis thus meant that there was a certain degree of overevaluation. It should also be mentioned, though without placing too much emphasis on the point, that half of the respondents who assessed their knowledge of Danish as "fluent" nevertheless asked that the interview be conducted in another language.

As mentioned in the introduction, it can be assumed that immigrants who came to Denmark as children have had greater opportunities to acquire Danish language skills than those who came to the country at a later age, while second generation immigrants, who were born in Denmark, can be assumed to have the best level of knowledge of the language of the three groups.

To check these assumptions, the responses in Table 3.4 were divided up according to the three groups; the results were as predicted. Irrespective of whether the analysis was based on respondents' own evaluations or those of the interviewers, there were few among the second generation immigrants and those who had arrived as children who had a poor knowledge of Danish (maximum 5-6%). The only exception was for immigrants from Turkey who arrived aged 12 or under; 14% of these respondents were categorised by the interviewers as speaking poor Danish, though only 4% placed themselves in this category.

In virtually all cases, a division of the responses in Table 3.4 according to gender revealed a lower assessment for women than for men, according to both respondents' and interviewers' assessments.

The following section seeks to elucidate the factors of particular significance for knowledge of Danish among those who arrived in the country aged 13 or older. As with the analysis of the educational level of the same group, the analysis was based on logistical regression. The dependent variable was assigned the value 1 if the respondent had fluent, good or average skill in speaking Danish, and 0 in the case of poor or very poor skills. The measure was a combination of the responses to how the interviewees assessed their Danish skills in five specific situations, for example in understanding the news or debates on TV or in expressing their views at a meeting. The analyses were made separately for men and women, because their Danish language skills were found to be at different levels.

Table 3.5 shows the explanatory variables included in the analyses. Variables above the dotted line relate to situations before and in connection with immigration, while variables below the line relate to the period in Denmark. In the case of the first group of variables there is no problem of causality, but in the second group of variables it is sometimes difficult to assess whether it is the language skill that affects the variable, or the reverse.

Explanations of why men and women had good or poor Danish language proficiency would appear to lie in part in different places, but there were also common trends.

The countries can be divided into two groups; it was particularly immigrants from Pakistan, Turkey and Vietnam who had difficulty with Danish. In general, there was a positive effect on the probability of having fluent, good or average Danish skills if a person had been a student or apprentice in his or her country of origin. This is a factor which could be expected to some extent to capture an effect of age at immigration, but which would primarily have meant that these people were used to studying.

For men, there was also a positive effect, all other things being equal, of having completed a high school education before immigration.

Table 3.5. Significant factors for level of Danish language proficiency for immigrants aged at least 13 on arrival in Denmark. Ages 16-70.

	Men	Women
Factors relating to the period before and in connection with immigration to Denmark		
Country of origin	***	***
Foreign education	***	Not significant
Primary occupation in country of origin	***	***
Basis for granting of residence permit	Not significant	Not significant
Age at time of immigration	***	***
Period in Denmark		
Length of residence	***	**
Single/married to another immigrant/married to a Dane	Not significant	**
Many/few immigrants resident in the neighbourhood	Not significant	***
Health	***	Not significant
Primary employment in Denmark	***	***
Danish language classes	Not significant	***
Danish education	***	***
Main language spoken in the home	***	***
Associates with Danes	Not significant	***
Has raised level of education in Denmark	Not significant	**

Note: Significant at *** = the 1% level, ** = the 5% level, * = the 10% level.
Source: Rockwool Foundation Research Unit interview survey conducted in 1999 among immigrants and second generation immigrants in Denmark.

There were a variety of factors related to the time spent in Denmark that had an effect on the Danish language proficiency of men and women. For women, it was of significance in the model if they associated with Danes, had taken Danish language courses, or lived in a neighbourhood with many or few other immigrants. However, this is also a good example of causality that could operate in both directions. If it is not a random matter where one lives or whom one speaks to, then the correlation detected here may actually be the result of certain factors (e.g. motivation and preferences) that may find expression in choice of place of residence and circle of acquaintances. In other words, it might be that living in the same place and participating in the same activities would not have the same effect on language proficiency for other people if factors such as motivation were different. These factors had no significant effect for men, for whom the most significant factors were to have taken a course of education in Denmark, to be in employment or a student, and to be in good health. For women, taking a course of education in Denmark and connection to the labour market were also of significance.

This does not necessarily mean that taking Danish language courses was of no importance for men. However, the effects of taking language courses may be obscured by the fact that those immigrants who acquire a certain level of Danish language proficiency, take courses of study in Denmark or otherwise use their professional qualifications are more likely than others to be able to obtain employment or be accepted on a course of study, and subsequently further improve their knowledge of Danish; and men do this more frequently than women.

With the reservations mentioned with regard to causality, it nevertheless appears on the basis of the analysis that it is important for Danish language skills whether immigrants participate in the life of the community in one way or another; whether they associate with speakers of Danish in everyday life is similarly important. Since having knowledge of Danish to a certain level has an effect on the chances of obtaining employment, it can be said that the effects of being in work or studying are to further improve Danish skills. For those women who are not active on the labour market, it is of significance whether they associate with speakers of Danish in their daily lives in some other way.

Length of residence in Denmark and age at time of immigration play a role for both sexes, and naturally the question of whether Danish is spoken in the home is also important.

3.2. The 2001 study

This section seeks to elucidate developments in the levels of education and Danish language proficiency among immigrants and second generation immigrants from the eight nationalities on the basis of the interview surveys of 1999 and 2001.

While in both surveys the interview was the only source of information about Danish language skills, in connection with the 2001 study it was also possible to obtain information about any foreign education from the registers at Statistics Denmark (see Larsen 2002). However, only around half of this information about education was based on actual reports; the remainder was based on estimates. A comparison at the individual level regarding information about foreign education in the statistical registers and in the interview surveys suggests that it was the more highly educated who were more likely to have submitted information about their qualifications to Statistics Denmark; others tended not to have reacted to the request to do so. Where the data used for the register were based on responses from the individuals concerned, the proportions of immigrants with further or higher education were more or less identical overall across the two surveys, even if there were discrepancies for some individuals. When the information about education taken from the statistical records was based on estimates, however, there was a greater difference between the surveys and the register data; and generally speaking, the level of education recorded in the register statistics was higher than that recorded in the interviews for the same individuals. Where the register records were based on actual responses, the information tallied at the individual level to a reasonable degree; that is to say, the two sources corresponded in 70-75% of cases. The figure was rather lower when the information was based on estimates. In order to allow comparisons with the 1999 survey, then, the 2001 survey also used responses regarding foreign education from the interview survey only.

Even though the level of education among non-Western immigrants and second generation immigrants remained lower than that of Danes – with large differences from one country of origin to another – an increase from 1999 to 2001 can be detected in the proportion of men with further or higher education. However, the increased proportion with further or higher education is not an indication that the level of education among young immigrants and second generation immigrants was approaching that of native Danes in 2001. The difference between Danes, and immigrants and second generation immigrants was larger in 2001 for those in the 16-35 age bracket than for older people.

The question of how much of the difference in education between Danes on the one hand and immigrants and second generation immigrants on the other was due to the best educated of the immigrants and second generation immigrants emigrating because of difficulty in finding suitable employment can be elucidated by examining whether those with further or higher education from Denmark were more likely to emigrate than Danes.

This appears not to have been the case. Both Danes and non-Western immigrants and second generation immigrants with further or higher education taken in Denmark were more likely to emigrate – especially for short periods – than others in their respective groups.

Knowledge of Danish among immigrants and second generation immigrants was found to be better in the 2001 survey than in the 1999 survey. This was the case regardless of whether the comparison was made on the basis of the interviewees' own assessments or those of the interviewers. The trend was most evident among those immigrants who had come to Denmark as children (aged 12 or under) and among second generation immigrants. The proportion of immigrants with poor Danish language skills found in the 1999 survey had almost completely disappeared in the 2001 survey, and the proportion with only moderately good Danish proficiency had grown smaller. The interviewers' assessments of levels of knowledge of Danish in 2001 are shown in Table 3.6.

Table 3.6. Interviewers' assessments of Danish language proficiency of immigrants and second generation immigrants, distributed by gender. 2001. Ages 16-70. Percent.

	Fluent	Good	Average	Poor	Total
Men					
All immigrants and 2nd gen. immigrants	28	29	26	16	100
Immigrants aged 13 or over on arrival in Denmark	15	31	33	21	100
Immigrants aged 12 or under on arrival in Denmark	62	29	7	2	100
2nd gen. immigrants	88	10	2	0	100
Women					
All immigrants and 2nd gen. immigrants	28	21	25	25	100
Immigrants aged 13 or over on arrival in Denmark	13	23	31	32	100
Immigrants aged 12 or under on arrival in Denmark	69	22	8	2	100
2nd gen. immigrants	88	9	2	1	100

Note: Weighted in accordance with the proportion of the Danish population of the national group.
Source: Calculations made by the Rockwool Foundation Research Unit on the basis of an interview survey in 2001 of immigrants and second generation immigrants in Denmark.

In all, more than 95% of the second generation immigrants and 90% of immigrants who came to Denmark as children had good or very good (fluent) Danish language skills. In contrast, half or less of the immigrants who arrived aged 13 or over had acquired these levels of Danish proficiency, with women having the least good command of the language.

3.3. The 2004 study

After several years of research into the integration of immigrants into the Danish labour market, the Rockwool Foundation decided in 2004 to start a project (reported in Tranæs 2008) that would focus exclusively on the use of the Danish education system by young non-Western immigrants and second generation immigrants. This section presents some results from the section of the project that was based on the use of statistics from Danish registers for 1997 and 2007.

While 36% of Danes aged 20-24 were registered on courses of education in 1997, the corresponding figures were 33% for second generation immigrants and 25% for immigrants who had been aged 0-14 on arrival. Ten years later, these proportions had risen to 46% for Danes, 41% for second generation immigrants and 39% for immigrants aged 0-14 on arrival. Thus the proportions of immigrants and second generation immigrants undergoing education remained significantly lower than the proportion of Danes, but the immigrants had closed the gap to some extent.

In 2007 there were also larger proportions of both Danes and immigrants who had completed a course of education that qualified them for a specific job; the increase was again greater among immigrants. In 1997, 66% of 30-year-old Danes had completed a course of education that qualified them for a job, whereas the proportion was only 23% among 30-year-old immigrants (aged 0-14 on arrival). In 2007 these figures had increased to 74% and 36% respectively, with 46% of 30-year-old second generation immigrants having completed such a course.

The differences between the groups were still very large, which is perhaps not so surprising. The parents of the young Danes had on average much stronger educational and professional backgrounds than the parents of the young immigrants and second generation immigrants, and parental background has a significant effect on children's education. If – as far as is possible – a comparison is made between young Danes and young immigrants with the same parental backgrounds, the probability of being registered on a course is in many cases greater for the first or second generation immigrants than for the Danes; and for the probability that 30-year-olds will have completed a course of education that gives a work qualification, the immigrants are clearly catching up with the Danes.

To the extent that the parents of immigrants and second generation immigrants come to resemble the parents of Danes, then, it might be expected that the patterns of education for these groups will also come to resemble those of Danes; but as yet this is far from being the case. At present there are few people among the two groups with comparable parental backgrounds; and the analysis suggests that as long as there are large differences between the two groups in terms of their social characteristics, there will also continue to be differences between them in their patterns of education as well – even though there are indications that the immigrants are better able to break away from their social inheritance than Danes.

3.4. Summary

This chapter has focused on the two variables, education and Danish language proficiency, which might be expected to be of crucial importance in determining the opportunities which immigrants and second generation immigrants have for participating in Danish society. Such participation includes integration into the labour market, which is the main theme of the studies described in this book.

The 1999 study was based on information regarding levels of foreign education and Danish language proficiency obtained solely via the interview survey.

Immigrants who came to Denmark as children aged 13 or over, or as adults, were asked about their level of education at the time of immigration and it emerged that it was only among immigrants from the former Yugoslavia, Iran and Poland that around half or more had completed a course of education before coming to Denmark. The smallest proportions were amongst immigrants from Pakistan, Somalia and Turkey, and it was these groups which also had the largest proportions – around 15% – with no formal education at all.

By combining the interview responses from the 1999 survey regarding education in immigrants' countries of origin with register information on education taken in Denmark, it was possible to build up an overall picture of immigrants' education. There were relatively more immigrants than Danes who only had education at the level of obligatory schooling, while the opposite was the case for vocational and higher education. Immigrants from the "old" immigrant source countries Turkey and Pakistan were particularly notable for their lack of vocational and higher education.

To conclude the analysis of the overall level of education, logistic regressions were used to elucidate the factors which had special significance for determining whether immigrants who had arrived in Denmark aged 13 or over had taken Danish and/or foreign courses of education. It was found, for example, that in addition to country of origin, the reason for granting a residence permit in Denmark was a significant factor for both sexes. Religion played a certain role for both sexes, in that strong associations with religious groups had a negative effect on the probability of having an education above the level of obligatory schooling.

With regard to Danish language skills, around one third of all Poles and Pakistanis assessed themselves as speaking fluent Danish. The poorest Danish language skills, as assessed by the respondents themselves, were among Somalis, of whom only one tenth thought that they spoke the language fluently.

The interview surveys were the only source of information on Danish language proficiency for both the 1999 and 2001 studies, but in connection with the 2001 study it was also possible to obtain register information from Statistics Denmark relating to foreign courses of education.

Knowledge of Danish among immigrants and second generation immigrants was found to be better in the 2001 survey than in the 1999 survey. This trend was most marked among those immigrants who had come to Denmark as children (aged 12 or under) and among second generation immigrants. The proportions of these groups having poor Danish language proficiency found in the 1999 survey had almost completely disappeared in the 2001 survey, and the proportions with only moderately good Danish proficiency had grown smaller.

In 2008 the Rockwool Foundation Research Unit published the results of a study of young non-Western immigrants' and second generation immigrants' use of the Danish educational system, based on Danish register statistics for the years 1997 and 2007.

While 36% of Danes aged 20-24 were registered on courses of education in 1997, the corresponding figures were 33% for second generation immigrants and 25% for immigrants who had been aged 0-14 on arrival. Ten years later, these proportions had risen to 46% for Danes, 41% for second generation immigrants and 39% for immigrants aged 0-14 on arrival.

In 1997, 66% of 30-year-old Danes had completed a course of education that qualified them for a job, whereas the proportion was only 23% among 30-year-old immigrants (aged 0-14 on arrival). In 2007 these figures had increased to 74% and 36% respectively, with 46% of 30-year-old second generation immigrants having completed such a course.

References

Blom, Svein and Agnes Aall Ritland. 1997. "Levekår blant ikke-vestlige-innvandrere", in Kåre Vassenden (ed.), *Invandrere i Norge. Hvem er de, hva gjør de og hvordan lever de?, Statistiske analyser* 20. Oslo/Kongsvinger: Statistisk sentralbyrå, 169-89.

Blom, Svein. 1998. *Levekår blant ikke-vestlige innvandrere i Norge, Rapporter* 1998:16. Oslo/Kongsvinger: Statistisk Sentralbyrå.

Hvidtfeldt, Camilla and Marie Louise Schultz-Nielsen. 2008. "Unge indvandreres brug af det danske uddannelsessystem", in Torben Tranæs (ed.), *Indvandrerne og det danske uddannelsessystem.* Copenhagen: Gyldendal.

Larsen, Claus. 2000. "Uddannelse og danskkundskaber", in Gunnar Viby Mogensen and Poul Chr. Matthiessen (eds), *Integration i Danmark omkring årtusindeskiftet*. Aarhus: Aarhus University Press, 48-95.

Larsen, Claus. 2002. "Uddannelse og danskkundskaber", in Gunnar Viby Mogensen and Poul Chr. Matthiessen (eds), *Indvandrerne og arbejdsmarkedet*. Copenhagen: Spektrum, 160-197.

4. Crime among immigrants

4.1. Introduction

Crime is an aspect of life, just like education, work, sickness and health, social and economic factors, and housing. Some of these aspects of life are discussed in the other chapters of this book. The relationship of crime to employment is perhaps less clear than is the case with some other factors such as education, but there is a link nevertheless, as is shown in Chapter 5. The exact direction of causality in this link may be difficult to determine. Just as it may be the case that a person engages in criminal activity because he or she cannot get a job, so conversely it may be the case that a person has difficulty in getting a job because he or she engages in criminal activity; employers may demand a clean criminal record in the same way as they may require a suitable educational background. For this reason, crime (measured in terms of convictions leading to custodial sentences within the previous five years) is also considered in Chapter 5 among the factors of significance for integration into the labour market.

This chapter seeks to evaluate the levels and patterns of crime among immigrants and second generation immigrants in comparison with those of Danes. It is based on Larsen (2000). Differences with respect to gender, age, residence and various other background factors are taken into account in these comparisons. To the extent that the data material allows it, comparisons are also made within the population of immigrants and second generation immigrants. The variable used is the crime rate, i.e. the size of the proportion of the various population groups recorded as having committed one or more offences. The crime rate used as a measure in this chapter is an average figure for persons aged 16-70 on 1 January in any year of the period 1993-1998. This means that it is impossible to capture the nuances that might exist in terms of variation in the rate from year to year, but on the other hand it does also mean that the results are based on a large number of individuals.

Only people with Danish residence permits are included in the analyses. Crime committed by tourists, by people who are only in Denmark for a short period in connection with their work or for other reasons, or by asylum seekers is thus not included. The types of crime analysed were violations of the criminal law (e.g. assault or theft), breaches of the traffic laws, and breaches of various special laws (e.g. the laws concerning euphoric substances or weapons). The figures must always be interpreted with reservations for the amount of unreported crime, for the degree of likelihood of crimes being solved, etc.

4.2. Convictions 1993-1998

Table 4.1 shows that the level of crime was lower among women than among men for immigrants, second generation immigrants and Danes. It also shows that the crime rate declined with increasing age. A separation of populations into Western and non-Western countries of origin shows that significant proportions of the populations of young male second generation immigrants in particular, but also immigrants from non-Western countries, were recorded as having committed one or more violations of the criminal, traffic or other special laws.

Table 4.1. Crime rates for men and women with one or more convictions for violation of the criminal, traffic or other special laws, shown by age group and immigrant status. Averages over the period 1993-1998. Percent.

Age	Immigrants from:		Descendants from:		Danes[3]
	Non-Western countries[1]	Western countries[2]	Non-Western countries[1]	Western countries[2]	
---------- Men ----------					
16-19	13.9	6.7	17.3	11.2	7.6
20-29	11.7	3.9	18.5	7.6	8.0
30-39	9.1	5.1	6.4	7.4	6.4
40-49	6.8	4.6	..	5.2	4.1
50-59	4.0	3.4	..	..	3.0
60-70	1.7	1.4	..	..	1.3
---------- Women ----------					
16-19	2.2	..	2.3	..	1.2
20-29	2.0	1.1	3.0	..	1.4
30-39	2.0	1.7	..	..	1.4
40-49	1.6	1.4	..	..	0.9
50-59	1.3	0.9	..	..	0.7
60-70	0.8	0.5	..	..	0.3

Note: Excluding cases resulting in acquittals or withdrawals of prosecution at trial under the Danish Criminal Justice Act §721 section 1 clauses 2 and 3.
"..": = Few or no observations
[1] Sum total of all non-Western immigrants and second generation immigrants as of 1 July 1998.
[2] A representative sample of 25% of Western immigrants and second generation immigrants as of 1 July 1998. [3] A representative sample of 2% of the population of Denmark as of 1 July 1998, excluding immigrants and second generation immigrants.
Source: Own calculations on the basis of register data from Statistics Denmark.

The table shows that for the same genders and age ranges there were systematic differences between the groups with respect to the rate of crime. For example, whereas male Danes aged 16-29 displayed a crime rate of around 8%, the rates for non-Western immigrants and non-Western second generation immigrants in the same age group were 12-14% and 17-19% respectively. In contrast, immigrant and second generation immigrant groups from Western countries had crime rates which roughly paralleled those of Danes of the same age, except in the case of young people aged 16-19.

In addition to gender and age, place of residence also has significance for the crime rate. Table 4.2 substantially confirms the existence of a positive correlation between density of population and crime, especially with respect to non-Western second generation immigrants. The tendency is not completely clear-cut, however, in that the crime rate was greater in medium-sized local authorities – i.e. those with over 10,000 inhabitants – than it was in the five largest local authorities outside the Greater Copenhagen area.

Table 4.2. Crime rates for men and women with one or more convictions for violation of the criminal, traffic or other special laws, shown by degree of urbanisation of place of residence and by immigrant status. Averages over the period 1993-1998. Percent.

Local authority	Immigrants from:		Descendants from:		Danes[3]
	Non-Western countries[1]	Western countries[2]	Non-Western countries[1]	Western countries[2]	
	Men				
Copenhagen, Frederiksberg	9.8	3.8	19.1	7.4	5.7
Remainder of Greater Copenhagen	9.0	3.5	16.0	5.9	4.9
Odense, Esbjerg, Randers, Aarhus, Aalborg	8.3	4.0	13.0	4.6	4.9
Medium-sized towns, >10,000 inhabitants	8.5	4.5	16.4	8.1	5.1
Others	6.8	4.7	12.1	7.9	5.1
	Women				
Copenhagen, Frederiksberg	2.0	1.0	2.9	..	1.2
Remainder of Greater Copenhagen	1.7	1.3	2.2	..	1.0
Odense, Esbjerg, Randers, Aarhus, Aalborg	1.8	1.0	2.2	..	0.9
Medium-sized towns, >10,000 inhabitants	1.9	1.2	2.4	..	1.0
Others	1.6	1.1	..	..	1.0

Notes and source: See table 4.1.

The fact that a significant proportion of non-Western second generation immigrants live in the Greater Copenhagen area in itself increases the average level of crime committed by that group. However, the overall pattern of crime seen in Table 4.1 is again found in areas with the same degree of urbanisation.

There were differences in the relative distributions of the various types of crime among the different groups. Amongst Danes, the most frequently recorded crimes were traffic violations, while violations of the criminal law predominated among non-Western second generation immigrants. This applied for both men and women. Among non-Western immigrants in total there were roughly the same numbers who were convicted of criminal law and traffic offences, but violations of the criminal code were predominant among women. The picture for Western second generation immigrants – and even more so, that for immigrants – closely resembled that for Danes. The picture is of course affected to a certain extent by differences in the age distribution of the groups.

The tables above were based on average rates of crime over the period 1993-1998, but the data also allow the possibility of tracking individuals throughout the period. Table 4.3 tracks individuals who were in the population

Table 4.3. Men and women in the population as of 1 January 1993 having one or more convictions for violation of the criminal, traffic or other special laws in the period 1993-1998, shown by age and immigrant status. Percent.

Age at 1 January 1993	Immigrants from:		Descendants from:		Danes[3]
	Non-Western countries[1]	Western countries[2]	Non-Western countries[1]	Western countries[2]	
------- Men -------					
16-19	43.3	10.1	51.5	28.2	30.4
20-29	38.3	14.5	39.8	25.9	28.6
30-39	31.6	20.4	23.6	21.1	23.5
40-49	24.6	17.3	..	18.9	17.6
50-59	14.8	14.0	..	26.3	11.7
60-70	7.8	6.8	..	..	6.2
------- Women -------					
16-19	9.7	3.4	11.0	9.5	6.0
20-29	9.4	4.5	13.9	10.2	6.9
30-39	8.8	7.3	12.9	4.7	6.3
40-49	6.9	5.5	..	..	4.5
50-59	5.9	3.9	..	..	2.7
60-70	3.6	3.1	..	..	1.7

Notes and source: See table 4.1.

and aged 16-65 on January 1 1993 throughout the period to 1998, when they would thus have been aged 21-70. Age has been selected as the criterion for grouping the populations, since one of the criteria for being included in the population on which the analysis is constructed is that an individual had to be between the ages of 16 and 70 in one of the years.

As is evident from the table, such an analysis reveals some rather high percentages. This is true not only for immigrants and second generation immigrants, but also for Danes. Of Danish men who were aged 16-29 at the beginning of the period, there were around 30% who were recorded as having one or more violations of the criminal, traffic or other special laws in the period 1993-1998. For male non-Western immigrants and non-Western second generation immigrants the corresponding figures were 38-43% and 40-52% respectively. Male second generation immigrants from Western countries displayed around the same level of crime as male Danes, while the level was slightly lower among immigrants from the same countries.

For women, too, the largest proportions were found among the non-Western immigrants and second generation immigrants, but as with all the women in the study these were at significantly lower levels than was the case for men. In the younger age groups the figures were lowest for immigrants from Western countries with levels around 3-5%, while female Danes were at a level around 6-7% and the others between 9% and 14%.

If we consider only breaches of the criminal law, the picture is as shown in Table 4.4. The greatest proportion of people with convictions was among young (ages 16 to 29) male second generation immigrants and non-Western immigrants; between a fifth and a third of these groups were recorded as having committed one or more crimes, whereas the figures for young Danes were between 7% and 13%. The rate among male Western immigrants was significantly lower. Among women, non-Western immigrants and second generation immigrants had a maximum rate of around 6-7% in the youngest age groups, while Danes and Western immigrants and second generation immigrants in these youngest groups were at a level of around 2-5%.

Taking an average over the period, we find that non-Western immigrants and second generation immigrants who had committed offences were the most likely to be punished with custodial sentences. The figure for this group was around 30%, as opposed to 22-23% for offenders among male Danes and male immigrants and second generation immigrants from Western countries. Among women who broke the criminal law, the proportion sent to prison was around 15-17%.

In order to analyse any connection between citizenship and crime rate, the sample populations were divided into those with Danish citizenship and those with foreign citizenship. There was a significant correlation between crime and citizenship in the case of the group with the highest crime rate, namely males from non-Western backgrounds. Among men with Danish citizenship in this group, an average of 7.7% were recorded as being convicted of breaches of criminal, traffic or other special laws, whereas the figure for those with foreign nationalities was 9.8%. For the other groups, the difference was just 0.1 of a percentage point.

Table 4.4. Men and women in the population as of January 1 1993 having one or more convictions for violation of the criminal law in the period 1993-1998, shown by age and immigrant status. Percent.

Age at 1 January 1993	Immigrants from:		Descendants from:		Danes[3]
	Non-Western countries[1]	Western countries[2]	Non-Western countries[1]	Western countries[2]	
Men					
16-19	27.2	5.9	34.0	19.2	12.8
20-29	19.0	5.4	19.8	8.4	7.3
30-39	15.2	5.7	6.1	7.5	4.9
40-49	9.3	4.5	..	..	3.1
50-59	6.3	2.1	..	..	1.8
60-70	4.7	..	..	..	1.6
Women					
16-19	7.0	2.6	6.2	4.8	2.7
20-29	6.6	1.5	6.9	4.1	2.2
30-39	5.9	2.4	5.0	..	1.6
40-49	4.3	2.1	..	..	1.4
50-59	4.2	2.0	..	..	0.8
60-70	3.2	1.5	..	..	1.0

Notes and source: See table 4.1.

An analysis of the patterns of crime for 2007 (Danmarks Statistik 2008) confirms in all significant respects the results of the studies that are presented in this chapter. Even after correction for age and socioeconomic status, immigrants and second generation immigrants from non-Western countries emerged in the analysis of the 2007 figures with a higher level of breaches of the criminal law than Danes or immigrants and second generation immigrants of Western origin.

4.3. Summary

This chapter presented an analysis of the levels and patterns of crime among immigrants and second generation immigrants compared with those of Danes. The variable used was the crime rate, i.e. the size of the proportion of the various population groups recorded as having committed one or more offences. The crime rate was an average figure based on the records for persons aged 16-70 on January 1 in each year of the period 1993-1998. Only people with the right of residence in Denmark were included in the analyses.

The crime rate was lower among women than among men in all groups – immigrants, second generation immigrants, and Danes – and it also decreased (for all groups) with increasing age. A separation of populations into Western and non-Western countries of origin showed that significant proportions of the populations of young male second generation immigrants in particular, but also immigrants from non-Western countries, were recorded as having committed one or more violations of the criminal, traffic or other special laws.

There were differences in the relative distribution of the various types of crime among the different groups. Amongst Danes, the most frequently recorded crimes were traffic violations, while violations of the criminal law predominated among non-Western second generation immigrants. This applied for both men and women. Among non-Western immigrants in total there were roughly the same numbers who were convicted of criminal law and traffic offences, but violations of the criminal code predominated among women. The picture for Western second generation immigrants – and even more so, that for immigrants – closely resembled that for Danes.

The statistics also made possible the tracking of individuals throughout the period 1993-1998. Of Danish men who were aged 16-29 at the beginning of the period, there were around 30% who were recorded as having one or more violations of the criminal, traffic or other special laws in the period 1993-1998. For male non-Western immigrants and non-Western second generation immigrants the corresponding figures were 38-43% and 40-52% respectively. Male second generation immigrants from Western countries displayed around the same level of crime as male Danes, while the level was slightly lower among immigrants from the same countries.

Among men from non-Western countries with Danish citizenship, an average of 7.7% were recorded in the period 1993-1998 as having been convicted of breaches of criminal, traffic or special laws, whereas the figure for those with foreign citizenship was 9.8%. For the other groups, the difference was just 0.1 of a percentage point.

An analysis of the patterns of crime for 2007 confirms in all significant respects the results of the studies that are presented in this chapter.

References

Danmarks Statistik. 2008. *Indvandrerne i Danmark 2008.* Copenhagen.

Larsen, Claus. 2000. "Kriminalitet", in Gunnar Viby Mogensen and Poul Chr. Matthiessen (eds), *Integration i Danmark omkring årtusindeskiftet.* Aarhus: Aarhus University Press, 252-278.

5. Labour market conditions

5.1. Introduction

This chapter discusses the integration of immigrants and second generation immigrants into the Danish labour market. The analyses are based on the work of Shultz-Nielsen 2000 and 2002, updated to 2007. The reason for giving special prominence to this topic is that employment is a key factor for the conditions of life of immigrants and second generation immigrants and for their overall integration into Danish society. In the first place, work provides an income that enables the recipient to be self-supporting. Employment also gives a person a sense of being useful, as well as providing a social network outside the family that can increase an immigrant's knowledge of Danish society and the Danish language. The integration of immigrants and second generation immigrants into the Danish labour market is important not only for the individuals concerned, but also for Danish society as a whole. The fewer people there are receiving transfer incomes and the more there are in employment, the more public resources there are available for other purposes. These economic effects of the status of immigrants in the labour market are presented in Chapter 7.

Integration into the labour market is taken in the following to mean being in employment. On the basis of this definition, there are of course a number of Danes who are not integrated into the labour market. Consequently, comparisons are made in the next section of the employment situations of immigrants and Danes; trends in the employment of both are examined for the period 1985 to 2007. The development is analysed separately for both Western and non-Western immigrants, and for second generation immigrants in both categories. There is also a special focus on some of the largest groups of non-Western immigrants in Denmark.

5.2. Trends in employment 1985-2007

This section is based on the rate of employment for persons aged 16-66, measured as the number of people in employment proportional to the number of people in this age range. The analyses are based on using register data for all Western and non-Western immigrants and second generation immigrants, and for Danes. The definitions of these terms are given in Chapter 1.

Among both immigrants and Danes in this age group there are people without work who may have been active previously on the labour market for many years, but who have now taken early retirement or are claiming incapacity benefit. Similarly, there will be a number of students who will eventually qualify for work as a result of their current courses of education. It would seem reasonable to ignore these categories of people, and limit the population studied to those actually in the labour force, i.e. people who are employed or who are available for work but unemployed. Doing this ignores a certain amount of hidden unemployment. There are for example immigrants receiving welfare benefits who have not yet registered with the employment service as being unemployed, because they are attending Danish classes or for some similar reason. It also ignores the fact that the existence of a large proportion of the population claiming incapacity benefits or early retirement benefits may be an indication that some people have been forced out of the labour market against their will. Nevertheless, wherever relevant, analyses are presented based solely on members of the labour force, that is to say, people who are either employed or formally registered as unemployed. In addition to the rate of employment, the analyses presented here are based on the level of participation in the labour force, i.e. the proportion in the labour force of all people aged between 16 and 66, and on the rate of unemployment, i.e. the measure of the unemployed as a proportion of the labour force.

Figures 5.1a and 5.1b show the fluctuations in the rate of employment for male and female immigrants and second generation immigrants from both Western and non-Western countries, and for Danes.

The figures show that the rate of employment for both male and female Danes has remained at a high and very stable level in comparison with that of non-Western immigrants in particular. The rate of employment for male Danes, which in general has reflected the business cycle in Denmark, increased from 80% in 1985 to 82% in 1986-88. It then fell during the period up to 1994, when it was only 76%. Since that date the rate has risen, reaching 80% in 2007 after an exceptionally long upswing in the economy.

At the same time, the rate of unemployment for male Danes fell to just 2% in that year. In 1988 unemployment was higher, at a level of 5%, and in the period up to 1994 it rose to 10%, whereafter it fell sharply. The fact that the rate of employment was nevertheless no higher in 2007 than in 1986-88 was due to the level of participation in the labour force being lower in 2007: 82%, as opposed to 86-87% in 1986-88. The reason for this was largely the lower average age of retirement, which had been made possible by the Danish early retirement scheme and the increase in the popularity of private pension schemes.

The rate of employment for Danish women was 13% lower than that for men in 1985. The level generally paralleled that for men thereafter, although with a narrowing of the gap between the two sexes, so that by 2007 the employment level for women had reached 74%. This narrowing was the result of a heavy reduction in the level of unemployment for women combined with a very modest reduction in the level of participation in the labour market.

Figure 5.1a. Rate of employment 1985-2007 among men aged 16-66.

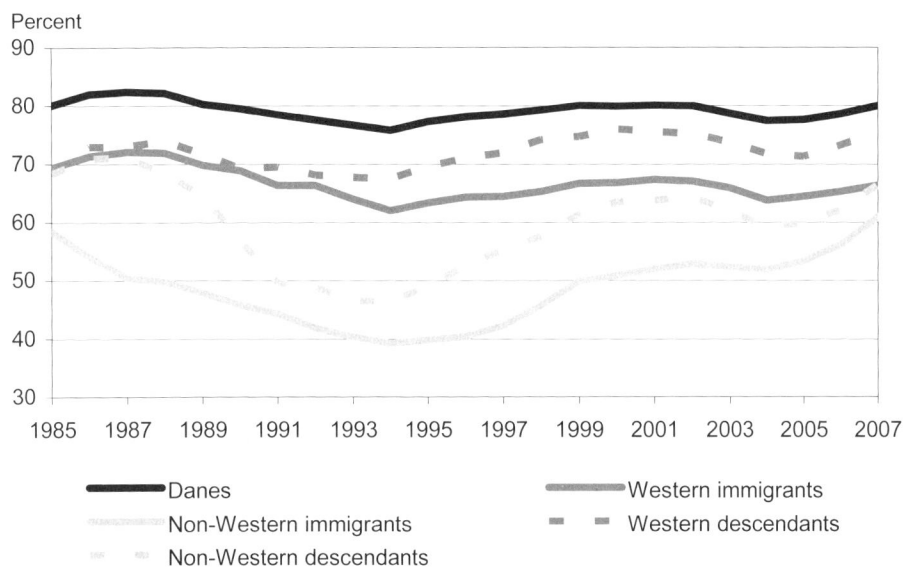

Source: Own calculations based on register data from Statistics Denmark.
Note: The ten new EU member states from Eastern and Southern Europe switched status in 2005 from non-Western to Western, and Romania and Bulgaria switched status from 2007. In the figure, these countries all retain their status as non-Western countries in 2005 and onwards.

Figure 5.1b. Rate of employment 1985-2007 among women aged 16-66.

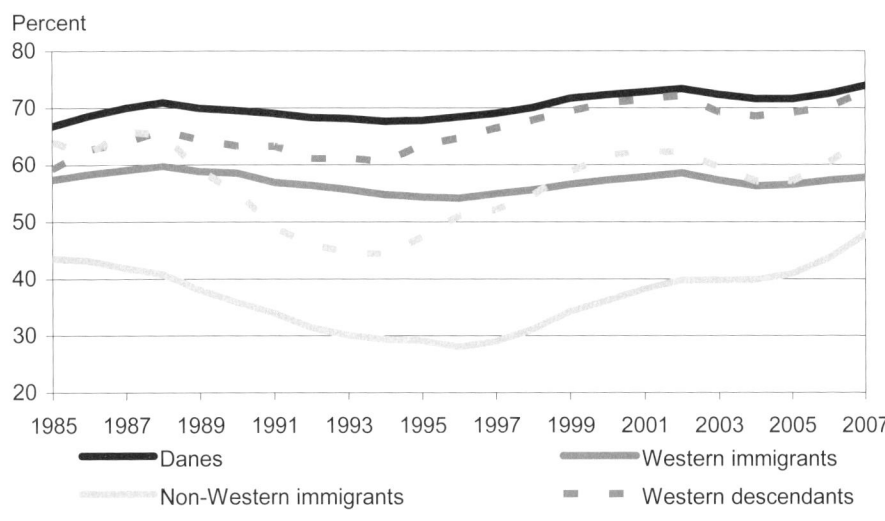

Source: Own calculations based on register data from Statistics Denmark.
Note: The ten new EU member states from Eastern and Southern Europe switched status in 2005 from non-Western to Western, and Romania and Bulgaria switched status from 2007. In the figure, these countries all retain their status as non-Western countries in 2005 and onwards.

The rate of employment for Western immigrants largely followed the trends for Danes, but at a lower level. The difference between the levels of employment for Danes and Western immigrants increased somewhat for both men and women between 1985 and 2007, rising from around 10 to around 15 percentage points. One of the reasons for the change was an increase in the number of students from Western countries.

With a single exception, the rates of employment recorded for both male and female second generation immigrants from Western countries were higher than those for immigrants from the same countries. The second generation immigrants were born in Denmark and thus have stronger ties with the country both linguistically and culturally than immigrants, many of whom arrived in the country as adults, and their higher rates of employment should be viewed in this light. Employment rates for second generation immigrants from Western countries saw a strong rise over the period, so that the level for men in 2007 was only five percentage points lower than that for Danes, as opposed to twelve percentage points in 1985; the corresponding differences for women were one and eight percentage points.

The employment rates for second generation immigrants from non-Western countries fluctuated considerably. The decline in employment rates for both genders from 1987 to 1994 can largely be attributed to a fall in the rate of participation in the labour market, while the subsequent increase was linked to both a rise in participation and a reduction in the rate of unemployment for both male and female second generation immigrants from non-Western countries from 15% and 17% respectively in 1994 to 5% in 2007.

The changes over time in the level of labour market participation by second generation immigrants from non-Western countries is largely the result of a fall in the average age of this group. The proportion of people aged 16-20 rose sharply from the end of the 1980s onward, and it was only some years later that these young people – like others in the same age group – began to participate seriously in the labour market. If a calculation is made of the rate of employment as if the age distribution of second generation immigrants from non-Western countries was the same as that of Danes, then the trends in this rate would very largely parallel those for second generation immigrants from Western countries, albeit at a slightly lower level of employment. In the cases of second generation immigrants from Western countries and both Western and non-Western immigrants, there is no significant change in the trends in the employment rates after standardisation of the age distribution.

Thus, it is not a change in the age distribution that can explain why employment rates for male non-Western immigrants fell so steeply from 58% in 1985 to 39% in 1994 for men and from 44% to 29% for women. By 2007 the rates for both sexes had risen again to 61% and 48% respectively. The business cycle had much to do with the changes; unemployment rates for men rose from 25% in 1985 to 38% in 1994, with a corresponding rise for women from 28% to 39%. By 2007 unemployment rates had fallen to 8% for men and 11% for women. There was a sharp reduction in the level of participation in the labour force for both male and female non-Western immigrants over the course of the period up until the second half of the 1990s, and this reduction was not completely offset by the subsequent rise in the period up to 2007.

The very steep decline in the labour force participation rate was in part due to the fact that many new non-Western immigrants arrived in Denmark during this period, and these newcomers tended to have little or no connection to the labour market at first. It may also have been the case that the most recently arrived immigrants during this period who did seek work were less successful in doing this than those who had arrived earlier. Analyses presented in the next section will cover this point.

As has been mentioned in previous chapters, ten Eastern and Southern European countries joined the EU on 1 May 2004, followed by Romania and Bulgaria in January 2007, and consequently these countries were re-categorised under the definitions used in these Danish studies of immigration from being non-Western to being Western countries. In order to maintain continuity in the analyses, in this chapter the 12 countries have not been counted as Western countries for the years 2005 and onward. However, calculations show that even if these countries were to be counted as Western countries, it would only alter the rate of employment for non-Western immigrants and second generation immigrants by a single percentage point.

Within the group of non-Western countries there are major differences in the rates of employment between the various individual countries, and substantial fluctuations in the rates over time, as can be seen in Table 5.1.

The variations in rates over time are of course linked with the number of new immigrants there were in each national group, since these must generally be expected to have a less strong connection to the labour market than the others.

The rate of employment for people from the former Yugoslavia fell from 59% in 1985 to 33% in 1998; this was due to the large influx of refugees during the period 1991-1993 as a result of the civil war in the region, with the total number of people in the age range 16-66 increasing from just over 8,000 in 1991 to almost 26,000 in 1998. The situation was somewhat similar with respect to people from Lebanon (in reality often stateless Palestinians), of whom the numbers in Denmark increased sharply between 1985 and 1991, with a corresponding decline in the rate of employment. Refugees from Iran, on the other hand, began to arrive in Denmark as early as 1984-85, and this factor is

Table 5.1. Rates of employment for immigrants and second generation immigrants aged 16-66 by country of origin for selected years (1 January).

	1985		1991		1998		2007*	
	%	No.	%	No	%	No.	%	No.
Former Yugoslavia	59	5,703	52	8,097	33	25,913	57	32,353
Iran	19	864	18	7,113	40	9,078	55	11,162
Lebanon	59	236	13	5,552	20	8,941	36	12,609
Pakistan	50	5,463	40	7,284	42	10,730	55	13,721
Poland	54	4,592	50	7,081	55	8,891	67	14,370
Somalia	39	121	14	522	9	6,648	35	8,538
Turkey	48	11,812	40	19,017	44	27,933	59	38,346
Vietnam	36	2,395	33	4,308	47	6,781	66	8,710
Other non-Western countries	56	19,517	45	33,728	43	57,870	55	113,057
Non-Western countries, total	52	50,703	40	92,702	40	162,785	55	252,866
Danes	74	3,301,018	74	3,333,738	75	3,342,217	77	3,294,223

Source: Own calculations based on register data from Statistics Denmark.
* The ten new EU member states as of 1 May 2004 plus Romania and Bulgaria are counted as non-Western countries here.
Note: The employment situation is linked to the start of the year and is calculated on the basis of register information for employment in November of the previous year.

reflected in the rate of employment for this group, which first reached a level of almost 40% in 1998. The greatest number of Somalis arrived in the 1990s, with the result that the rate of employment for this group was still relatively low in 1998.

For Poles, the rate of employment was among the highest of the eight national groups during the period 1985-1998, reflecting the fact that Polish immigrants and second generation immigrants have a relatively high level of participation in the labour market and a low rate of unemployment. The rate of employment was also relatively high among people from Turkey, Pakistan and the former Yugoslavia (in the last case, up until the middle of the 1990s). Guest workers from these countries came to Denmark in the period up until 1973. In 1985, Turks, Pakistanis and Yugoslavs had a rate of participation in the labour market that was only marginally lower than that of Danes; however, a rather higher rate of unemployment meant that their rate of employment was in fact somewhat lower than that for Danes. The proportion of second generation immigrants was also highest for these three groups; second generation immigrants increased the overall rate of employment by a couple of percentage points for their national groups, because, as Figure 5.1 shows, second generation immigrants had a significantly stronger attachment to the labour market than people from the same groups born outside Denmark.

The table shows that all groups benefited from the economic upswing of the first years of the new century, although the rate of employment among immigrants and second generation immigrants from Lebanon and Somalia remained very low.

The total rate of employment was affected by the extent to which the women from the various countries had a connection to the labour market which matched that of the men. In this respect, there remained great differences between the countries even in 2007, as Figure 5.2 shows. While the proportions of men and women in employment were approximately the same for Danes and Poles, there were around 20% more men than women in employment from the former Yugoslavia, Vietnam and Iran, and double the number of men in employment in comparison to women in the case of Somalis and Lebanese. However, for nearly all groups the differences in employment rates between men and women had diminished in 2007 in comparison with the situation in 2001.

Figure 5.2. Ratios of the percentage of men in employment to the percentage of women in employment, by country of origin. 2007.

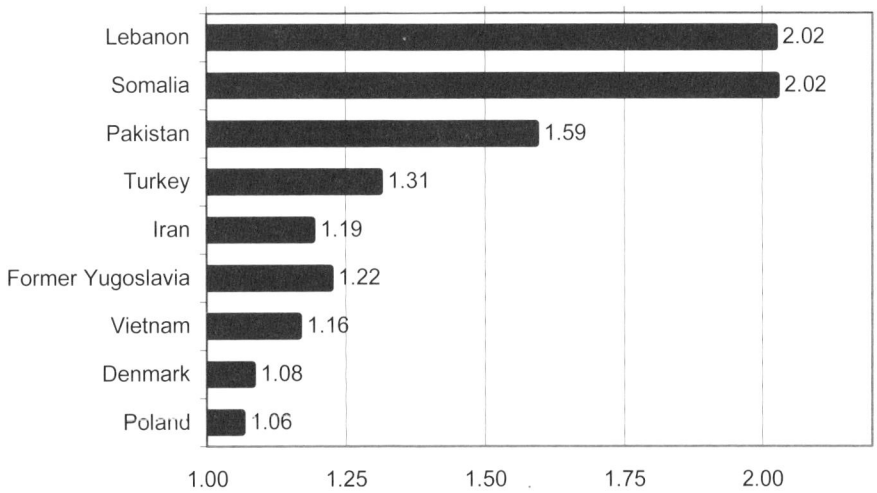

Source: Own calculations based on register data from Statistics Denmark.

5.3. The link between year of immigration and participation in the labour market

It is apparent from the foregoing section that if strength of connection to the labour market is measured in terms of rate of employment, then the connection was relatively weak for non-Western immigrants. It may be difficult to see to what extent this was due to an increasing number of new immigrants, who often tended to have a rather limited connection to the labour market at the outset of their stay in Denmark, and to what extent it was due to differences in how well people arriving in Denmark at different points in time succeeded on the labour market. However, Denmark possesses register data covering a long period, and this can be used to elucidate this issue. One method of doing this is exemplified in Figure 5.3, which shows the rates of participation in the labour market according to the number of years immigrants have resided in Denmark.

Figure 5.3. Rates of participation in the labour market for men aged 16-66 (inclusive) from non-Western countries according to date of immigration to Denmark and duration of residence.

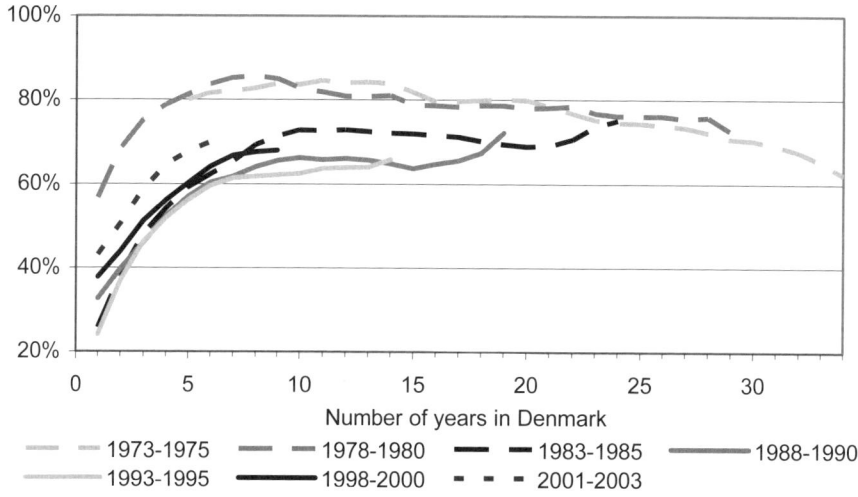

Source: Own calculations based on register data from Statistics Denmark.

The reason for showing the rate of participation in the labour market rather than the rate of employment is that the rate of employment is very sensitive to the business cycle. A comparison of the degrees of attachment to the labour market for various cohorts of immigrants identified by year of entry to Denmark therefore requires the rate of employment to be viewed in relation to the general level of employment for Danes for each year. This can be achieved in an almost equivalent way by keeping the unemployment rate out of the picture and examining the level of participation in the labour force.

Calculations were made of the rate of participation in the labour market for immigrants who arrived in Denmark during the period 1973-75 from their 5th to their 33rd years after arrival, using data from the period 1980-2007. The calculations were based on data for all immigrants who were between the ages of 16 and 66 during the relevant years. In the case of the cohorts of immigrants arriving from 1978 to 1980, calculations were made from the 1st to the 29th years after arrival.

The figure shows that non-Western male immigrants who came to Denmark in the period 1973-75 had a high level of participation in the labour market from their fifth to their thirty-third years of residence, after which the rate slowly declined. This fall may simply be age related, in that the average age in the group aged between 16 and 66 rose from 33 early in the period to almost 50 at the end of it. Men who arrived in the period 1978-80 also had a high level of participation in the labour market, this being at over 80% from their fifth to their fourteenth years after arrival in Denmark.

The rate of participation in the labour market for male non-Western immigrants who arrived in Denmark between 1983 and 1985 was very different from that of the earlier arrivals. While the non-Western men who immigrated to Denmark between 1978 and 1980 had a high level of participation in the labour market from as early as the first year after their arrival, those who immigrated between 1983 and 1985 took significantly longer to find their feet as members of the workforce. Only after nine years in Denmark did the rate of participation in the labour market rise just above 70%. For any given duration of residence in the country, the rate was lower than for those who arrived in 1978-80.

A very similar pattern can be observed for men from non-Western countries who arrived in Denmark between 1988 and 1990, in that even after 18 years their rate of participation in the labour market remained lower than that for male immigrants who arrived in the period 1978-1985. This trend continued among male immigrants who arrived in 1993-95; after 13 years in Denmark, they still had a lower rate of participation in the labour market than those who arrived in 1988-1990.

Over the short period that it has been possible to observe the two subsequent cohorts of immigrants, the results suggest that the trend towards an ever-declining level of participation in the labour market among the most recently arrived immigrants has been halted. Explanations for this apparent change in the pattern may lie in the upswing in the business cycle and the decline in the number of immigrants from non-Western countries arriving in Denmark after 2002. In addition, there have been more intensive efforts by politicians to get immigrants out into the labour market.

Nevertheless, there remains a large gap between the rate of participation in the labour market for the recently arrived cohorts and that of the non-Western male immigrants who arrived in Denmark in the 1970s. The level of participation in the labour market among non-Western males who arrived in 2001-2003 was actually 12 percentage points lower after six years of residence than for those who arrived in 1973-75 after the same length of time.

An equivalent study of non-Western women shows that the rate of participation in the labour market was lower for women than for men, but that for women as well as men the immigrants who arrived earliest in Denmark had the highest rate of participation in the labour market. Moreover, the trend towards a declining level of participation again seems to have been halted with the more recent arrivals.

The correlation found between the rate of participation in the labour market and the duration of residence for non-Western immigrants is not altered to any significant degree depending on whether the 12 new EU countries from Eastern and Southern Europe are counted as Western or non-Western countries.

5.4. Distribution of employment categories among immigrants from non-Western countries

Among those who were in employment in 1996, over 40% of immigrants and second generation immigrants were unskilled workers. This was a significantly higher proportion than that among Danes. On the other hand, the proportion of immigrants and second generation immigrants who were employed in white-collar positions – and especially in more senior posts – was lower than that of Danes. In the case of male immigrants, there were also fewer skilled workers than among Danes. An analysis of employment categories for 2001 showed that Danes continued to be in a clear majority among senior management and professionals, while immigrants were often to be found in jobs that required fewer qualifications or skills.

Immigrants were more frequently employed in the manufacturing sector than Danes, but the proportion did fall significantly between 1985 and 2001, when this sector accounted for just over 23% of the immigrants in employment. The proportion of immigrants employed in almost all other sectors increased, but at the same time the pattern of employment shifted away from immigrants and second generation immigrants being employed in large organisations. While over half of the non-Western immigrants, both men and women, were employed in workplaces with at least 100 employees in 1985, that figure had fallen by more than 12 percentage points by 1998, when more immigrants were employed in small and medium-sized companies. The proportion of men employed in very small workplaces – i.e. workplaces with 1-4 employees – almost doubled between 1985 and 1998, from 5.5% to 10.8%.

Self-employed immigrants and second generation immigrants mostly worked within retailing, repair workshops and the hotel and restaurant sector. The proportion of self-employed people among non-Western immigrants and second generation immigrants between the ages of 16 and 66 was around 5%, and was thus approximately equal to the proportion of self-employed Danes. In relation to the number of people in employment, however, the proportion in self-employment was much higher for immigrants and second generation immigrants than for Danes, simply because the proportion of immigrants in employment was smaller.

5.5. Discrimination

The aim of this section is to detail the discrimination that immigrants and second generation immigrants from non-Western countries report to have experienced. A question in the 2001 survey asked of respondents who had applied for a job within the previous five years was "Have you been turned down for a job for which you applied within the past five years?" If the response was in the affirmative, interviewees were then asked if they believed they had been discriminated against on grounds of age, gender, ethnic origin or anything else, and for each form of discrimination to say whether discrimination was "definitely" or "possibly" involved. In all, 47% of immigrants who had applied for jobs had not been rejected at all, while 31% answered "Yes, definitely" when asked if they had suffered discrimination, and a further 12% answered "Yes, possibly". The remaining 10% had been rejected for a job, but did not believe that there was any question of discrimination. The distribution of the responses is shown in Table 5.2.

Table 5.2. "Have you been turned down for a job for which you applied during the past 5 years, and if so, was it because of discrimination?"

	Immigrants and 2nd gen. immigrants from non-Western countries, 2001	Danes 2001
Yes, definitely	31	15
Yes, possibly	12	10
No, but have been turned down for a job	10	35
No, have not been turned down for a job	47	40
Total	100	100
Number of individuals	1,573	412

Source: Own calculations based on interview data.

The table also shows the results from a representative random sample of 891 Danes resident in Denmark in 2001, of whom 412 had applied for jobs within the previous five years. Of the Danes who had applied for jobs, 40% had not been rejected, while 35% had been turned down but did not feel they had suffered discrimination. On the other hand, 15% of the Danes who had applied for jobs were quite certain that they had been discriminated against, and 10% suspected that this might have been the case.

Table 5.3 shows the distribution of forms of discrimination, and it can be seen that the primary basis of discrimination perceived by immigrants was ethnicity. Of immigrants who applied for jobs, 35% felt they had been discriminated against primarily on grounds of their ethnic origins. If the category "A mixture of several reasons for discrimination", with 2% of the responses, is added to this, then 37% of the immigrants who had applied for jobs in the previous five years believed that they had been turned down primarily on grounds of ethnicity. The results for 2001 were on a par with those from the first interview survey in 1999, where a slightly but not crucially different question formulation was used. In the 1999 survey, 39% of immigrants felt they had experienced discrimination in connection with a job application during the previous five years.

Table 5.3. "Have you been discriminated against on grounds of age, gender, ethnic origin or any other factor?" Responses from immigrants and Danes who had applied for jobs within the previous five years. Percent.

	Immigrants and 2nd gen. immigrants from non-Western countries 2001	Danes 2001
Yes, primarily age discrimination	2	11
Yes, primarily gender discrimination	1	3
Yes, primarily ethnic discrimination	35	1
Yes, primarily other form of discrimination	3	8
Yes, a mixture of several types of discrimination	2	2
No, but have been turned down for a job	10	35
No, have not been turned down for a job	47	40
Total	100	100
Number of individuals	1,573	412

Source: Own calculations based on interview data.

The table also shows how perceptions of discrimination by Danes were distributed. Over 25% of those Danes applying for jobs felt they were discriminated against in being rejected, but for other reasons than those cited by immigrants. Over 11% of the Danes who had applied for jobs gave age as the ground for discrimination, while under 3% reported gender discrimination. The 8% of job applicants who reported "other form of discrimination" were apparently referring to factors such as disability, overweight or a particular dialect.

Overall, the results indicate that while a significant proportion of non-Western immigrants perceived discrimination on ethnic grounds in applying for jobs, the elimination of all ethnic prejudice would not completely remove the perception of experiencing discrimination from the labour market. Many people would still feel unreasonably prevented from obtaining a job, but the reasons would be primarily discrimination based on age, gender, disability, etc.

It can therefore be concluded that discrimination apparently plays a role in the problems that immigrants experience in integrating into the Danish labour market. The survey data show that while 36% of those in employment said that they had experienced discrimination in applying for jobs, the figure for those who were not in employment was 52%. Furthermore, 49% of the respondents who had felt discriminated against at some time did actually have jobs at the time of the survey. Of those immigrants who stated that they had not experienced discrimination during the relevant period, 64% were in employment at the time of the survey. Thus, the employment rate of the immigrants who felt that they had experienced discrimination was 75% of the employment rate of the immigrants who stated that they had not perceived any discrimination.

5.6. Incentives to work

One factor that can be decisive in determining whether a person really wants to find employment is the question of whether a reasonable financial gain is involved. A calculation of the disposable income which a person would have if in full-time employment (37 hours per week) on the one hand and if receiving full unemployment benefit on the other shows that 36% of the non-Western immigrants and second generation immigrants interviewed in the questionnaire surveys would have gained less than DKK 500 in extra income per month by working, in both 1999 and 2001 (see Table 5.4). If the costs of child care were left out of the calculation, the proportion of immigrants for whom the difference was DKK 500 or less was reduced to 31% in 2001. The corresponding figures for Danes, calculated in exactly the same way as for immigrants, were 15% and 11% respectively.

The reason that the incentive problem is so much greater for immigrants is primarily that they usually earn a relatively low hourly wage, which means that the difference between unemployment benefits and income from paid employment is modest.

This is also the main reason why the incentive problem is generally greatest for women. Of the women from the eight non-Western countries included in the 2001 questionnaire survey, over 40% would not have gained more than 500 kroner extra per month through working – even if child care costs were not taken into account. On the one hand, this implies that there were many who worked despite the very small financial gains involved. On the other hand, however, research into the Danish labour market shows that the lack of financial incentives to work means that in the long run, fewer of the unemployed take jobs, and that more and more of those who are in employment, leave it. A study

Table 5.4. Shares of employed members of unemployment funds among immigrants, second generation immigrants and Danes whose disposable income when employed full time was less than it would have been if full-time unemployed. Ages 15-59. Percent.

	Excluding child care costs		Including child care costs		
	Difference < 0 kr.	Difference < 500 kr.	Difference < 0 kr.	Difference < 500 kr.	Number of individuals
In total					
Immigrants and 2nd gen., 1999	17	30	21	36	798
Immigrants and 2nd gen., 2001	19	31	26	36	913
Danes, 2001	5	11	9	15	1,210
Men					
Immigrants and 2nd gen., 1999	14	26	18	34	488
Immigrants and 2nd gen., 2001	15	25	22	30	537
Danes, 2001	5	9	6	11	584
Women					
Immigrants and 2nd gen., 1999	21	35	26	41	310
Immigrants and 2nd gen., 2001	25	41	33	44	376
Danes, 2001	5	14	11	19	626

Source: Own calculations based on interview data and register data from Statistics Denmark.

conducted by the Rockwool Foundation showed that the probability of still being in employment after two years was highest among those for whom it was financially worth working at the time the study started. Similarly, job search activity and mobility were greatest among the unemployed who could expect to gain financially by obtaining employment, and these were also the people who were most likely to get a job during the two year period (Smith 1998). These statistics were reanalysed in 2001 in an article which showed that financial incentives play a decisive role for both the likelihood of employed people remaining in their work and the probability of the unemployed finding work, even when differences in background factors are taken into account (Pedersen and Smith, 2001).

Thus, even though incentives are not taken into account in the next section – because the analyses of incentives were only carried out for those in employment whose salaries were known – incentives must be assumed to have played a role for all the immigrants and second generation immigrants in the study.

5.7. Comparative analyses for employed and unemployed immigrants

Analyses of the factors over and above incentives and discrimination that were of significance for the probability of immigrants being in employment were carried out in connection with both the 1999 and the 2001 studies, using logistical regressions. The analyses were made separately for men and women, since it was apparent that different factors were significant for the two genders. The results are shown in Table 5.5 for men and Table 5.6 for women. The analyses were made on the basis of data from both registers and the questionnaire surveys, thus allowing for an assessment of the interviewees' proficiency in Danish to be taken into account. Students were not included in the analyses because they are in the process of becoming qualified for the labour market, and have an atypical pattern of employment. This could potentially distort and blur the picture that emerged for the other respondents.

For men, the probability of being in employment was greatest for those who were between the ages of 25 and 50, and for those in good health and with good Danish language skills. Associating with native Danes and reading Danish newspapers also increased the chances of being in employment. All else being equal, immigrants from Pakistan, Poland and Turkey had the best chance of having work both in 1999 and in 2001. However, having a Danish partner or having completed a course of education that resulted in a job qualification only made statistically significant differences in 2001. Only in 1999 did religious beliefs and year of immigration make a statistically significant difference.

For women, too, the chances of being in employment were clearly greater for those between 25 and 45 years of age, for those in good health, for those with good Danish language skills, and for those who had been in Denmark for a fair length of time. It was advantageous to have an education which gave a job qualification, to associate with Danes, and not to have small children. All else being equal, women from Poland, Vietnam and Turkey had the greatest likelihood of being in employment. In 2001 there was a statistically significant correlation between being in employment and reading Danish newspapers, though this was not the case in 1999.

A comparison of the decisive factors for immigrant men and women finding employment gives the impression of a more stable picture over time in the case of women. For women, it was especially the young, the well-qualified, and those who had strong connections with Danish society who had the greatest chance of being in work. The picture for men was similar, especially in 2001, but the slightly smaller significance of Danish language skills, for example, is indicative of the fact that among men in employment there continued to be a larger number who had jobs despite limited qualifications. This difference may have been due

Table 5.5. Significant factors for the integration into the labour market of immigrant men aged 16-66.

	Significance 1999	Significance 2001	Factors associated with greater likelihood of employment
Age	***	***	Being aged 25-50
Children	Not significant	Not significant	-
Has a Danish spouse/partner	Not significant	**	Having a Danish spouse/partner
Health	***	***	Good health
Language	***	***	Good Danish language skills
Danish contacts	***	**	Associating with Danes
Reads newspapers weekly	***	***	Reading Danish newspapers
Religious affiliation	**	Not significant	Not being a practising Muslim
Education	Not significant	***	Having completed a course of education leading to a job qualification
Crime	Not significant	*	No criminal record
Length of residence in DK	***	Not significant	Long period of residence
Basis for residence permit	Not significant	Not significant	-
Phase of business cycle at date of immigration	Not significant	Not significant	-
Employment in country of origin	Not significant	Not significant	-
Country of origin	***	***	Being Pakistani, Polish or Turkish
Log likelihood	-672	-596	
Percentage in employment	54%	61%	
Number of individuals	1,330	1,214	

Note: *** indicates correlation at the 1% level, ** indicates correlation at the 5% level, * indicates correlation at the 10% level.
Source: Own calculations based on interview data and register data from Statistics Denmark.

Table 5.6. Significant factors for the integration into the labour market of immigrant women aged 16-66.

	Significance 1999	Significance 2001	Factors associated with greater likelihood of employment
Age	***	***	Being aged 25-45
Children	***	***	Not having young children
Has a Danish spouse/partner	Not significant	Not significant	-
Health	***	***	Good health
Language	***	***	Good Danish language skills
Danish contacts	***	***	Associating with Danes
Reads newspapers weekly	Not significant	***	Reading Danish newspapers
Religious affiliation	Not significant	Not significant	-
Education	***	***	Having completed a course of education leading to a job qualification
Crime	Not significant	Not significant	-
Length of residence in DK	***/**	***/*	Long period of residence
Basis for residence permit	Not significant	Not significant	-
Phase of business cycle at date of immigration	Not significant	Not significant	-
Employment in country of origin	Not significant	Not significant	-
Country of origin	**	***	Being Polish, Vietnamese or Turkish
Log likelihood	-588	-570	
Percentage in employment	36%	42%	
Number of individuals	1,262	1,194	

Note: *** indicates correlation at the 1% level, ** indicates correlation at the 5% level, * indicates correlation at the 10% level.
Source: Own calculations based on interview data and register data from Statistics Denmark.

to more traditional patterns of gender roles where the man is expected to be the family bread-winner regardless of level of qualifications, while women's participation in the labour market was to a greater degree the norm only for those who had adopted a more Danish pattern of attitudes to work.

Education played a significant role in employment for women in both 1999 and 2001, but only in 2001 in the case of men. This may have been due to a combination of supply and demand effects.

The fact that education was already a significant factor for immigrant women's employment in 1999 may be due to the fact that there were a larger number of well-educated women who broke the traditional pattern of gender roles and sought employment. The increase between 1999 and 2001 in the significance of education in the case of men may be an indication of an increased interest in immigrants' qualifications amongst employers at a time when there was very little unemployment among native Danes, and when employment was also on the increase for the immigrant population.

The fact that a trend in the direction of a more "Danish" pattern for immigrants of the probability of being in employment started to emerge as early as 2001, rather than a couple of years later as might have been expected, may have been because well-qualified immigrants were slightly over-represented in the questionnaire survey of that year, thus making the effect more evident.

The complete analysis, as already mentioned above, shows a strong link between proficiency in Danish and employment in both 1999 and 2001. It has been difficult to determine in previous studies whether it was knowledge of Danish that brought about employment, or whether employment brought about a good knowledge of Danish. In the 2001 study, however, a large number of immigrants and second generation immigrants who participated in the 1999 survey were interviewed again. It was thus possible to track their progress over time with respect to both Danish proficiency and employment. An analysis of these data showed that of those people who did not have a job in 1999, those who had found employment by 2001 possessed a higher level of Danish language skill on average in 1999 than those who were still without work in 2001. In other words, it seems that it was more a matter that Danish proficiency helped in finding a job than *vice versa*.

5.8. Summary

The rate of employment among Danes remained at a high and relatively stable level throughout the period 1985-2007 in comparison with that for non-Western immigrants. The rate of employment for Western immigrants generally followed the trends for Danes, though at a somewhat lower level. The rates of employment were higher for second generation immigrants in the case of both

Western and non-Western immigrant groups. There were marked differences between the eight countries in the survey, and major fluctuations in the employment rates over time. Fluctuations were closely linked to the number of newly arrived immigrants in a given group, since these people could be presumed to have a weaker connection to the labour market than those who had been in Denmark for longer periods. All groups obtained an advantage from the continued upturn in the Danish economy during the early years of the new century.

Over the short period through which it has been possible to track the most recently arrived cohorts of immigrants, the results suggest that the trend towards a steadily declining level of participation in the labour market among the most recently arrived male immigrants has been halted. Equivalent analyses for non-Western women show that the rate of participation in the labour market is lower for women than for men. Just as is the case for men, it appears that the trend for the most recently arrived cohorts of women to have a progressively weakening connection to the labour market has been halted in the available data up to 2008.

The results indicate that while a significant proportion of non-Western immigrants believed they had experienced discrimination on ethnic grounds when applying for jobs, the elimination of all ethnic prejudice would not completely remove all perception of discrimination from the labour market. Many people would still feel unreasonably prevented from obtaining a job, but the reasons would be primarily perceived discrimination based on age, gender, disability, etc. However, discrimination does appear to play a role in the problems that immigrants have in becoming integrated into the Danish labour market. The interview surveys also show, though, that three out of four immigrants who felt they had experienced discrimination still managed to achieve the same status in the labour market as those who did not feel discriminated.

A calculation of the amounts of disposable income which a person would have if in full-time employment (37 hours per week) on the one hand, and if receiving full unemployment benefits on the other, shows that 36% of non-Western immigrants and second generation immigrants interviewed in the questionnaire surveys would have gained less than DKK 500 per month in extra income by working. Analyses showed that financial incentives play a decisive role both for willingness of the employed to remain in work and for the likelihood of the unemployed finding work.

Logistical regression analyses were carried out for both the 1999 and 2001 surveys to determine the factors which were important for the likelihood of immigrants being in employment. For both surveys, the analyses revealed a strong link between Danish language proficiency and being in employment. A comparison of the two surveys seems to demonstrate that it was more the case that good Danish language skills led to obtaining employment than *vice versa*.

References

Pedersen, Peder J. and Nina Smith. 2001. *Unemployment Traps: Do Financial Disincentives matter? Working Paper 01-01*. Aarhus: Centre for Labour Market and Social Research.

Schultz-Nielsen, Marie Louise. 2000. "Integrationen på arbejdsmarkedet" and "Hvilke individuelle faktorer har betydning for integrationen på arbejdsmarkedet?", in Gunnar Viby Mogensen and Poul Chr. Matthiessen (eds), *Integration i Danmark omkring årtusindeskiftet*. Aarhus: Aarhus University Press, 96-126 and 127-159.

Schultz-Nielsen, Marie Louise. 2002. "Indvandrernes tilknytning til arbejdsmarkedet 1985-2001" and "Hvorfor er så mange indvandrere uden beskæftigelse?", in Gunnar Viby Mogensen and Poul Chr. Matthiessen (eds), *Indvandrerne og arbejdsmarkedet*. Copenhagen: Spektrum, 80-117 and 117-159.

Smith, Nina.1998. "Betyder økonomiske incitamenter noget?" in Gunnar Viby Mogensen (ed.), *Beskæftiget – ledig – på efterløn*. Copenhagen: Spektrum.

6. Immigrants and the Danish Welfare System

6.1. Introduction

In the majority of European countries there are social welfare systems in place which, to a greater or lesser degree, provide income transfers from the state to individuals to enable them to maintain a certain standard of living if for one reason or another – such as unemployment or illness – they are unable to support themselves for a period of time.

There are, however, major differences with respect to the amounts and types of the payments available. There are also large differences in the ways in which the social welfare system is financed. The main principles of the Danish welfare system, which is of the Scandinavian type, are that everyone has equal rights to the various benefits, that the levels of benefit are more or less the same for all recipients, and that the system is publicly financed through taxation. The Danish model thus transfer wealth from high income groups to low income groups. There is also a redistribution of income over the course of a lifetime, in that those who are in employment contribute to the support of the young and the elderly.

The analyses reported in Chapter 5 showed that despite the improvement in the employment situation in recent years, the labour market participation of immigrants, particularly non-Western immigrants, remains relatively weak. Immigrants can therefore often be expected to be in the low income group and to be relatively often recipients of social welfare benefits – not only benefit payments related to the labour market, such as unemployment pay or sickness benefits, but a wide range of other benefits too. A brief account of these will be given in the sections below, based on the descriptions of Danish welfare benefit payments found in *Forsikringsoplysningen* (Danish Insurance Association) (2000). This account will by no means be exhaustive; it is simply intended to provide sufficient background information to enable the reader to understand the analyses of transfer incomes to immigrants and Danes. Benefits related to education, housing and child support will not be covered in this chapter.

6.2. Welfare payments

6.2.1. Long-term benefits

Old age pension: To qualify for old age pension it was necessary in 2000 to have reached the age of 67 (lowered to 65 in 2004), to be domiciled in Denmark and have Danish citizenship, and also to have been resident in Denmark for a period of three years between the ages of 15 and 67. The Danish citizenship requirement could be waived if, for example, a person had lived in Denmark for at least ten years between the ages of 15 and 67, of which five years should have been immediately prior to pension payments starting. People with refugee resident status are entitled to old age pension irrespective of the duration of residence in Denmark.

Incapacity benefits: Payable to people aged 18-66 (64 after 2004) if they have a permanent loss of ability to work due to physical, psychological or social causes. The same rules regarding residence and citizenship apply as for the old age pension.

Early retirement benefits: People who reached the age of 60 prior to 1 July 1999 were able in certain cases to claim an early retirement pension up until the age of 67 if they wished to stop working. To be eligible for this benefit, it was necessary to have been domiciled in Denmark and to have been a member of an unemployment fund for a total of twenty years out of the previous 25. Claimants had to be entitled to unemployment benefit, and should not receive any other welfare payment. Those who reached the age of 60 after 1 July 1999 were only entitled to claim the benefit up until the age of 65.

Transitional benefits (abolished in 1995): The most important requirements for receipt of this benefit were to have reached the age of 50, but not 60; to be resident in Denmark; and to have received unemployment benefits for at least 12 months out of the previous 15. Recipients also had to have been members of an unemployment fund for a total of 20 years out of the 25 prior to claiming the benefits, and should not receive any other benefit payments.

6.2.2. Short-term benefits

Unemployment pay: To qualify for unemployment pay, a person normally has to have been a member of an unemployment fund for a minimum of one year, to have worked for a minimum of one year within the previous three, and to be available for work. Unemployment pay is payable for a maximum of four years. After one year of benefit, recipients are entitled and obliged to participate in job centre activation programmes for the remaining three years.

Job centre activation programmes: These are a series of measures aimed at increasing the chances of obtaining employment; they are initiated after a maximum of one year of unemployment pay.

Sickness benefits: The general requirement for receipt of this benefit is residence in Denmark. Wage earners who do not receive wages while ill have the right to sickness pay from their employers in accordance with detailed regulations concerning length and amount of employment. If a wage earner is not entitled to payments from the employer, the local authority is obliged to pay sickness benefits in accordance with the detailed regulations. This benefit can normally be paid for a maximum of one year.

Maternity/paternity benefits: Entitlement to maternity/paternity benefit is generally speaking identical with entitlement to sickness benefit. Parents can receive benefits for a total of 28 weeks between them after the birth of a child.

Social security benefits: To receive social security benefits a person must have experienced some change in his/her life, for example loss of employment or the ending of a marriage or cohabitation relationship with a partner, which means that he or she can no longer support him/herself and his/her family, and that his or her needs cannot be covered by any other benefit payments.

In principle there is no limit to how long one can receive social security payments.

Since 1 July 2002 there has been a requirement that a person should have been resident in Denmark for at least seven of the eight years prior to applying for social security benefits. If this requirement is not fulfilled a person can receive *starting out benefits*, which are paid at a lower rate than social security benefits.

Rehabilitation benefits: In order to qualify for this benefit, recipients must not only already be receiving social security benefits, but also have a limited/reduced capacity to work and no other means of returning to a position whereby they can be fully or partially self-supporting other than through some programme of rehabilitation. The benefit is normally payable for a maximum of five years.

Local authority activation programmes: This form of activation scheme is provided for recipients of social security benefits, who are regarded as being a weaker group in their relation to the labour market than recipients of unemployment pay.

Leave: Parental leave and educational leave payments may be available in accordance with detailed regulations.

6.2.3. Entitlements

Immigrants who are foreign nationals generally have the same entitlements to social security payments as Danes. However, in the cases of the old age pension and incapacity benefits there are certain differences in the rules relating to Danes and to foreign nationals, in that Danish citizenship is normally a requirement for receipt of these benefits, together with three years of residence in Denmark between the ages of 15 and 65 (67 prior to 2004) in the case of the old age pension. Nevertheless, foreign nationals are also entitled to a Danish old age pension if they have been legally resident in Denmark for a minimum of ten years between the ages of 15 and 65 (67), of which five years must have been immediately before reaching the retirement age. Refugees are entitled to an old age pension irrespective of length of residence, and they can count the time of residence in their home country in the calculation of their pensions. Citizens of the former Yugoslavia, Pakistan and Turkey are also exempt from the ten year rule if they came to Denmark as guest workers and have worked in the country for at least a year, and have lived in the country for at least five years.

6.3. Transfer payments to immigrants

6.3.1. Long-term benefits

The data material in this chapter is largely based on the Danish *Sammenhængende Socialstatistik* ("Coherent Social Statistics"), a database containing information on benefit payments made and their duration during a given year, duration being indicated with a figure between 1 and 360. This information is particularly important, since a person may have received different types of benefits in the course of a year. In order to take this into account, the concept of the *predominant* benefit payment is used. If an individual has received several types of benefits during a given year, the predominant benefit payment is defined as the one that the person has received over the longest period in that year. When the concept of the predominant benefit payment is used, it means that an individual can only appear once in each of the tables below. The chapter also makes use of interview data, but only to a limited extent (Pedersen 2000 and Nielsen 2002).

As set out in Chapter 1, the age and gender profiles of the immigrant population differ from those of the Danes; the immigrant population is generally younger, and in certain age groups has a greater proportion of men than the Danes. This factor obviously affects the numbers who receive particular benefits, for example incapacity benefits. In Table 5.1 below a weighting procedure is therefore used to standardise the figures, so that we can see the percentage of people who have received incapacity benefits *if* the immigrant population had had the same age distribution as the population of Danes.

Table 6.1 shows the percentages of the populations in receipt of old age pension, incapacity benefits, early retirement benefits or transitional benefits as the predominant payment, distributed by country of origin for the year 2000. For all types of benefit, the table relates only those people in the relevant age brackets.

As is evident from the table, there are sizeable differences in the proportions of the groups receiving old age pensions. The "old" immigrant source countries such as Pakistan and Turkey had relatively large proportions in receipt of old age pensions – 74% and 84% respectively out of those in the relevant age brackets received Danish state pension benefits. People from the other countries, such as Iran and Lebanon, were predominantly refugees, and the proportions for these countries varied more. The proportion of people with an Iranian background receiving old age pensions was as low as 41%, while for people with a Polish background the proportion reached almost 81%. Figures for the former Yugoslavia, an area from which Denmark has received both guest workers and refugees, are just below the level for Pakistan and Turkey.

These large differences in the proportions receiving old-age pensions can in part be explained by differences in the durations of residence among immigrants. The three countries with the longest average period of residence among their nationals were Pakistan, Poland and Turkey, and many of the immigrants from these countries received a pension.

Table 6.1. Proportions of immigrant populations and Danes receiving long-term benefits in 2000, distributed according to the predominant form of benefits and country of origin. Percent.

	Old age pension (ages 67-70)	Incapacity benefits[1] (ages 18-66)	Incapacity benefits[2] (ages 18-66)	Early retirement benefits (ages 60-66)	Transitional benefits (ages 51-59)
Former Yugoslavia[3]	70.0	9.6	14.4	15.5	3.3
Iran[3]	41.2	7.8	13.9	4.3	1.4
Lebanon[3]	61.8	7.9	16.9	8.0	0.9
Pakistan[3]	73.8	5.5	8.4	44.9	11.9
Poland[3]	80.5	6.4	7.3	36.3	4.1
Somalia[3]	58.3	1.8	7.6	5.5	0.9
Turkey[3]	84.0	6.1	12.3	47.2	18.2
Vietnam[3]	45.8	6.8	14.5	10.2	2.9
All non-Western immigrants[3]	69.5	4.4	10.5	29.1	6.7
Western immigrants[4]	80.4	5.9	5.8	33.2	3.3
Danes[5]	87.0	7.6	7.6	43.4	3.2

[1] Actual percentages. [2] Percentages calculated for the age group 18-66 as if the various immigrant groups had the same gender and age distributions as Danes in a 2% random sample of the population. [3] Sum total of all non-Western immigrants and second generation immigrants. [4] A representative sample of 25% of Western immigrants and second generation immigrants. [5] A representative sample of 2% of all Danes.
Note: The age limits are related to age on 1 January 2001, and are inclusive of the ages given. Rounding of figures means that the columns do not necessarily add up to 100.
Source: Own calculations on the basis of register data from Statistics Denmark.

Where there was a relatively large proportion of those aged 67-70 who were not receiving the old age pension, many of the people in the group would have been receiving social security payments. For example, 48% of immigrants from Vietnam were receiving social security benefits, as opposed to just over 12% of all non-Western immigrants. Among people originating from Iran and Lebanon there were also considerable shares, over 30% and nearly 25% respectively, receiving social security benefits.

The second and third columns of Table 6.1 show the percentages receiving incapacity benefits. The second column shows the actual percentages, while the third column shows the weighted figures, i.e. the percentages who would have received incapacity benefits if the immigrant groups had had the same gender and age profiles as Danes. The unweighted figures show that overall, a smaller proportion of non-Western immigrants than Danes received incapacity benefits. The proportions were 7.6% for Danes, as opposed to only 4.4% for non-Western immigrants. However, this picture is altered if we consider the weighted figures. If the total non-Western immigrant population had had the same gender and age distribution as Danes, then 10.5% of them would have been receiving incapacity benefits. Incapacity benefits are given to people who have permanently lost the ability to work, and who therefore cannot be active on the labour market. The figures are thus an indication that a relatively high proportion among the immigrant population were in a very weak position in relation to the labour market.

The proportion of the population receiving early retirement benefits or transitional benefits depends on the number of people who have been members of unemployment funds. For immigrant groups, the length of period of residence would have been of significance in this respect, as well as the level of attachment to the labour market, since the longer a person had been in Denmark, the easier it would have been for them to fulfil the requirements concerning long-term membership of an unemployment fund. People who came to Denmark as guest workers, and who have therefore typically been in the country for a relatively long period, are more likely to be receiving early retirement benefits; this is evident in the table, where immigrants from countries such as Turkey and Pakistan display relatively high percentages receiving these benefits. Among Poles, too, there were relatively many recipients of early retirement benefits; the explanation is that many Poles have also been in Denmark for a relatively long period and, as shown in Chapter 5, Poles have consistently maintained a relatively high level of employment.

The distribution of payments of transitional benefits is naturally enough reminiscent of the pattern described for early retirement benefits, since both benefits are dependent upon having been a member of an unemployment fund for a considerable number of years. The percentages are highest among immigrants from Turkey and Pakistan, as a result of their longer average period of attachment to the labour market.

Table 6.2 shows the average amounts of payments for old-age pension, incapacity benefits, early retirement benefits and transitional benefits. It shows that people from Somalia received the largest amounts in old age pensions, despite their having been in Denmark for the shortest period on average. This is because people who were resident in Denmark on the basis of having refugee status were allowed to count the years of residence in their home countries in the calculation of their pensions. Turks and Iranians, on the other hand, had typically come to Denmark as ordinary immigrants (in the legal sense), and consequently could not obtain so much in pension. The same explanation applies to the differences in the amounts of incapacity benefits, where immigrants from Pakistan and Turkey again received the smallest amounts. For example, immigrants of Turkish origin received 15-20% less in payments than the average for non-Western immigrants. People from refugee source countries such as Iran and Somalia were at the other end of the scale.

The figures provide clear evidence that, from the point of view of the individual, the precise category of residence permit given is very important. In the period 1997-2001, 33%, 31%, 22%, 20% and 26% (figures for each year) of "spontaneous" asylum seekers actually already had the right of residence in Denmark (and some had even been born in the country), but wanted to obtain the more advantageous refugee status (Danmarks Statistik 2002).

Table 6.2. Average annual amounts paid to immigrant groups and Danes in receipt of old age pension, incapacity benefits, early retirement benefits or transitional benefits in 2000, distributed according to the predominant benefit payment received and country of origin. DKK.

	Old age pension	Incapacity benefits	Early retirement benefits	Transitional benefits
Former Yugoslavia	62,864	88,782	115,847	119,578
Iran	70,915	103,046	..	..
Lebanon	72,103	95,089	..	..
Pakistan	37,255	73,450	115,877	118,122
Poland	63,153	90,873	116,225	119,600
Somalia	90,397	107,071	..	..
Turkey	39,720	72,342	118,034	118,836
Vietnam	74,793	99,542	120,661	..
All non-Western immigrants	58,036	87,557	115,479	117,828
Western immigrants	62,080	93,174	108,804	115,002
Danes	68,785	105,071	109,684	114,421

See notes for Table 6.1. Note: ".." = Few or no observations.
Source: Own calculations based on the Coherent Social Statistics.

The variation was significantly less in the amounts paid in early retirement benefits and transitional benefits. This is because both types of benefits are calculated according to rates for unemployment pay, and typically do not vary very greatly.

With respect to receipt of long-term benefits, the non-Western immigrants displayed a pattern that deviated from that of Danes, though not very greatly. There were smaller percentages of immigrants receiving all these benefits than there were Danes. If, however, corrections are made for gender and age distributions among the non-Western immigrants receiving incapacity benefits, the percentages for that benefit are greater than for Danes.

6.3.2. Short-term benefits

Table 6.3 shows the percentages of the populations who received various short-term benefits in both 1998 and 2000. The figures for the two years are shown in order to indicate any effects of the improving employment situation in Denmark on the uptake of short-term benefits.

One of the principal benefits related to the labour market is *unemployment pay*. It is to be expected that a large proportion of non-Western immigrants would be receiving unemployment benefits because of the high level of unemployment among them (see Chapter 5), and indeed the table indicates that the percentage for the group was well above that for Danes. In 2000, for example, 11% of non-Western immigrants were receiving unemployment pay, as opposed to just over 8% of Danes. The percentage of Western immigrants was on a par with that of Danes, being again just over 8%. The improvement in the employment situation between 1998 and 2000 resulted in fewer claims for unemployment pay in the latter year for all groups.

The reason that the difference between non-Western immigrants and Danes was not greater with respect to unemployment benefits was that a proportion of the non-Western immigrants could not fulfil the employment record requirements for receipt of unemployment pay, and received social security benefits instead. Consequently, as Table 6.3 shows, there were much larger percentages among non-Western immigrants and second generation immigrants who received social security benefits than among Danes and Western immigrants and second generation immigrants.

An improvement is observable between 1998 and 2000 for non-Western immigrants, of whom the proportion receiving social security benefits fell from around 25% to under 21%. Immigrants from Somalia and Lebanon stood out in this respect, as the proportions receiving social security benefits as the predominant benefit in 2000 were at levels of 52% and 40% respectively.

Table 6.3. Proportions of the populations of immigrants, second generation immigrants and Danes aged 18-66 (inclusive) who were receiving short-term benefits in 1998 and 2000, distributed by the predominant benefit and country of origin. Percent.

	Non-Western				Western				Danes	
	Immigrants		Descendants		Immigrants		Descendants			
	1998	2000	1998	2000	1998	2000	1998	2000	1998	2000
Unemployment pay	13.4	11.0	10.8	8.9	9.9	8.2	10.4	8.2	9.8	8.2
Sickness benefits	4.1	5.1	4.6	5.1	5.4	6.2	5.6	7.2	7.5	8.8
Maternity/paternity benefits	1.8	2.1	2.6	3.1	2.2	2.4	2.8	3.0	2.7	2.9
Social security benefits	24.9	20.9	8.4	9.1	3.6	3.4	5.3	5.1	2.6	2.4
Rehabilitation benefits	3.6	4.5	0.8	0.8	0.5	0.5	0.7	..	0.7	0.8
Local authority activation programmes	6.6	8.3	8.4	6.4	1.5	1.6	2.4	2.2	1.5	1.5
Job centre activation programmes	2.1	2.5	1.3	1.0	1.1	1.2	1.4	1.2	1.0	1.1
Leave	2.6	1.5	1.6	1.7	2.2	1.5	2.3	1.5	2.2	1.5
Short-term benefits in total	58.9	55.9	38.4	36.0	26.3	25.0	30.9	29.1	27.8	27.3
Short-term benefits in total, including incapacity benefits	65.3	62.2	39.5	37.3	32.8	30.8	37.3	35.7	35.9	34.9

See notes for Table 6.1.
Source: Own calculations based on the Coherent Social Statistics and Pedersen (2000).

The percentages of non-Western immigrants and second generation immigrants receiving rehabilitation benefits and local authority activation allowances are larger than for Danes or Western immigrants and second generation immigrants. This is because local authority activation and rehabilitation are the local government instruments for getting recipients of social security benefits out into the labour market. If we combine payments to non-Western immigrants of social security benefits, local authority activation allowances and rehabilitation benefits, the reduction in the proportion receiving social security benefits in 2000 is partially offset by increases in the other two types of benefits.

In contrast to many of the other short-term benefits, the proportions of non-Western immigrants and second generation immigrants receiving sickness benefits or maternity/paternity benefits are actually smaller than or equivalent to the proportions for Danes. The explanation is obviously that immigrants are less likely than Danes to be able to fulfil the employment requirements for these benefits. It is also the case that immigrant populations are generally younger on average, and thus probably have less need for sickness benefits. For the remaining benefits, i.e. job centre activation allowances and leave allowances, there is little difference between immigrants and Danes. The percentage receiving job-centre activation allowances was a little higher for non-Western immigrants than for Danes, which can be attributed to the difference in the proportions receiving unemployment pay.

If we consider short-term benefits all together, then there were around 56% of all non-Western immigrants who received such benefits at some point in the course of 2000, as opposed to around 27% of Danes. For non-Western second generation immigrants the proportion was 36%. For Western immigrants and second generation immigrants the proportions were approximately the same as those for Danes.

It is thus clear that non-Western immigrants in particular, and to a certain extent second generation immigrants, were more frequently recipients of short-term benefits than Danes or Western immigrants or second generation immigrants.

Table 6.4 shows the amounts paid out in short-term benefits to non-Western and Western immigrants and second generation immigrants and to Danes. In general, immigrants from non-Western countries received somewhat more than other groups in short-term benefits. The differences were overwhelmingly due to differences in the duration of the payments. There are some benefits, for example social security benefits, for which the daily amount may vary from person to person depending on their current situations; but given the generally standardised payments which typify the Danish social security system, differences in the benefit rates cannot be expected to be a crucial factor in accounting for differences in total amounts.

The relatively higher amounts paid in social security benefits to non-Western immigrants, taken together with the fact that this group received this benefit relatively more often than others, meant that the group, which made up only 5% of the Danish population at the time, received around 35% of the total amount of the benefits paid out in 2000. The situation was more or less unaltered in comparison with 1998, despite the fact that the rate of employment had improved more for immigrants than for Danes since then.

Table 6.4. Average annual amounts paid in short-term benefits to immigrants, second generation immigrants and Danes in 2000. DKK.

	Non-Western		Western		Danes
	Immigrants	Descendants	Immigrants	Descendants	
Unemployment pay	63,741	52,789	56,349	54,087	49,325
Sickness benefits	36,571	20,360	25,320	22,332	22,363
Maternity/ paternity benefits	44,878	50,188	37,941	38,311	41,977
Social security benefits	78,471	36,732	56,984	59,922	58,786
Rehabilitation benefits	47,627	47,228	39,166	..	39,704
Local authority activation programmes	73,236	28,658	60,843	57,126	53,422
Job centre activation programmes	58,340	44,022	59,985	44,022	56,919
Leave	46,172	46,920	38,774	..	38,031
Short-term benefits in total [1]	75,914	46,516	52,724	51,944	46,323

[1] Includes all payments received by an individual in 2000. ".." = Few or no observations
Source: Own calculations based on the Coherent Social Statistics.

6.4. Duration of benefit payments

The analyses in the previous section presented an overview of the benefits which immigrants received and the amounts involved. This section examines the duration of social welfare payments to immigrants viewed over a number of years. The duration of payments related to immigrants' future attachment to the labour market is of particular interest. Short-term benefits are relevant in this context, particularly social security benefits, because many more non-Western immigrants receive these benefits than Danes.

As mentioned above, the Coherent Social Statistics, in addition to recording the amounts paid, register the portion of the year for which an individual receives social security benefits. This makes it possible to total the durations of benefit payments over several years. Table 6.5 shows the total duration of social security benefit payments for a period of five years, from 1996 to 2000. The analysis is inspired by Filges (2000), who analysed the duration and number of periods of receipt of social security benefits over various five-year periods. In this analysis, however, a simple summation of the duration of receipt of benefits

Table 6.5. Number of years of receipt of social security benefits in the period 1996-2000, shown for non-Western immigrants and second generation immigrants, Western immigrants and second generation immigrants, and Danes, distributed by gender. Ages 18-66. Percent.

	Non-Westerners[1]		Westerners[2]		Danes[3]	
	Men	Women	Men	Women	Men	Women
Did not claim benefit	50.5	50.7	87.7	88.1	90.8	89.6
Up to one year	23.7	18.4	8.1	7.3	6.2	6.6
1-2 years	10.5	9.5	1.9	2.0	1.4	1.7
2-3 years	7.5	8.7	1.1	1.3	0.7	1.0
3-4 years	4.3	6.1	0.5	0.7	0.5	0.6
4-5 years	2.6	4.9	0.4	0.5	0.3	0.3
Entire period	0.8	1.8	0.2	0.1	0.1	0.2
Total	100.0	100.0	100.0	100.0	100.0	100.0
Number of individuals	89,406	88,306	10,624	9,938	31,125	30,497

Note: [1] Sum total of all non-Western immigrants and second generation immigrants. [2] A representative sample of 25% of Western immigrants and second generation immigrants. [3] A representative sample of 2% of all Danes.
Source: Own calculations based on the Coherent Social Statistics.

is used. This means that if a person received social security benefit payments for a total of, say, two years, this does not necessarily mean that this was a continuous period.

First and foremost, the table shows that there were major differences between the groups with respect to the proportions who did not receive any social security benefits at all over the five year period. Only a little more than half of non-Western women and men received no benefit payments at all during the period, while the corresponding proportions for Western immigrant populations were around 90%. Of the half of non-Western immigrants and second generation immigrants who did receive benefits, most were in receipt of social security benefits for up to one year. Of Western immigrants and second generation immigrants who claimed social security benefits, the typical duration of benefits was of maximum one year. The proportions of the populations who received social security benefits payment for the entire period were insignificant for all groups. Non-Western women had the largest share, 1.8%.

The periods of receipt of social security benefits described in the table may either refer to payments for reason of unemployment (which means that recipients had to be available for the labour market) or for other reasons. As indicated in section 6.2.2, social security benefits are paid in the event of social circumstances that require it, such as unemployment or sickness. For people who receive social security benefits over a prolonged period, there exist certain supplementary benefits paid to help these people get out of the social security system, namely local authority activation allowances and rehabilitation benefits. A person can thus be receiving benefits under more than one scheme, while still being governed by the legislation on Denmark's active social policy. It is therefore relevant to take into account local authority activation and rehabilitation in connection with the duration of benefits.

However, the inclusion of social security benefits, local authority activation and rehabilitation benefits in the calculation of the duration of benefits would make no significant differences to the proportions of Western and non-Western immigrants and Danes who claimed no benefits: in no group would the proportion fall by more than a couple of percentage points. On the other hand, the inclusion of the other benefits would affect the proportion who claimed benefits over an extended period. In the case of non-Western women, there were 15% who claimed one of the three social welfare benefits for at least four years out of the five-year period.

If all short-term welfare benefits are included in the calculation, then naturally the proportions of the populations who did not claim any welfare benefits are significantly reduced. In the case of non-Western immigrants and second generation immigrants the share is reduced by half, so that only one in four did not claim any benefits.

Table 6.6 shows the distribution by country of origin, gender and age of those of the populations who received social security benefits, local authority activation allowances or rehabilitation benefits for at least four years during the five-year period 1996-2000. The percentages of immigrants and second generation immigrants from Lebanon and Somalia stand out. Of women with a Lebanese background, 56% were either claiming social security benefits or receiving local authority activation allowances or rehabilitation benefits for a minimum of four years during the period. Almost one out of every three Lebanese men was a claimant in four out of the five years, while these benefits were also claimed by significant numbers of immigrants and second generation immigrants with Iranian and Vietnamese backgrounds.

The table divides the populations into three age groups: 18-29, 30-49 and 50-66. Within the separate age groups the patterns are somewhat similar to those described above, in that Lebanon and Somalia stand out in particular. The figures for the Western immigrant population are again similar to those for Danes, with differences of only one or two percentage points between the groups. It is striking that in many cases the largest proportions receiving benefits were in the age group 30-49, where the majority could be expected to be active on the labour market.

Table 6.6. Proportions of populations who claimed social security benefits, local authority activation allowances or rehabilitation benefits for at least four years during the period 1996–2000, by country of origin, gender and age. Percent.

	Men	Women	Age at 1 January 2000		
			18-29	30-49	50-66
Former Yugoslavia	9.4	14.6	5.1	16.3	11.1
Iran	13.5	23.3	5.9	19.3	25.0
Lebanon	30.5	56.2	27.0	51.6	36.7
Pakistan	2.8	9.6	1.5	10.1	6.7
Poland	3.9	8.4	2.8	9.3	6.3
Somalia	29.4	36.6	21.0	40.0	33.1
Turkey	2.9	9.4	3.4	7.7	8.0
Vietnam	8.3	19.8	6.4	16.3	28.3
Other non-Western countries	8.9	11.9	6.0	13.6	8.4
All non-Western countries	9.8	15.4	6.8	16.7	10.8
Western countries	1.4	1.7	0.6	2.2	1.1
Danes	1.1	1.7	1.7	2.0	0.5

Source: Own calculations based on the Coherent Social Statistics.

6.5. The average level of public support

This section focuses on the trends over time in claims for various welfare benefits. As was shown in the analyses in Chapter 5, the business cycle increased employment rates for both immigrants and Danes for the first years of the 21st century. It is to be expected that this increase would have led to lower welfare payments such as unemployment pay and sickness benefits, and also social security benefits, since more people would be in a position to support themselves without full or partial assistance from public funds. In the following section, we will examine the extent to which there was a reduction in the number of people who were passive recipients of public support.

For this, we create a variable which represents the proportion of the days in a year when a person has been *passively supported*. This variable is calculated by taking the total number of days in a year for which a person has received unemployment pay, sickness benefits, social security benefits or incapacity benefit. If the proportion of the year is greater than 80%, the person is said to have been passively supported in that year. A person who was passively supported in a given year can thus have been employed for a maximum of 10 weeks in that year, since $(1-0.8)*52$ = approximately 10.

Clearly, the level of employment will be a crucial factor in determining trends in the proportion of the population who are passively supported. For immigrants, however, there is another important factor to take into account, namely that throughout the period under consideration (1985-2000) there was a constant stream of arrivals of new immigrants. As was shown in Chapter 5, the rate of employment among newly arrived immigrants is lower than that among those who have been in the country for a long time. Newly arrived immigrants will therefore often be passively supported, and will thus distort the picture when comparisons are made with the population of Danes. In order to take this factor into account, Figure 6.1 only includes people who were resident in Denmark throughout the period 1985-2000. Furthermore, a limited age group was used for the calculations for the figure, which only included people aged 25-59. This was to avoid distortions in the material resulting from the inclusion of young people receiving a maintenance grant for education and people aged over 59 claiming early retirement benefits. Western immigrants were also omitted from the figure, since their pattern of receipt of welfare benefits – unlike that of non-Western immigrants – closely resembled that of Danes.

Figure 6.1. The proportion of non-Western immigrants who lived in Denmark for the entire period and Danes aged 25–59 who were passively supported during the period 1985–2000, by gender. Percent.

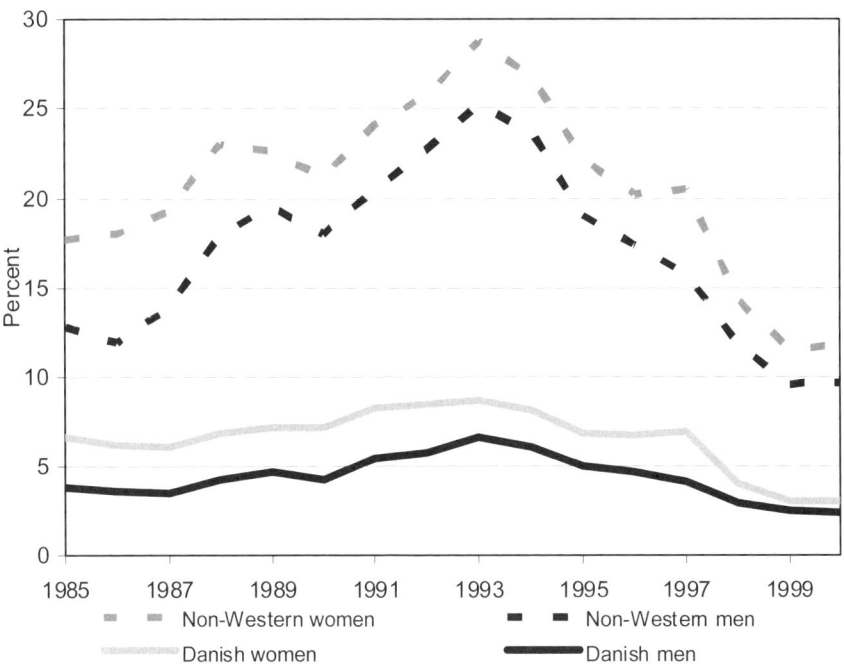

Source: Own calculations based on the Coherent Social Statistics.

The figure shows clearly that even though the differences varied over time, there was always a marked contrast between non-Western immigrants and Danes. A much larger proportion of non-Western immigrants were passively supported, because of their limited degree of attachment to the labour market. After the mid-1980s the Danish business cycle began a downturn, which resulted in a lower level of employment and higher rates of unemployment for the whole population. The effects of this can be seen in the graph lines for both Danes and immigrants, but the hard times clearly hit the immigrants harder, with the proportions of non-Western men and women who were passively supported both rising steeply. Both lines peaked around 1993/1994.

Throughout the period, non-Western women were the group with the largest share who were passively supported. In 1985 the proportion was 18%, rising to a peak of nearly 29% in 1993 – a rise of around 11 percentage points.

The proportion of male and female Danes who were passively supported peaked at roughly the same time, but the rise was more moderate. The highest proportion for Danish women was 10%, in 1993, while in 1986 it was around 7%. The level for Danish men was even lower. The gender differences were naturally connected to the fact that men had a stronger attachment to the labour market than women, a fact which applied to both Danes and immigrants. After 1993 the proportion of non-Western immigrants who were passively supported fell, again very steeply, while the fall for Danes was much more modest.

An interesting development can be detected towards the end of the period (1998–2000). As mentioned above, the number of non-Western immigrants who were passively supported fell dramatically after 1993, but the curve flattens out at a relatively high level compared to that for Danes. This would appear to conflict with the increase in employment levels that was observed for the period 1998–2000. A possible explanation is the introduction of a new law on integration in 1999. This legislation extended a special integration measure from applying only to refugees to covering immigrants who came to Denmark in connection with family reunification. This may have resulted in a *take-up effect* – i.e. a larger proportion of the people who were entitled to benefits deciding to claim them.

Another explanation could be that the proportion of people supported passively had reached such a low level that only a small group of people with very little prospect of finding employment remained.

6.6. Likelihood of receiving welfare benefits

Table 6.7 shows the results of an analysis based on a logistical regression model in which the dependent variable is whether a person is claiming social security benefit or not. The analysis has been carried out for non-Western immigrants covered by the main surveys in 1998 and 2000 (interview surveys supplemented with register data). Descendants were not included in the analysis, primarily because variables such as date of immigration and employment in the home country are not relevant for them.

Table 6.7. Significant factors for the likelihood of immigrants being in receipt of social security benefits in 2000 and 1998. Ages 18-66.

	All in 2000	All in 1998	Factors increasing the likelihood of being in receipt of social security benefits
Country of origin	***	***	Being from Lebanon or Somalia
Gender	**	***	Being a woman
Age	***	***	Being aged between 18 and 40
Evaluation of own health	***	***	Poor health
Region	***	***	Living outside North Jutland
Education	Not significant	***	No education/not completed obligatory schooling
Children in Denmark from date of arrival	**	**	Having children in Denmark from date of arrival
Employment in country of origin	Not significant	*	Not having been a student
Year of immigration	**/***	***	Being a new arrival
Gross household income, 1999	***	***	Low household income
Home occupier status	***	***	Being a tenant
Evaluation of Danish proficiency	***	***	Having poor Danish language proficiency
Number of children between the ages of 0 and 17 living at home	***	***	Having many children
Religious convictions	Not significant	Not significant	-

Note: *** indicates that the variable is significant at the 1% level; ** indicates that the variable is significant at the 5% level; * indicates that the variable is significant at the 10% level.
Source: Main surveys.

The analysis shows that the country of origin did have significant effects, even after correction for a large number of factors such as gender, age, education, language proficiency, etc. There was a greater likelihood that immigrants from countries such as Somalia and Lebanon would be in receipt of social security benefits. Women were more likely than men to be receiving social security benefits. Surprisingly, education did not have an effect in the analysis for 2000, though it did in the analysis for 1998. There appear to be two explanations for this. In the first place, there was obviously an interaction with other variables. For example, people who were highly educated usually also tended to have good language skills. Language proficiency had a large influence on the likelihood of receiving social security benefits, in that good language skills reduced the probability of receiving benefits. In the second place, the composition of the group of recipients changed between 1998 and 2000. The proportion of people who received social security benefits due to unemployment fell, making employment-related variables less significant.

The older a person was, the greater the likelihood of their being in receipt of social security benefits, though only up until the age of 40. After that the likelihood declined with increasing age – clearly because after that point many immigrants were receiving incapacity benefits. Self-evaluation of state of health was also included as an explanatory variable, and an evaluation that a person was in poor health also increased the probability of his or her being in receipt of social security benefits.

It appears that to a large extent, the variables that resulted in immigrants having a greater probability of being in receipt of social security benefits should be interpreted from the perspective of relationship to the labour market. Other than education, there is no variable that shows any surprising values. The inevitable conclusion must be that it was immigrants' weak ties to the labour market which constituted the main explanation for the relatively high share in receipt of social security benefits.

6.7. Summary

This chapter has clarified the use of the social security system by immigrants in comparison with the use by Danes. Special focus has been given to non-Western immigrants and second generation immigrants, as the results of analyses have consistently shown that it is these groups whose patterns of use of the system deviate significantly from those of Danes. This is in contrast to Western immigrants and second generation immigrants, whose use of the system is very reminiscent of the patterns of use by Danes.

The relationship of welfare benefits to the main theme of this book, integration into the labour market, seems to be clear. Given their weaker attachment to the labour market, there is a much greater likelihood of non-Western immigrant populations needing the social welfare system for support.

Fundamentally, immigrants in Denmark are entitled to receive the same welfare assistance as Danish citizens. There are, however, certain exceptions, especially with regard to old age pensions and incapacity benefits. Rights to these benefits are only available to foreign nationals who have been resident in Denmark for at least ten years.

In the case of the old age pension, the proportions of the immigrant groups who received this pension varied in the data, because of the different periods of residence in Denmark. A relatively high proportion of people with Turkish, Pakistani or Polish backgrounds and who fell into the relevant age categories received old age pensions. People from Iran, for example, were at the other end of the scale.

The proportion of non-Western immigrants and second generation immigrants who received incapacity benefits was over 4%, whereas the figure for Danes was nearly 8%. However, if the population of non-Western immigrants and second generation immigrants had had the same gender and age distribution as that of the Danes, around 10% of them would have been receiving incapacity benefits.

The weaker ties to the labour market of non-Western immigrants – and to a certain extent of non-Western second generation immigrants – were the reason that around 11% of them received unemployment benefits in 2000, in contrast to 8% of Danes. The relatively modest difference was due to the fact that many immigrants received social security benefits instead. Thus, in 2000, one in five non-Western immigrants received social security assistance, whereas the figure for Danes was only slightly above 2%. Taking all short term benefits together (unemployment pay, social security benefits, sickness pay, etc.) showed that around 56% of non-Western immigrants received some form of support from the social security system in any given year, as opposed to 27% of Danes. If incapacity benefits are included in the calculation then there were more than 62% of non-Western immigrants who received some form of benefit, as opposed to 35% of Danes.

When the duration of receipt of social security benefits over a five-year period (1996-2000) was examined, it was found that among non-Western men and women there were only half who did not receive any benefit at all, while the corresponding figure for male and female Danes was around 90%.

To obtain an overview of the changes in immigrants' use of the social security system over time, an analysis was made of the proportions of the population who were passively supported by the benefits system over the period 1985-2000. A person was defined as passively supported if he or she was dependent on unemployment pay, sickness benefits or social security benefits. The analysis showed that the proportion of non-Western immigrants who were passively supported during the entire period was higher than the proportion of Danes. The weakness of the Danish economy from the mid-1980s to the early 1990s had a great influence on the extent of passive support. Whereas the proportion of non-Western men who were provided for passively was 11% in 1986, the figure rose to 38–39% in 1993. The corresponding figures for native Danish men were 4% and 7% respectively. The weak economy thus had the greatest impact on immigrants. However, the greatest positive impact of the improved employment situation after 1993/1994 was also on immigrants.

A concluding analysis of the factors which had significance for the likelihood of being in receipt of social security benefits suggested that immigrants' weaker attachment to the labour market was the primary explanation as to why so relatively many of them received social security benefits.

References

Danmarks Statistik. "Asylansøgninger og opholdstilladelser 2001", *Statistiske Efterretninger. Befolkning og valg* nr. 2002: 7. Copenhagen.

Filges, Trine. 2000. *De langvarige kontanthjælpsmodtagere.* Copenhagen: Socialforskningsinstituttet.

Forsikringsoplysningen. 2000. *Sociale ydelser 2000.* Copenhagen.

Nielsen, Niels Kenneth. 2002. "Overførselsindkomster til indvandrere", in Gunnar Viby Mogensen and Poul Chr. Matthiessen (eds), *Indvandrerne og arbejdsmarkedet*. Copenhagen: Spektrum, 198-258.

Pedersen, Søren. 2000. "Overførselsindkomster til indvandrerne", in Gunnar Viby Mogensen and Poul Chr. Matthiessen (eds), *Integration i Danmark omkring årtusindeskiftet*. Aarhus: Aarhus University Press, 160-207.

7. Immigrants and the public exchequer

7.1. Introduction

This chapter deals with the effects of immigration on public finances in Denmark. It is based on a number of studies conducted within the Rockwool Foundation project on immigration to Denmark: Wadensjö (1999, 2000 & 2002); Wadensjö and Orrje (2002); Wadensjö and Gerdes (2004 & 2006); and Wadensjö (2007).

The inhabitants of a country contribute in various ways to public income. People with incomes pay income-related taxes (direct taxes such as income tax) and taxes on their purchases (indirect taxes, including Value Added Tax). Direct taxes are easy to link to individuals, and indirect taxes can be calculated approximately as a certain proportion of disposable income. Company taxes, on the other hand, can be difficult to ascribe to individuals.

Public sector expenditures on individuals can be worked out similarly. The simplest expenditures to calculate are transfer incomes, which are made directly to individuals, for example in connection with sickness, unemployment or old age. As far as costs associated with public consumption and public investments are concerned, some of these costs can also be attributed to individuals fairly easily. These are the costs of individual public consumption, which are in fact like transfer incomes, but take the form of services rather than cash. Using information on actual use of these services by individuals, it is possible to attribute the costs to the relevant people. There are other costs which cannot be directly related to individuals, even though they are dependent on the overall size of the population. In some cases, these costs can be divided equally between all the individuals in the country. This would be appropriate, for example, for expenditure on the road network: the larger the population, the greater the number of homes there are and the more local traffic, and thus the higher the costs of the municipal road system. A third group of expenditures is – up to a certain point at least – independent of the size of the population and of any changes in it. This concerns, for example, expenditure on defence and the foreign service.

The Finance Ministry's Law Model, described earlier in this book (Section 2.2.5), which operates with a random sample of one thirtieth of the population of Denmark, contains detailed information about public receipts and expenditures. These are individualised in the model to a considerable extent. This makes it possible to calculate net transfers to and from the public purse for those members of the population who are included in the sample. Since there is also information available on the countries in which the various people in the sample, and their parents, were born, it is possible to calculate net transfers to and from public funds for different immigrant groups. It is also possible to analyse the ways in which various factors affect the size of the net transfers.

7.2. Changes over the period 1991-2001

Table 7.1 shows the average net transfers to the public exchequer per person aged 18 or over for various groups in 1991 and for each year between 1995 and 2001. Transfers to and from children under 18 are attributed to their parents.

Table 7.1. Net transfers to the public exchequer per person aged 18 or over for different groups during the years 1991 and 1995-2001. Amounts in DKK at contemporary prices (amounts adjusted to 1997 prices in *italics*).

Group	1991	1995	1996	1997	1998	1999	2000	2001
Danes	13,400 *14,800*	14,800 *15,600*	18,600 *18,600*	22,300	24,500 *23,800*	26,700 *25,200*	29,000 *27,500*	30,400 *28,200*
Western immigrants	14,800 *15,600*	14,100 *14,800*	11,100 *11,100*	12,600	23,800 *23,000*	25,200 *23,800*	39,300 *37,100*	40,800 *37,100*
Western 2nd generation	19,300 *21,500*	8,900 *9,700*	26,700 *27,500*	34,200	19,300 *19,300*	40,100 *37,900*	50,500 *46,800*	55,700 *50,500*
Western immigrants and 2nd generation	14,800 *16,300*	14,100 *14,800*	11,900 *12,600*	14,800	23,800 *23,000*	26,000 *25,200*	40,800 *37,900*	42,300 *38,600*
Non-Western immigrants	-49,000 *-53,500*	-65,300 *-68,300*	-66,100 *-67,600*	-60,900	-54,200 *-53,500*	-55,700 *-53,500*	-58,600 *-54,900*	-57,900 *-52,700*
Non-Western 2nd generation	700 *700*	-19,300 *-20,000*	-16,300 *-16,300*	-18,600	-700 *-700*	-19,300 *-18,600*	-14,100 *-13,400*	-4,500 *-3,700*
Non-Western immigrants and 2nd generation	-48,300 *-52,700*	-63,800 *-66,100*	-63,800 *-65,300*	-58,600	-52,000 *-50,500*	-54,200 *-52,000*	-55,700 *-52,000*	-54,200 *-49,700*
All members of the population	11,900 *13,400*	12,600 *12,600*	14,800 *15,600*	19,300	21,500 *20,800*	23,000 *22,300*	25,200 *23,800*	26,700 *24,500*

Source: Finansministeriets Lovmodel.

As can be seen from the last row of the table, the average transfer values for the entire population were positive, and increased throughout the 1990s. This does not mean, however, that the Danish public exchequer had an ever-increasing surplus, but is due to a larger proportion of the tax income being attributed to individuals than the expenditures on public consumption and investment. The reason for this is that a significant proportion of the spending by the public sector (for example on defence and the foreign service) is not affected by marginal changes in the population size.

For Western immigrants, transfers to the public exchequer were positive in every year of the study. The downturn in the Danish economy reduced the value of these transfers between 1991 and 1996, but the amounts then rose steadily until 2001. The figures were even higher for Western second generation immigrants, except in 1995 and 1998. For Danes, too, the transfers were positive in every year of the study, and they increased during the course of the period.

In contrast, there was an average net transfer from the public exchequer to non-Western immigrants. Transfers per capita increased markedly between 1991 and 1995, and indeed until 1996, when DKK 66,000 was transferred annually per non-Western immigrant aged 18 or over. These net transfers from the public exchequer diminished noticeably between 1996 and 1998 as the employment situation improved. Since the upswing in the economy continued into 1999, one might have expected a further reduction in net transfers to non-Western immigrants; instead, there was no substantial change.

In the case of non-Western immigrants who had been resident in Denmark for ten years or more, the average net transfer from the public exchequer amounted to DKK 47,000 in 1999 (figures not shown in the table). Transfers were greatest, at DKK 74,000 annually, for those who had been in the country for 3-5 years. Even those non-Western immigrants who had been in the country for a long time continued to receive transfer incomes from the public exchequer.

Table 7.1 shows that the figures fluctuated a great deal for second generation immigrants with both Western and non-Western backgrounds. This was in part due to the fact that these were young groups, particularly the non-Westerners. Most of them were at an age when they were on their way to becoming established on the labour market (and being established on the labour market usually means that net transfers change from being negative to being positive). A small shift in the age composition of the sample could therefore have considerable impact. In addition, a single extreme value could have major consequences for the average in a group with few observations. The large differences in net transfers between 1998 on the one hand and 1997 and 1999 on the other for non-Western second generation immigrants were thus due to one extreme value in the 1998 sample (one individual with an exceptionally high positive value). If this outlying value is omitted from the sample, the average figure for 1998 is roughly on a par with the figures for 1997 and 1999.

However, it is the total net transfers which are most relevant in assessing the overall economic effects. These total net transfers, as shown in Table 7.2, reflect average net transfers per person and the total number of people in a group.

Table 7.2. Total net transfers to the Danish public exchequer from different groups during the years 1991 and 1995-2001. Amounts in DKK millions at contemporary prices (amounts adjusted to 1997 prices in *italics*).

Group	1991	1995	1996	1997	1998	1999	2000	2001
Western immigrants	1,046 *1,151*	1,143 *1,188*	913 *928*	1,054	2,101 *2,064*	2,205 *2,163*	3,460 *3,229*	3,601 *3,289*
Western 2nd generation	126 *134*	67 *67*	208 *208*	252	141 *134*	304 *290*	401 *379*	453 *408*
Western immigrants and 2nd generation	1,173 *1,284*	1,203 *1,255*	1,121 *1,143*	1,307	2,242 *2,198*	2,509 *2,405*	3,868 *3,608*	4,040 *3,705*
Non-Western immigrants	-4,855 *-5,338*	-8,753 *-9,206*	-9,488 *-9,763*	-9,132	-8,790 *-8,597*	-9,436 *-9,191*	-10,631 *-10,060*	-11,077 *-10,149*
Non-Western 2nd generation	1 *1*	-82 *-82*	-74 *-74*	-104	15 *15*	-148 *141*	-141 *134*	-37 *-30*
Non-Western immigrants and 2nd generation	-4,788 *-5,338*	-8,835 *-9,206*	-9,562 *-9,763*	-9,235	-8,775 *-8,597*	-9,577 *-9,191*	-10,772 *-10,060*	-11,114 *-10,149*
All immigrants and 2nd gen.	-3,682 *-4,046*	-7,624 *-7,951*	-8,449 *-8,827*	-7,929	-6,533 *-6,399*	-7,068 *-6,785*	-6,904 *-6,451*	-7,060 *-6,444*
Western immigrants and 2nd generation; transfers as a percentage of GDP	+0.13	+0.11	+0.10	+0.12	+0.19	+0.21	+0.30	+0,30
Non-Western immigrants and 2nd generation; transfers as a percentage of GDP	-0.54	-0.88	-0.89	-0.83	-0.75	-0.79	-0.84	-0.83
All immigrants and 2nd generation, transfers as a percentage of GDP	-0.41	-0.76	-0.79	-0.71	-0.56	-0.58	-0.54	-0.53

Source: Finansministeriets Lovmodel.

There were considerable net transfers from the Western immigrant population to the public exchequer in all the years listed. The level dropped a little during the first half of the 1990s in parallel with the downturn in the economy, but it then increased again gradually until it reached a figure of DKK 3.6 billion in 2001.

The picture was very different for the non-Western immigrant population. There were major net transfers to these immigrants from the start of the 1990s, and these transfers had more or less doubled by 1996 to something approaching DKK 10 billion. The amount of the transfers then declined gradually in 1997 and 1998 before rising once more in the period up to 2001, by which time the amount totalled in excess of DKK 11 billion, primarily because of the increase in the number of immigrants in the country.

The sizes of the transfers are also given in the table as percentage of the Danish GDP. In 1991 transfers to immigrants – Western and non-Western – totalled 0.41% of GDP. This proportion increased to 0.79% in 1996. Between 1996 and 1998 it fell to 0.56%, and it declined a trifle more to 0.53% of GDP in 2001. For non-Western immigrants alone, the corresponding figures were -0.54% in 1991, -0.89% in 1996, -0.75% in 1998 and -0.83% in 2001.

Costs associated with asylum seekers are not included in the calculations, since these expenditures are regarded as part of the cost of border policing. They amounted to DKK 546 million in 1991, DKK 2,433 million in 1995 and DKK 907 million in 1999. In 2007, however, the figure had shrunk to DKK 441 million.

One major finding that is evident from Tables 7.1 and 7.2 is that net transfers differ substantially for the different immigrant groups. There is a net transfer *from* Western immigrants *to* public funds, and a net transfer *to* non-Western immigrants *from* public funds. It is also clear that in total, net transfers go from public funds to immigrants.

7.3. Factors affecting the amount of net transfers to or from individuals

Up to this point, we have considered the amount of net transfers per person and the total amounts of net transfers to various groups. We will now turn to the issue of how different factors affect the amounts of these net transfers.

It is typical for all societies that money is transferred from people of active working age to people outside the active working age. Transfers are also made between people in the active age groups, for example from those in employment to the unemployed. Such transfers can take place in several ways, for example within families, through private arrangements (insurance, saving, charities) or via the public sector. It is characteristic of industrialised countries – and most particularly welfare states such as Denmark – that a very large proportion of this redistribution takes place via the public sector.

Net transfers between groups are heavily dependent on the age structures of the groups in question. Among immigrants, there are few old people – especially in the case of immigrants from non-Western countries – while there are a relatively high number per immigrant of children under the age of 18. The low number of elderly people would tend to promote net transfers from immigrants to the public exchequer, while the high rate of fertility would lead us to expect net transfers to the immigrant population.

We can illustrate the significance of these demographic factors by first considering how net transfers vary with age and then examining how these patterns affect the various groups. In the data material used in this analysis, children are regarded as independent individuals; in other words, net transfers related to children are not added to the incomes of parents in this section.

Figure 7.1 shows that for all three groups, there are net transfers from the public exchequer to children and young people, and similarly to the elderly. For both Danes and Western immigrants, the switch from positive to negative transfers takes place around the age of 60, in contrast to the situation for non-Western immigrants, where the transfers are negative at all age levels except one. Net transfers from the public exchequer increase gradually with age, primarily because of the costs associated with illness and care for the elderly. Since there are few immigrants over the age of 68, the expenditures on Danes are taken as being representative for immigrants, in order to avoid very large random variations. In the figure, random variation is reduced for all three groups by using averages for three consecutive ages in years, so that, for example, the figures for age 42 are actually an average for people aged 41, 42 and 43.

A comparison of the figures for the age group 20-60 reveals both similarities and differences between the groups. The pattern is essentially the same for Danes and Western immigrants. In the case of young adults, the figures for Western immigrants were rather lower than for Danes, since a proportion of such immigrants had come to Denmark to study. Students have little or no income, and therefore pay less in tax. The most noticeable difference is between Danes and Western immigrants on the one hand and non-Western immigrants on the other. For non-Western immigrants, there was a net transfer *from* public funds in virtually all age categories, including people of active working age.

A detailed analysis based on the figures for 1999 shows that the large differences in net transfers between Danes and non-Western immigrants cannot be explained in terms of differences in the age or family structure of the populations, but is primarily attributable to the lower rate of employment among non-Western immigrants. This leads to lower average incomes from work and thus to the payment of less taxes, and to substantial transfers from public funds in the form of unemployment benefits. This effect is intensified by the fact that non-Western immigrants typically earn lower wages, and the income for self-employed non-Western immigrants is also lower than is the case for the self-employed in the other two groups.

Figure 7.1. Net transfers to the public exchequer, by age (average of three consecutive ages in years), DKK thousands annually. 1999.

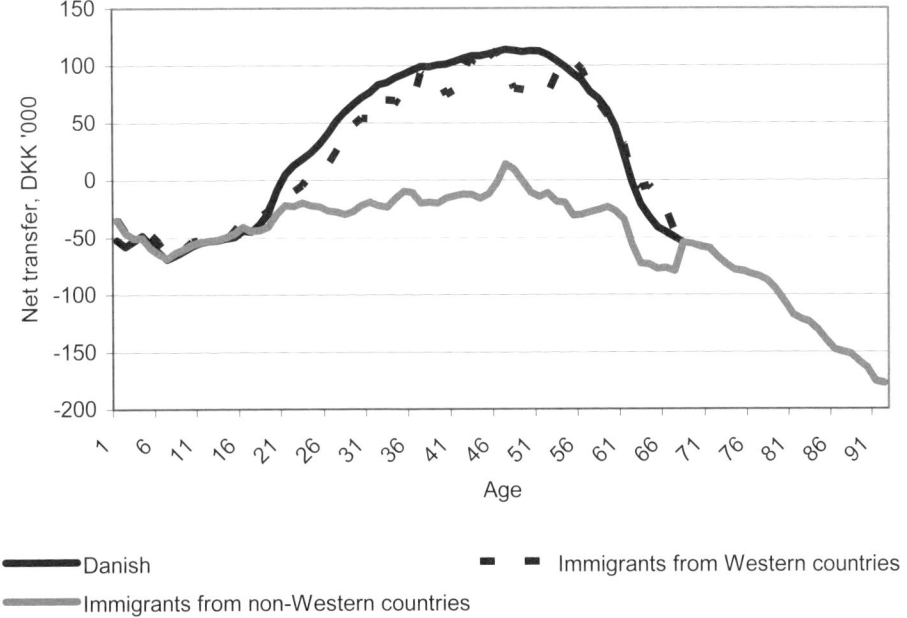

Source: Gunnar Viby Mogensen and Poul Chr. Matthiessen (2002).
Note. Actual average amounts are used for each group for people aged 0-67. For those aged 68 and over, the values for Danes are used for all three groups, since there are so few data for older immigrants.

7.4. A cohort analysis: The long-term effects of one year's immigration

So far we have considered net transfers in single years and compared various years. Another approach would be to consider the consequences that immigration in a given year has for the public finances in that and subsequent years. This can be done by analysing a hypothetical immigration of 10,000 people from Western and 10,000 from non-Western countries.

The immigration we will analyse is presumed to have taken place at the beginning of 1998. Each immigrant group is assumed to have the same age distribution as the immigrants from the cohort who actually did arrive in 1998. The number of these immigrants remaining in Denmark will gradually diminish over time, since we will only take the first generation into account. The rates of remigration and the age structures of the groups are assumed to continue unchanged from the pattern in 1998, and the mortality rates in the various age groups are assumed to mirror those of the population of Denmark in general. It is also assumed that the levels of net transfers by age continue in the future in a pattern for each group identical to that seen in 1998.

The value of money changes over time. This means that the amounts of net transfers must be discounted. This is done using four different rates (Table 7.3). As the table shows, the Western immigrants make a significant transfer *to* public funds, whatever discount rate is adopted. Immigrants in this group are largely of active age in terms of work, and many of them remigrate relatively quickly, so that they do not reach the retirement age in Denmark. For non-Western immigrants, in contrast, there are sizable net transfers *from* public funds, regardless of the discount rate applied. Like the Western immigrants, the non-Western immigrants are of active working age, but their rate of employment is considerably lower. Furthermore, the remigration rate is lower, so that a larger proportion remain in the country after the retirement.

Table 7.3. Total net transfers to public funds in DKK millions as a result of an immigration of 10,000 people from Western countries and 10,000 people from non-Western countries in 1998. Equivalent values for 1995 in parentheses.

Discount rate	Western immigrants	Non-Western immigrants
0	6,718 (4,152)	-15,446 (-26,027)
1	6,314 (4,087)	-11,062 (-19,187)
2	5,697 (3,482)	-8,325 (-11,490)
3.5	4,717 (3,306)	-5,864 (-10,882)

Note. Age structure is taken as being the same as for actual immigrants in the year in question. For assumptions regarding remigration and mortality rates, see the text.
Source: Gunnar Viby Mogensen and Poul Chr. Matthiessen (2002).

The results of this type of calculation are highly dependent upon the year that is chosen as a basis for the calculation. The figures in brackets show the results of a calculation based on an immigration at the beginning of 1995 using that year's patterns for calculating the net transfers. The results are affected by the lower rate of employment in that year. The transfers from the Western immigrants are lower, and the transfers to the non-Western immigrants are considerably larger.

7.5. Studies in other countries

As discussed in Wadensjö and Orrje (2002), a number of countries have carried out cross-sectional studies of the fiscal effects of immigration. The quality of the data used for these studies is variable, except in the case of those from the Nordic countries.

A Norwegian study in 1998 showed that refugees received substantial income transfers, but there was a net positive transfer to public funds from other immigrants. The situation with respect to refugees was primarily due to their poor connection to the labour market.

A number of studies were carried out in Sweden between the 1960s and the 1990s, with very varied results. There was a shift from the immigration of labour to immigration by refugees over the period, combined with major changes in the Swedish economy. While in the 1960s and 1970s there were net transfers from immigrants to public funds, the situation was much changed in the 1990s as a result of the poor economic situation and the substantial influx of refugees. A study conducted in 1999 showed that the net negative transfers to immigrants in 1994 were equivalent to 2% of Swedish GDP.

However, in a number of countries, such as the UK, Australia and Canada, the studies carried out appear to show a positive contribution to public funds from immigration.

The fiscal effects of immigration thus vary between different countries and also within individual countries, depending on the period selected for analysis. A common factor in all these studies is that immigrant populations are found to have an age structure that could be expected to contribute to a positive net transfer to public funds. However, immigrants have a lower rate of employment and lower earnings than those of native populations. This means that while there is one factor – the age distribution – which has a positive fiscal effect, there is another factor – employment – which has a negative effect. In some cases it is the first factor which is dominant, while in others it is the second. The results are also dependent on whether the calculations include only the first generation of immigrants, or whether they also include second generation immigrants.

7.6. Summary

This chapter has examined the effects on the public exchequer of immigration to Denmark in the period 1991-2001.

The inhabitants of a country contribute in various ways to public income. People with incomes pay income-related taxes (direct taxes such as Income Tax) and taxes on their purchases (indirect taxes, including Value Added Tax). Most of these amounts can be linked to individuals.

Public sector expenditures on individuals can be worked out similarly. The simplest of these expenditures to calculate are transfer incomes, which are made directly to individuals, for example in connection with sickness, unemployment or old age. As far as costs associated with public consumption and public investments are concerned, some of these costs can also be attributed to individuals fairly easily. These are the costs of individual public consumption, which are in fact like transfer incomes, but which take the form of services rather than cash. Other costs, on the other hand, cannot be directly attributed to individuals, even though they are dependent on the overall size of the population (for example, the costs of the roads). A third group of expenditures are those which, within certain limits, are not dependent on the size of the population (for example the costs of defence and the foreign service).

For Western immigrants, transfers to the public exchequer were positive in every year of the study described in this chapter. The downturn in the business cycle reduced the value of transfers between 1991 and 1996, but after that they increased gradually until 2001, when they amounted to over DKK 41,000 per capita. The figures were even higher for Western second generation immigrants, except in 1998. Transfer incomes from Danes were positive in all years between 1991 and 2001.

In contrast, there was an average net transfer from the public exchequer to non-Western immigrants. Transfers per capita increased markedly between 1991 and 1995, and indeed until 1996, when DKK 66,000 was transferred annually per non-Western immigrant aged 18 or over. These net transfers from the public exchequer diminished noticeably between 1996 and 1998 to DKK 54,000 as the employment situation improved.

Since the upswing in the economy continued into 1999, one might have expected a further reduction in net transfers to non-Western immigrants; instead, there was a slight increase in the amount, which reached just under DKK 58,000 per capita in 2001.

However, it is the total net transfers which are most relevant in assessing the overall economic effects. There were considerable net transfers from the Western immigrant population to the public exchequer in all the years listed. The level dropped a little during the first half of the 1990s with the downturn in the economy, but it then increased again gradually until it reached a figure of DKK 3.6 billion in 2001.

The picture was very different for the non-Western immigrant population. Major net transfers were made to these immigrants from the start of the 1990s, and these transfers had more or less doubled by 1996 to something approaching DKK 10 billion. The amount of the transfers then declined gradually in 1997 and 1998 before again rising in the period up to 2001, by which time the amount had reached over DKK 11 billion, primarily because of the increase in the number of immigrants in the country.

In 1991 transfers to all immigrants – Western and non-Western – totalled 0.41% of GDP, and this amount had increased to 0.79% in 1996. Between 1996 and

1998 it fell to 0.56%, and it declined a trifle more to 0.53% of GDP in 2001. For non-Western immigrants the corresponding figure for 2001 was 0.83%.

For Danes, Western and non-Western immigrants alike, there are net transfers from public funds to children and young people and to the elderly. While for Danes and non-Western immigrants there is a positive net transfer to the public exchequer for people in the age range 20-60, there is a net transfer from public funds to non-Western immigrants in this age category, primarily because of their poor situation with respect to employment.

The fiscal effects of immigration vary between different countries and also within individual countries, depending on the period selected for analysis. Immigrant populations have an age structure which should in itself promote positive net transfers to the state. However, immigrant populations generally have a lower rate of employment and lower earnings than those of native populations. This means that there is one factor – the age distribution – which has a positive effect, and another factor – employment – which has a negative effect. In some cases it is the first factor which is dominant, while in others it is the second.

References

Gerdes, Christer and Eskil Wadensjö. 2006. *Immigration and the Welfare State: Some Danish Experiences.* AMID Working Paper Series 60/2006.

Viby Mogensen, Gunnar and Poul Chr. Matthiessen with contributions by Claus Larsen, Niels-Kenneth Nielsen, Marie Louise Schultz-Nielsen and Eskil Wadensjö. 2002. *Indvandrerne og arbejdsmarkedet. Mødet med det danske velfærdssamfund.* Copenhagen: Spektrum.

Wadensjö, Eskil. 1999. "Ekonomiska effekter av indvandringen", in David Coleman and Eskil Wadensjö, with contributions by Bent Jensen and Søren Pedersen, *Indvandringen til Danmark. Internationale og nationale perspektiver.* Copenhagen: Spektrum.

Wadensjö, Eskil. 2000. "Omfördeling via offentlig sektor: En fördjupad analys", in Gunnar Viby Mogensen and Poul Chr. Matthiessen (eds), *Integration i Danmark omkring årtusindeskiftet.* Aarhus: Aarhus University Press.

Wadensjö, Eskil. 2002. "Ekonomiska effekter av invandringen", in Gunnar Viby Mogensen and Poul Chr. Matthiessen (eds), *Indvandrerne og arbejdsmarkedet.* Copenhagen: Spektrum.

Wadensjö, Eskil. 2007. "Immigration and net transfer within the public sector in Denmark", *European Journal of Political Economy* 23/2, 472-485.

Wadensjö, Eskil and Helena Orrje. 2002. *Immigration and the Public Sector in Denmark.* Aarhus: Aarhus University Press.

Wadensjö, Eskil and Christer Gerdes. 2004. "Immigrants and the Public Sector in Denmark and Germany" and "Some Socioeconomic Consequences of Immigration", in Torben Tranæs and Klaus F. Zimmermann (eds), *Migrants, Work and the Welfare State.* Odense: University Press of Southern Denmark.

8. The geographical distribution of non-Western immigrants in Denmark

8.1. The residential pattern of non-Western immigrants, 1985-2004

8.1.1. Introduction

In the course of the work on the Rockwool Foundation immigration project, it became increasingly clear that there was an important spatial aspect of immigration and its consequences, and that this had been under-researched. The Board of the Research Foundation therefore allocated funds to a project that would focus on the geographical distribution of non-Western immigrants and the implications of this for a variety of factors related to integration.

Since non-Western immigrants tend to have low incomes and frequently to be recipients of welfare benefits, other questions arose as well: how do the living conditions and the geographical distribution of non-Western immigrants differ from those of other low-income groups, and how do these low-income groups' patterns of residence and home-occupier status differ from those of other social groups?

As the project progressed, its aims became broader. The analysis was extended to cover the residential situation of the entire population, as the title of the book that came out of the project suggests: *En befolkning deler sig op?* (A Dividing Population?) (Damm, Schultz-Nielsen and Tranæs, 2006). The book compares the patterns of residence in 1985 and 2003. The immigrant group also includes second generation immigrants (see also Anna Piil Damm and Marie Louise Schultz-Nielsen (2008)). This chapter is primarily concerned with describing the research on the geographical distribution of non-Western immigrants and the implications of this in relation to integration.

Patterns of residence that follow social and ethnic boundaries are often seen as social segregation. This study was based primarily on two key measures of residential segregation, namely *Evenness* and *Exposure*. To assess these, the study followed the recommendation of Massey and Denton (1988) in using two classic indices of segregation, the Dissimilation and Isolation indices.

Evenness refers to the difference in the distributions of two social groups across area units in a town, for example in terms of districts of the town. A minority group such as non-Western immigrants is said to be segregated if its members are distributed very differently across area units in comparison with the majority population (Blau 1977). Evenness is maximised, and segregation minimised, when all area units have the same relative proportions of members of the minority and majority groups as the town or city as a whole.

Exposure refers to the degree of potential contact or the opportunities for social interaction between the members of the minority and majority groups within geographical districts of a town. Exposure indices measure the extent to which the members of the minority and majority groups may potentially meet each other physically if they live in the same residential district.

8.1.2. The Dissimilation Index

The index for unevenness of housing settlement is called the Dissimilation Index. It measures the degree to which a minority group is distributed in the same way as a majority population across various residential districts in a geographical area such as a town. The index value is designated D, and it measures the degree of unevenness in how the members of the two groups are distributed across the residential districts. The value of D varies between 0 and 1 and indicates the proportion of the minority population who would have to move to another district of the town so that the distribution of the minority population in the town in question is in line with the distribution of the majority population.

The Dissimilation Index is calculated as follows (Cutler *et al.*, 2005; Echenique and Fryer 2005):

$$D = \frac{1}{2}\sum_{i}^{I}\left|\frac{x_i}{X} - \frac{t_i - x_i}{T - X}\right|$$

where

I = the number of residential districts in the town,

x_i = the number of minority group members in residential district *i*,

t_i = the number of inhabitants of residential district *i*,

X = the number of minority group members living in the town, and

T = the total number of inhabitants in the town.

The formula operates as follows. For every residential district, a calculation is made of the difference between the proportions of the majority and minority populations that live there. The numerical values of these differences for all the housing districts are then added together and the total divided by two, since every overrepresentation of the minority group in one housing district must be counterbalanced by an underrepresentation somewhere else. As it is the difference in the relative distributions of the two population groups that is calculated, it makes no difference to the Dissimilation Index value whether the town as a whole is home to many or few members of the minority group.

According to Massey and Denton (1988), an index value under 0.3 indicates a relatively high level of integration, a value of 0.3-0.6 indicates a moderate degree of segregation, and a value over 0.6 is evidence of a high level of segregation. However, the index values are affected by the size of the housing districts used in the calculation. The smaller the housing districts, the larger the values will be (Cutler *et al.*, 2005). This means that the district boundaries cannot be used too rigidly. This is because the finer the division into districts, the greater are the requirements for the evenness of the distribution of the homes of the majority and minority populations.

In this chapter, the D values are multiplied by 100 so that the results can be read in terms of a percentage proportion of the minority population that would have to move from one residential district to another in order to obtain a uniform population distribution.

8.1.3. The Isolation Index

The Isolation Index is a measure of the proportion of the members of the minority group in a housing district which a typical minority group member will encounter in the town or country. The index values range between 0 and 1, and in slightly simplified terms the value can be said to be an expression of the probability that a random member of the minority group in a country or town will meet coincidentally with another member of the same ethnic group in his or her housing district.

The Isolation Index is calculated as follows (Massey and Denton 1988):

$$_xP^*_x = \sum_i^I \frac{x_i}{X} \frac{x_i}{t_i}$$

The calculation is based on the members of the minority group in a town. If there are x_i members of the group who live in residential district i, the probability of a randomly selected resident of district i being a minority group member will be x_i/t_i. The probabilities for all the residential districts are then weighted according to the proportion of the total town membership of the minority group who live in the residential district in question, i.e. x_i/X. The weighted probabilities for all the residential areas are then added together to produce the Isolation Index value for the town.

Unlike the Dissimilation Index, the Isolation Index value is highly dependent on the relative sizes of the majority and minority populations. The Dissimilation

Index describes the proportion of the minority group who would need to move to another residential district to even out the distribution of the population, and the size of the minority group makes no difference to this. In contrast, the Isolation Index measures the probability of being able to move around the area where one lives without contact with a member of the majority population, and of course this probability increases the more members of the minority group there are.

8.1.4. Delimitation of residential districts

A key issue in an analysis of the residential distribution of a population is how the residential districts are delimited, and what factors are taken into account in doing this.

In this study, the aim was to define residential areas for the entire population of Denmark which would reflect the geographical areas within which each individual had most contact with the other residents. In addition, it was necessary that these residential districts should be stable over time, which ruled out the use of administrative divisions such as parishes or school districts. Finally, it was necessary that the residential districts could be linked to information from administrative registers.

The residential districts were delineated on the basis of the National Square Grid – Denmark, which is a national system of vector grids constructed by the National Survey and Cadastre (Kort & Matrikelstyrelsen), Statistics Denmark and other organisations. The grid uses a rectangular coordinate system to divide Denmark into cells measuring 100 x 100 metres. It is possible to link data to each of these hectare cells, and these data can then be presented in aggregate form. In order to obtain access to such data from Statistics Denmark, however, it was necessary to observe their confidentiality requirements, which follow the principle that the more detail one wants about the people in a specific area, the more households there must be in that area. For this reason, cells had to be merged to create residential districts.

Small residential districts comprise a minimum of 150 households. These districts were used for the calculation of the Dissimilation Index and also as an explanatory variable in the statistical analyses. The larger residential districts were used for descriptive data and consisted of a minimum of 600 households.

The districts were constructed from the 431,233 hectare cells in Denmark which were inhabited on either 1 January 1985 or 1 January 2004. Table 8.1 shows the distribution of households and residents in the hectare cells on these two dates. The 10.1% of the cells included in the table despite being uninhabited in 1985 are included because they were inhabited in 2004; similarly, 3.9% of the hectare cells that were listed as uninhabited in 2004 were inhabited in 1985.

Table 8.1. Distribution of households and residents in Denmark in hectare cells in 1985 and 2004. Percent.

	Distribution of households		Distribution of residents	
Number of households/residents in the cell	1985	2004	1985	2004
0	10.1	3.9	10.1	3.9
1-4	63.9	65.7	44.1	46.8
5-9	14.2	15.5	16.0	16.4
10-19	8.0	9.9	11.5	13.2
20-49	2.5	3.4	15.0	16.0
50-99	1.0	1.1	2.1	2.3
100-149	0.3	0.3	0.7	0.7
150-	0.2	0.2	0.6	0.6
Total	100.2	100.0	100.1	99.9
Total number of inhabited hectare cells	431,233	431,233	431,233	431,233

Source: Anna Piil Damm, Marie Louise Schultz-Nielsen and Torben Tranæs (2006).

The table shows that only 0.2% of the hectare cells had sufficient households in both 1985 and 2004 not to require merging with other cells to form residential districts with at least 150 households. On the other hand, 65% of the cells had fewer than 5 households in both years. In other words, it was necessary to carry out a comprehensive process of merging cells.

In merging cells into suitable residential districts it was decided to emphasise certain criteria, namely that the residential districts should:

- comprise a minimum of 150 households
- remain unaltered over time
- use any local physical barriers as borders
- consist of contingent cells
- be compact in shape
- be homogenous with respect to the ownership and type of housing
- be physically relatively small
- be of roughly the same size.

The criteria are presented above in order of priority, and they were used for the creation of both small and large districts. An additional criterion used in the creation of the large residential districts was that they should respect the boundaries of the small districts: a small residential district could not be divided across two or more larger districts.

8.1.5. Trends in the two indices, 1985-2004

The proportion of non-Western immigrants in the Danish population rose sharply during the period 1985-2003, as Chapter 1 of this book describes. Figure 8.1 shows how the proportion of non-Western immigrants to Danes in the population increased from 1.5% in 1985 to 5.9% in 2003. This trend is reflected in the Isolation Index, which rose from 9.2% in 1985 to 23.4% in 2003. By the end of the period, a randomly-selected non-Western immigrant had a greater chance of randomly encountering another non-Western immigrant in his or her residential district than a recipient of welfare benefits had of encountering another person receiving welfare benefits, for whom the Isolation Index value in 2003 was 20.5% There were, however, many fewer non-Western immigrants than there were recipients of welfare benefits. This means that the homes of immigrants must have been more concentrated into a smaller number of residential districts than was the case for recipients of employment-related transfer incomes, i.e. benefits such as unemployment pay, social security benefits, incapacity benefits, activation allowances, etc. as described in Chapter 6. The same picture can be seen from the Dissimilation Index, which stood at 54.1% in 2003 for non-Western immigrants, as against 27.3% for recipients of transfer incomes. The Isolation Index value for a division of the population according to education and gross income was only 21%.

Figure 8.1. Index calculations. Non-Western immigrants and second-generation immigrants, 1985-2003.

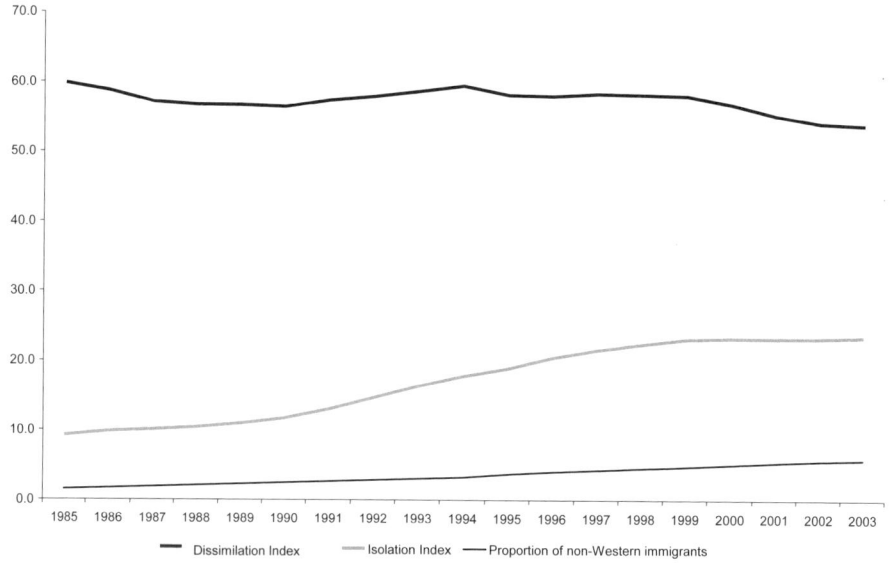

Source: Own calculations based on register data from Statistics Denmark and Geomatic.

One of the explanations for the high index value probably lies in the marriage patterns of non-Western immigrants, which are briefly described in Chapter 1. Non-Western immigrants (unlike recipients of welfare benefits) usually marry within their national group, and this in itself can contribute to increasing the concentration of immigrants in a given area.

Even though the Dissimilation Index for non-Western immigrants was high in 2003, Figure 8.1 shows that it was even higher at the start of the period covered by the study, at 60.1%. After that, the Dissimilation Index, which measures unevenness in residential distribution, exhibited a slightly downward trend, especially in the periods immediately subsequent to 1994 and 1999. Part of the explanation for this was undoubtedly the government's new housing policy, whereby newly arrived refugees were deliberately placed in housing spread over much of Denmark. However, the fact that this policy, which gave rise to a very widespread distribution of refugees, only brought about such a modest decline in the value of the index was probably a reflection of the fact that many refugees subsequently chose to move to the larger towns.

To help elucidate this issue, Table 8.2 shows the residential patterns for people originating from various countries. The figures presented are for the last day of each of the years 1994, 1998 and 2003.

Table 8.2. Patterns of places of residence for the largest national groups among non-Western immigrants in Denmark.

	Dissimilation Index			Isolation Index			Number of individuals	
	1994	1998	2003	1994	1998	2003	1994	2003
Afghanistan	97.5	95.0	84.7	2.3	2.5	3.0	1,180	10,192
The former Yugoslavia	80.9	69.8	66.7	4.6	7.6	8.2	13,451	44,037
Iraq	87.6	83.4	73.7	3.7	5.8	6.7	6,378	25,492
Iran	76.7	74.1	69.8	3.3	2.9	2.5	11,039	14,065
Lebanon	85.7	86.4	84.5	15.1	20.6	22.7	15,057	21,620
Pakistan	87.0	86.2	84.1	6.9	7.7	7.5	14,585	19,082
Somalia	90.9	86.9	86.5	3.5	7.0	10.7	5,237	16,708
Sri Lanka	87.5	86.3	83.1	4.6	6.1	5.3	7,148	10,307
Turkey	80.2	79.5	75.9	13.2	15.9	15.5	39,113	53,979
Vietnam	87.0	84.9	80.4	5.4	6.5	6.3	9,138	12,411

Source: Own calculations based on register data from Statistics Denmark and Geomatic.

It was not possible to obtain figures for people with different types of residence permit, so it is not known exactly which of these people were refugees, family members reunited with previous immigrants, or guest workers. If we consider the immigrants and second generation immigrants from the former Yugoslavia, we can assume that most of the people included in the statistics at the end of 1994 were guest workers and family members or second generation immigrants born in Denmark. In 1994 the Dissimilation Index for this group was at a level of 80.9%, but it fell to 69.8% in 1998 after the arrival in Denmark of a very large group of refugees from the region.

The Dissimilation Index also fell over time for the other nationalities, but in general not particularly steeply in the period from 1994 to 1998. On the other hand, the index dropped very sharply between 1998 and 2003 for Afghans and Iraqis, many of whom arrived as refugees after 1999. Since there were very few people from these countries living in Denmark in 1994, it is necessary to interpret the Dissimilation Index values for this year with caution. In general, however, the index values were very high for all groups, which is strong evidence of a high level of residential segregation for each individual group.

The values for the Isolation Index reflect the fact that people from the former Yugoslavia were spread significantly more thinly across the country than the Turks, who were certainly a larger group, and therefore had a greater chance of randomly encountering a fellow countryman. However, it was people from Lebanon – in reality, often stateless Palestinians – who were most likely to encounter a fellow countryman in their residential districts. The index value rose in step with the increase in the number of Palestinians in Denmark, whereas the Dissimilation Index value for this group did not change very much.

The proportion of immigrants in the population is generally greatest in the larger towns in Denmark, but even for towns with very similar proportions of immigrants in the population there were significant differences in 2003 in the extent to which immigrants and Danes lived in the same residential districts. A comparison between the four largest cities in Denmark (Copenhagen, Aarhus, Odense and Aalborg) showed that even though the proportion of immigrants in the population was a little higher in Copenhagen than in Aarhus and Odense, the probability of a non-Western immigrant encountering another non-Western immigrant by chance in his or her residential district was 40-41% in Aarhus and Odense as against only 26% in Copenhagen. This was because the homes of immigrants were more widely dispersed geographically in Copenhagen than in the other two cities. In Copenhagen, Isolation Index values of the same level were only found in certain districts, such as Nørrebro, Brønshøj, Ishøj and Brøndby, where the proportions of immigrants in the population were far higher than those found in Aarhus and Odense.

Of the immigrants living in the medium-sized towns of Denmark, i.e. towns other than the four largest but with populations in excess of 10,000, most had homes in towns close to Copenhagen such as Farum, Frederiksværk and Helsingør, where the proportion of immigrants in the population was greater than 10% in all cases. However, it was in the towns of Haderslev, Ikast and Korsør, all of them far from Copenhagen, that the housing pattern of non-Western immigrants was most different from that of the remainder of the population. Of the medium-sized towns, Ikast was the one where a non-Western immigrant had the greatest chance of randomly encountering another immigrant in his or her residential district.

A convenient explanation for immigrants' very unusual patterns of residence might seem to lie in their weak connection with the labour market. If that were the case, then it could be expected that their patterns of residence would resemble those of others with similarly low incomes. However, a comparison of the residence patterns of immigrants and of Danes with the same level of income indicates that this is not the case. Among those immigrants who were in the top 25% of income earners in the population, 59% would have had to move in order to create an even distribution of residence in districts where Danes with the same income level live. Among the immigrants in the lowest 25% of income earners in the population, 50% would have had to move for their residence distribution to be the same as that of Danes with the same income level.

8.2. Where do non-Western immigrants live?

Non-Western immigrants live more frequently than Danes in multi-storey flats owned by non-profit, state subsidised cooperative housing associations. One reason for this is clearly that immigrants generally have lower incomes than Danes, and therefore a relatively cheap rented flat for which it is possible to claim housing benefits is an attractive solution. In addition, local authorities in Denmark have the right to allocate a proportion of all vacant flats owned by these housing associations to tenants of their choice, which means that they can often help people to find a home regardless of their position on a waiting list. However, even taking socioeconomic factors such as income into account, immigrants still exhibit a disproportionately high likelihood of being tenants in large blocks of flats.

The fact that immigrants are rarely tenants in houses or small apartment blocks is presumably connected with the fact that they often live in the larger towns. However, it can also be difficult to obtain access to the most attractive homes owned by small housing associations, as there may be long waiting lists. Networks also play a role, especially in the case of housing associations, since these homes are often passed from one owner to another without a formal queue. Discrimination may also be a factor.

The most transparent section of the housing market is for owner-occupied housing. Paradoxically, however, it is where immigrants are most rarely represented. This may be connected with the fact that immigrants often live in towns, where house prices are higher. Living in towns is often a matter of choice. Studies of the refugees who were placed in different parts of the country under the government's policy on refugee housing have shown that they frequently choose to move into the towns. Reasons for this choice might be that it is in towns that their countrymen and other immigrants live, and that in towns they have access to a support network, shopping facilities, etc. that make it easier for them to maintain their accustomed life style.

The preference for living in large towns, where it is difficult to find a privately rented or private housing association apartment, and where owner-occupied accommodation is expensive, means that many immigrants live in flats owned by state subsidised cooperative housing associations. Their relatively low incomes and short period of stay in Denmark imply that the other options in the towns where they wish to live are not as practicable.

Analyses also show that immigrants, all else being equal, have a preference for moving to housing areas where there are many other immigrants. For Danes, the greater the proportion of immigrants there are in a housing area, the lower the probability of their moving there. Similarly, it is more likely that people will move away from rather than into an area with a large proportion of people living on welfare benefits.

This latter tendency applies to immigrants as well as to Danes, all else being equal. In the light of this fact, it might seem surprising that there is such a high concentration of benefit recipients in certain housing areas. The explanation is that all else is *not* equal, and factors such as level of income or changes in family circumstances mean that some people have to live in these areas anyway.

There is no clear point at which an area has so many resource-poor residents that it must be regarded as a "vulnerable" district. But if vulnerability of districts is assessed in terms of crime rate, then it can be seen that the problems of crime increase with the proportion of immigrants in the area and especially with the proportion of people receiving welfare benefits. A reasonable definition of a "vulnerable" district would appear to be one where the proportion of people living on transfer income exceeds 40% and the proportion of immigrants exceeds 30%. Most such areas in Denmark are now situated, as indeed they were previously, in the Greater Copenhagen Area; but as early as 1991 Aarhus, Denmark's second-largest city, also had housing districts which would be categorised as "vulnerable" using this definition. The increasing number of immigrants in the population and the increased emphasis on the policy of distributing refugees all over the country has meant that the phenomenon of vulnerability has spread to a number of medium-sized provincial towns; by 2003, Odense, Esbjerg, Horsens, Nakskov, Korsør, Slagelse and Svendborg also had vulnerable residential districts.

8.3. The effects of living in a municipality with many other refugees on refugees' employment prospects and salary

Is it a good or a bad thing for integration into the labour market if immigrants live close to many of their countrymen? This important question is the focus of analyses, presented in the last chapter of the book *En befolkning deler sig op?* A comprehensive presentation of the analyses, with all the assumptions, data documents and a full explanation of the methodology, is contained in Damm (2006).

The answer to the question is sought in an analysis of the effects of the number of immigrants from the same country living in a municipality on the integration into the labour market. However, it has only been possible to answer this question in the case of refugees, and not for immigrants generally. It should also be noted that the units considered are municipal authorities, not the small residential districts described earlier in this chapter. In addition to specifically analysing the effects of the number of fellow-countrymen, an examination is made of the effect of the number of refugees of all origins in the municipality.

An immigrant's prospects of employment might be positively affected by the proximity of many fellow countrymen through two mechanisms. First, there are likely to be better opportunities to make use of a tight ethnic network which provides its members with access to extra resources in the host country to promote their economic integration. Second, members of an ethnic minority who consume a high proportion of ethnic products and services are often willing to accept jobs with a lower rate of pay if the workplace is close to or within an ethnic enclave. This willingness to accept less pay reduces the waiting time for receiving an acceptable job offer, thus increasing the probability of obtaining employment, though at a lower wage.

In contrast, there are several mechanisms whereby living close to many fellow countrymen may negatively affect the prospects of employment. First, it is likely to reduce the speed of acquisition of the language and norms of the host country, and these things are generally necessities for a person to be fully functional as a member of the labour force. Second, separation of housing into ethnic enclaves may promote prejudice towards ethnic minorities. Finally, the quality of public institutions such as job centres may be poorer in ethnic enclaves where there are few native people and many immigrants.

It is, however, difficult to determine cause and effect. If the refugees who live in municipalities with many of their fellow countrymen frequently cope badly on the labour market, is this because the presence of the fellow countrymen hinders integration – or is it rather that immigrants who have difficulty coping on the Danish labour market also have a preference for living close to their compatriots? Many of the problems that immigrants have with the labour market can be explained in terms of factors such as gender, age, education, duration of residence, country of origin, or whatever other variables researchers have data for. However, even when research takes into account the significance of all these observable characteristics, there still remain differences between how well immigrants perform on the labour market in different Danish municipalities. The question is, then, whether these remaining differences can be explained in part or even entirely in terms of the number of the immigrants' fellow countrymen living in the same municipality.

The basic problem is to separate out the "neighbourhood effect" from the effect of relevant personal characteristics which are not observable to researchers but which mean that immigrants who cope badly on the Danish labour market also wish to live in close proximity to many of their fellow countrymen. In reality this only becomes a problem if it is mainly those immigrants who cope least well – out of all the immigrants from the same country and with otherwise similar characteristics – who choose to live in close proximity to many of their countrymen. It appears, however, that this is indeed the case, which means that there is a causality problem.

It is therefore necessary to use a research method which will take into account the fact that immigrants are "sorted" between municipalities on the basis of personal characteristics which researchers have no information about, but which might have independent significance for integration into the labour market. This requires the use of a suitable additional dataset. The study described here uses just such a method. It so happens that the Danish authorities have unintentionally brought the necessary data into existence, since at a certain time they implemented a practical "experiment" by randomly distributing a particular group of immigrants – namely refugees – across the entire country. It was in 1986 that the Danish authorities decided that at the outset, refugees should be spread out across the entire country, and that their place of residence should not be governed either by their own wishes or those of the local authorities.

The data on which the study was based consisted solely of individual level data on refugees extracted from the administrative registers at Statistics Denmark on all immigrants for the period 1984-2000. In addition, an age criterion was used in selecting the individuals to be included. Only individuals aged 18-59 among immigrants from refugee source countries were included in the analysis. The final criterion was that the selection was limited to individuals for whom there were observations in the register for each year of a seven-year period from the date of their being granted asylum. The use of these criteria resulted in a sample consisting of 13,927 individuals. The likelihood of each of these individuals being in employment was then calculated. A further analysis was then made of whether income from paid work correlated with whether there were many or few of their fellow countrymen in the municipality where they lived. This stage of the analysis covered only those individuals who had a positive income from work seven years after they had been granted asylum, who were 5,647 in number.

Table 8.3 shows the statistics for every ethnic group separately, and for the whole sample. Most of the individuals were of Middle Eastern origin. It has already been noted that rate of employment, annual work income and the number of fellow countrymen living in the same municipality vary greatly from one ethnic group to another. Taking the information presented in Table 8.3 as the point of departure, a statistical regression model was used to calculate the likelihood of a refugee being in employment seven years after asylum was granted. Similarly, a statistical regression model was used in connection with calculations concerning immigrants' wages from employment seven years after being granted asylum.

Table 8.3. Descriptive statistics for selected variables seven years after the granting of asylum, for each ethnic group and for the entire sample. Average (Standard Deviation)

Country of origin	Number of individuals	Rate of employment		Annual income from work		Average number of fellow countrymen in municipality of residence
		Men	Women	Men	Women	All
Poland	393	0.52 (0.50)	0.42 (0.49)	76,945 (49,689)	61,798 (42,985)	731 (957)
Iraq	2,213	0.32 (0.47)	0.13 (0.33)	54,308 (49,890)	50,685 (49,582)	1,407 (1,496)
Iran	2,829	0.34 (0.47)	0.19 (0.39)	42,663 (37,633)	37,168 (33,315)	1,063 (999)
Vietnam	1,331	0.48 (0.50)	0.24 (0.43)	64,571 (39,421)	48,410 (31,288)	770 (687)
Sri Lanka	1,770	0.54 (0.50)	0.34 (0.47)	58,716 (39,770)	41,381 (28,571)	161 (154)
Stateless (Palestinians)	3,867	0.24 (0.43)	0.06 (0.24)	40,872 (41,075)	47,940 (41,119)	1,280 (1,307)
Ethiopia	146	0.25 (0.44)	0.26 (0.44)	50,673 (41,275)	41,696 (21,366)	180 (136)
Afghanistan	268	0.37 (0.48)	0.16 (0.37)	47,594 (43,023)	50,977 (39,075)	223 (205)
Somalia	872	0.29 (0.46)	0.09 (0.29)	52,591 (42,401)	42,506 (38,891)	1,482 (1,165)
Romania	216	0.56 (0.50)	0.50 (0.50)	76,283 (52,911)	57,547 (35,849)	83 (82)
Chile	22	0.36 (0.50)	0.50 (0.53)	64,003 (45,290)	50,448 (19,319)	156 (146)
Entire sample	13,927	0.35 (0.48)	0.18 (0.38)	24,450 (40,025)	12,211 (28,117)	1,010 (1,177)

Source: Anna Piil Damm, Marie Louise Schultz-Nielsen and Torben Tranæs (2006).
Note: An individual is counted as being employed if he/she is a wage earner with at least 9 hours of work per week on average over the course of a year, or if he/she is self-employed. Annual income is standardised to 1980 prices. Average annual employment income is calculated for individuals with a positive income from work seven years after being granted asylum.

The results show that there is a *negative* correlation between the likelihood of a refugee having employment and the number of fellow-countrymen living in his/her municipality. There is similarly a negative correlation between refugees' average annual income from employment and the number of fellow countrymen living in the same municipality.

These correlations cannot, however, be interpreted as being causal, i.e. empirical evidence that living in proximity to one's fellow countrymen damages one's chances of integration into the Danish labour market. They would be equally consistent with the fact that refugees with certain (unobservable) personal characteristics that hinder economic integration have a tendency to move to municipalities where many of their fellow countrymen live, while refugees with certain (unobservable) personal characteristics which are favourable to employment have a preference for living in municipalities where there are few of their fellow countrymen.

However, the data created by the random placement of refugees at the time they were granted asylum makes it possible to test for causality. The results of this analysis show that living in proximity to many fellow countrymen, all else being equal, *improves* the likelihood of being in employment and of having a higher income.

The economic importance for the integration of refugees into the labour market of the number of fellow countryman living in the same municipality appears to be considerable. Seven years after the granting of asylum, the difference between living in a municipality with the average number of fellow countrymen, which is around 1,000 people, and living in a municipality with twice as many, is that a refugee living in the latter type of municipality earns 21% more than one living in a municipality with few fellow countrymen. In addition, the rate of employment is four percentage points higher for refugees in municipalities with many fellow countrymen. These comparisons are for refugees with the same observable characteristics and the same preferences for living in the vicinity of fellow countrymen.

The results reported above are averages for refugees. The great majority of refugees have less than twelve years of schooling and thus neither matriculation qualifications for entry to higher level study nor educational qualifications for specific employment. It would seem reasonable to suppose that refugees with little education would in particular benefit from having many fellow countrymen in the vicinity for integration into the labour market. The analysis confirms this. The results were driven by the uneducated; it was not possible to obtain statistically robust results for educated refugees alone.

It is important to note that the positive labour market effect only arises when there are many fellow countrymen living in the same municipality, and not refugees of mixed origins; the latter situation probably has a negative effect on the integration of refugees into the labour market.

Future studies should examine whether the results also apply when we consider the number of fellow countrymen living not just in the same municipality, but in the same housing district. It would also be valuable to discover whether the results apply to immigrants in general, and not just to refugees. It should be noted that a proportion of refugees – as mentioned in Section 6.3.1 – may originally have had a different basis for residence in Denmark.

It is important to emphasise that the positive effect of having many fellow countrymen living in the same municipality only applies to wages and rates of employment, and not to integration in general. It is very possible that it has a negative effect on other conditions of life that populations are not mixed, and that newcomers do not find themselves obliged to have much to do with the citizens of the host country in their everyday lives, because they can manage with the help of previous arrivals from the same country who live close by.

8.4. Summary

Overall, the analyses of the patterns of residence of the population of the country today compared with those of twenty years ago show that Denmark was and continues to be a country where people from different backgrounds often live in the same residential district, whether one is talking about differences in education, income or social welfare payments.

The only dimension where differences in residential patterns are very pronounced is with regard to the patterns of residence of non-Western immigrants in comparison with the residence patterns of Danes. The proportion of non-Western immigrants who would have had to move to another residential district for the population to be evenly distributed between the two groups was 54% in 2003. This actually represents a fall in comparison with 1985, when the proportion was 60%. This change is attributable in part to the policy of distributing refugees around the country which was in force during the period.

The proportion of immigrants in the population is generally greatest in the larger towns in Denmark, but even for towns with very similar proportions of immigrants in the population there are significant differences in the extent to which immigrants and Danes live in the same residential districts.

Most of the immigrants living in medium-sized towns in Denmark are found in towns close to Copenhagen such as Farum, Frederiksværk and Helsingør, where the immigrant population exceeds 10% of the residents. However, it is in the towns of Haderslev, Ikast and Korsør, all of them far away from Copenhagen, that the housing patterns of non-Western immigrants are the most different from that of the remainder of the population.

A convenient explanation for immigrants' very unusual patterns of residence might seem to lie in their weak connection with the labour market. However, a comparison of the residence patterns of immigrants and of Danes with the same level of income indicates that this is not the case. Of immigrants in the 25% of the population with the highest incomes, 59% would have to move if their patterns of residence were to become the same as those of Danes in the same income bracket. Among the immigrants in the lowest 25% of the income distribution, 50% would have to move for their residence distribution to be the same as that of Danes with the same income level.

There are major differences between non-Western immigrants and Danes with regard to their type of residence. Non-Western immigrants live more frequently than Danes in multi-storey flats owned by state-subsidised housing cooperatives. A contributory cause of this is that immigrants' incomes are generally lower than those of Danes, making these relatively cheap rented apartments more attractive. Moreover, the local authorities' right to allocate a proportion of vacant housing owned by these cooperatives to tenants of their choice means that they can help immigrants find such a home.

The fact that immigrants rarely rent houses or apartments in smaller blocks is probably linked to the fact that they often live in the larger towns and cities. In addition, this form of accommodation is less accessible to immigrants because of the long waiting lists and the need to have a network. Finally, immigrants are least often to be found living as owner-occupiers.

The separation process is further fuelled by the fact that immigrants – all else being equal – have a tendency to move to areas where there are high proportions of other immigrant residents, while Danes seek to move away from areas with large immigrant populations.

If the *vulnerability* of districts is measured in terms of the crime rate, then the problems increase with the proportion of immigrants in a housing area and especially with the proportion of people receiving welfare benefits. If a vulnerable area is then defined as an area where the proportion of recipients of benefits in the population exceeds 40% and the proportion of immigrants 30%, then most such areas are to be found now, as they were previously, in the Greater Copenhagen Area. However, the increasing number of immigrants in the population and the increased emphasis on the policy of distributing refugees all over the country has meant that the phenomenon has spread to a number of medium-sized provincial towns; by 2003, Odense, Esbjerg, Horsens, Nakskov, Korsør, Slagelse and Svendborg also had "vulnerable" residential districts.

Even though a municipal authority is too large an area to be described as an ethnic enclave, living in a municipality with many fellow countrymen is a factor which has both advantages and disadvantages for the economic integration of immigrants in a host country. The advantages concern having a network; the disadvantages include slower learning of the local language and norms.

Do the advantages outweigh the disadvantages, or *vice versa*? This question has been studied specifically for refugees in Denmark, but not for immigrants in general.

There is in general a negative correlation between the number of refugees who live within a municipality and those refugees' rate of employment and wage income, both when the refugees are fellow countrymen and when they are from different countries of origin. This negative correlation for refugees who are fellow countrymen, however, is due to the fact that refugees who have difficulty in coping on the Danish labour market, over and above difficulties that can be explained by factors such as age, education and duration of period of residence, display a strong tendency to live in close proximity to their fellow countrymen. If this propensity is taken into account, it turns out that for refugees with a low level of education, living in a municipality with many fellow countrymen actually appears to have a positive effect on labour market integration. In the case of better educated refugees, who are few in number, it is not possible to calculate any effect with statistical certainty. It should be noted that a proportion of refugees – as mentioned in Section 6.3.1 – may originally have had a different basis for residence in Denmark.

However, further analyses indicate that living in a municipality with many refugees of mixed origin is harmful to the rate of employment and wage income.

It is important to note that the positive effect of having many fellow countrymen living in the same municipality only applies to wages and rates of employment, and not to integration in general. It is possible that it has a negative effect on other conditions of life that populations are not mixed, and that newcomers do not find themselves obliged to have much to do with the citizens of the host country in their everyday lives, because they can manage with the help of previous arrivals from the same country who live close by.

References

Blau, Peter M. 1977. *Inequality and Heterogeneity: A Primitive Theory of Social Structure.* Free Press.

Cutler, David M., Edward L. Glaeser and Jacob L. Vigdor. 2005. *Is the Melting Pot still Hot? Explaining the Resurgence of Immigrant Segregation.* Working Paper no. 11295. National Bureau of Economic Research.

Damm, Anna Piil. 2006. "Ethnic Enclaves and Immigrant Labour Market Outcomes: Quasi-Experimental Evidence". *Journal of Labor Economics.* 2009.

Damm, Anna Piil, Marie Louise Schultz-Nielsen and Torben Tranæs. 2006. *En befolkning deler sig op?* Copenhagen: Gyldendal.

Damm, Anna Piil and Marie Louise Schultz-Nielsen. 2008. "Danish Neighbourhoods: Construction and Relevance for Measurement of Residential Segregation". *Danish Journal of Economics.* 146(3), 241-263.

Echenique, Frederico and Roland G. Fryer. 2005. *On the Measurement of Segregation.* Working Paper No. 11258. National Bureau of Economic Research.

Massey, Douglas S. and Nancy. A. Denton. 1988. "The Dimensions of Residential Segregation". *Social Forces.* 67(2), 281-315.

9. The integration of non-Western immigrants in Denmark and Germany

9.1. Introduction

In order to obtain a deeper understanding of the factors which influence the integration of non-Western immigrants, the Rockwool Foundation Research Unit (RFF) and the Institute for the Study of Labour (IZA) carried out a comparative analysis of integration in Denmark and Germany. The project was based on two representative questionnaire surveys, carried out in parallel in the two countries, as described in Chapter 2 of this book. The German survey, the Rockwool Foundation Migration Survey – Germany (RFMS-G), covered immigrants from Iran, the former Yugoslavia, Lebanon, Poland and Turkey. The Danish survey, RFMS-D, covered the same groups and in addition a representative group of immigrants from Pakistan, Somalia and Vietnam. Together, the two data sets obtained from these surveys formed a unique tool for comparative analyses in the area of immigrant integration. The results of the study were published in 2004 in a book entitled *Migrants, Work, and the Welfare State*, edited by Torben Tranæs of RFF and Klaus F. Zimmermann of IZA. Since that book was completed later than the two Danish studies of 1999 and 2001, it was possible to carry the research forward a couple more years in a number of areas.

The study examines the historical development of immigration and immigration policy during the post-war period. A great many more immigrants came to Germany than Denmark, a fact reflected in the larger proportion of foreigners in the population. However, there have been some differences in the patterns of immigration between the two countries. Traditionally, Denmark has pursued a more liberal policy with respect to immigrants from the Nordic countries and asylum seekers. In Germany, people of Turkish origin make up a much larger percentage of the immigrant population than is the case in Denmark. EU citizens also comprise a much larger proportion of the immigrant population in Germany than in Denmark, while Pakistanis are relatively more numerous in Denmark than in Germany.

Like many other Western European countries, both Denmark and Germany – and especially Germany – recruited guest workers in the 1960s to meet the demand for more labour, which continued until the economic downturn began in 1973. Subsequently, immigration continued at a substantial level, largely because of family reunifications. The 1980s saw a significant influx of asylum seekers and refugees. In the 1990s Germany permitted the immigration of labour from Eastern Europe, while Denmark has allowed a large increase in immigration of people coming to work or study since the start of the 21st century. In both countries immigrants have tended to establish their homes in urban areas, but in Denmark immigrants have shown a more marked preference for settling in the larger towns and cities.

9.2. Educational attainment and training

Human capital is of paramount importance for enhancing economic performance. While most previous studies in the literature concentrated on the labour market outcomes of immigrant education, this study considered the post-migration human capital investments of immigrants. Starting with a thorough review of the educational systems in Denmark and Germany, the study showed that there are many similarities between the two educational systems with regard to structure, years of education, and lengths of various programmes. Major differences are the early differentiation of pupils in the German school system, as opposed to the comprehensive principle applied in Denmark, and the extension in Germany of compulsory education beyond primary and lower secondary school to include an introduction to vocational training.

The analysis showed that immigrants in Denmark were on average less well educated upon arrival, but that they acquired more schooling once they were in Denmark than was the case for immigrants in Germany. This might be related to a more vigorously applied integration policy in Denmark. Second generation immigrants fared better than the immigrants in both countries; especially with regard to primary and secondary schooling choices. However, the immigrants had managed to narrow the educational gap between themselves and the total population. More immigrants in Germany finished vocational training than in Denmark, indicating the importance of vocational training in Germany. However, this was not sufficient, given the well-known difficulties of German migrants, for them to perform well on the labour market. There were also significant differences in the educational achievement among the five nationalities considered in the study: Poles and Iranians acquired more human capital in Denmark than other groups, while Lebanese and Turks ranked the lowest. Iranians also stood out for their high level of schooling achievement in Germany, while the Turks were again at the bottom. This is particularly worrying, as the Turks are by far the largest immigrant group in Germany and also in Denmark.

A careful econometric analysis investigated the determinants of educational attainment and vocational training, and identified the nature of the observed differences in both countries. The analysis of the educational levels in Denmark showed that younger, healthier males from Poland and Iran, those who had acquired a Danish passport, or those who had better educated fathers had a greater probability of finishing *Folkeskole* (obligatory secondary schooling) or *Gymnasium* (high school)/university as opposed to not finishing their schooling in Denmark. Pre-migration work experience, religiosity, and growing up in a small town acted as barriers to finishing schooling. Apparently the incentive structure in Denmark does not seem to encourage those with low skills to take advantage of the Danish educational system.

The analysis of the educational levels in Germany indicated that those male immigrants who were healthier, arrived in Germany at a younger age, lived in Germany for a long time, had no pre-migration schooling, and had educated fathers had a greater probability of completing *Haupt-/Realschule* (obligatory secondary schooling) or *Gymnasium* (high school)/university as opposed to not going to school in Germany. Most importantly, the analysis showed that there was intergenerational transmission of human capital. Nevertheless, the educational attainment of immigrants in Germany was found to depend on gender and ethnicity. While it is not surprising that German citizens have higher probabilities of finishing schooling in Germany than do immigrants on average, it is surprising that immigrants who were born in Germany were found to have a lower likelihood of finishing schooling in Germany than immigrants born abroad.

The following conclusions were reached concerning vocational training. In Denmark, it was found that the older immigrants with pre-migration education who had acquired a Danish passport, or foreign nationals who came from Poland or Iran, or immigrants whose fathers were in upper-level white collar-jobs, all had greater chances of finishing vocational training, irrespective of gender. In Germany, younger age on entrance to the country, more years since migration, upper secondary pre-migration education, no pre-migration education, family background, and citizenship were all significant positive determinants of finishing vocational training. Immigrant women and second generation immigrants invariably had smaller chances of completing vocational training. Gender differences in the vocational training system in Germany may have been the cause of the differences in career paths and the occupational segregation of women. The authors could not explain why immigrants born in Denmark and Germany had the same and lower chances respectively of completing vocational training than immigrants born abroad, but this finding certainly suggests that integration problems lie ahead. One reason, however, could be the less satisfying return on vocational training for immigrants, which was also one of the findings (see Section 9.5 below).

Making a comparison across the two countries, there were greater ethnic differences in Germany than in Denmark for both educational attainment and vocational training. However, the Iranians fared consistently better than the Turks in educational attainment, and the Lebanese fared worse than the Turks. Compared to Turks, Poles had greater chances of finishing vocational training, while the Lebanese did worse.

9.3. Employment trends

An important measure of integration into the labour market is the employment rate. Both Denmark and Germany displayed a severe level of under-employment among immigrants. Only 54% of immigrants from non-Western countries in Germany were in employment, as opposed to 67% of native Germans (henceforth simply "Germans", in parallel with the use of "Danes" in this book to indicate members of the native population). In Denmark, 46% from the same non-Western countries were in employment, compared to 76% of Danes. The employment rate for non-Western foreigners was thus lower in Denmark than it was in Germany, although Danes were more attached to the labour force in Denmark than Germans in Germany. The employment of immigrants was quite simply much more successful in Germany than in Denmark.

The fact that Germany was more successful than Denmark in this respect does not indicate that Germany had no problem with low employment rates for immigrants. Germany had experienced a downward trend in employment rates, documented in the study, since the mid 1980s, a phenomenon that can be traced back to the beginning of the 1970s. This fall in employment had a clear parallel in Denmark. However, immigrants to Denmark have been substantially less employed over the years, especially in the early 1990s.

Despite the difference in employment levels for foreign citizens in Germany and Denmark, the patterns of employment for the various nationalities were fairly similar across the two countries. Poles exhibited the highest rate of employment in both countries, while employment levels were the lowest for migrants from Lebanon. The relative employment rates for male and female immigrants were also more or less the same in Denmark and Germany. Thus, the generally higher employment rate among women in Denmark did not seem to have influenced the employment behaviour of immigrants in Denmark.

9.4. Employment incentives

The analysis goes a step further, studying and identifying the reasons why immigrants generally had a weaker labour market attachment than the native populations, especially in Denmark. A potentially important cause of low employment rates was that financial incentives for taking up work were low: the proportion of immigrants in the labour force between 25-55 years of age who gained less than €100 extra per month from working was between 17% and 18% in Germany and between 35% and 41% in Denmark. The financial incentives to work were lower in Denmark primarily because the unemployment benefit system paid a higher replacement rate to the low-paid groups, which included many immigrants. In Germany, the lowest paid workers received relatively lower benefits than in Denmark, and the middle- and high-income earners received relatively higher benefits. Hence, it is not surprising that large shares of the immigrants in Denmark who were unemployed were in fact unavailable to the Danish labour market. It is striking that the proportion of unemployed immigrants who met the ILO's availability criteria was 60% in Germany and 51% in Denmark, compared to 66% of unemployed workers in general in Denmark in 2002.

The study demonstrated through econometric analyses that female immigrants were relatively less likely to be in the labour force in Germany than in Denmark. However, once they were participating in the labour force, they had a relatively better chance of being employed in Germany than men, indicating a serious commitment to the labour force on their part. The analyses also showed that human capital factors were important for immigrants' labour market attachment in both Denmark and Germany. The likelihood both of participating in the labour force and of being employed was positively related to good health, good language skills, and a good educational background, either from the home countries or, even better, from the host country. Educational qualifications acquired in the home country played a greater role in immigrants' labour market attachment in Germany than in Denmark.

Vocational training exerted a positive effect on the labour market attachment and chances of employment in both countries. However, as mentioned above, it was found that relatively few second generation immigrants finished vocational training. The labour market benefits from having a university degree were less clear-cut. Employment seemed to be higher for immigrants with a university degree solely because it increased their labour force participation, while the employment chances for these immigrants were not better than those for immigrants with no education. In fact, the risk of unemployment for vocationally-educated immigrants was lower than for immigrants with a university degree in both countries.

The analyses also showed strong ethnic disparities whereby Polish immigrants had the highest likelihood of participating in the labour force and of being employed in both Denmark and Germany. Lebanese immigrants had the lowest likelihood of participating in the labour market in Germany. In Denmark, while Lebanese immigrants were particularly poorly represented among the employed, Iranians had the lowest likelihood of participating in the labour force.

9.5. Earnings dispersion

Once immigrants are working, one objectively-measurable key indicator of their successful labour market integration and performance is earnings. The study investigated the monetary dispersion of paid employment using the *Rockwool Foundation Migration Survey* for Denmark (RFMS-D) and Germany (RFMS-G) and focusing on the same five common immigrant groups in both countries. Analytical innovations made possible by the dataset included the use of a direct measure of the labour market experience in the host country and an objective measure of language proficiency. Migrants who had become citizens of the host country were treated as a separate group. The earnings data exhibited substantial variation for both countries among people from the former Yugoslavia, Poles, Iranians, Lebanese, Turks, and the naturalized immigrants. Naturalized citizens of both sexes in both countries had the highest earnings. In both countries males earned more than females. More remarkable, immigrants in Denmark earned more than immigrants in Germany, both on a general level and for each separate migrant group.

Utilization of multivariate analyses led to deeper structural results: Danish immigrants earned more throughout their working lives than comparable immigrants in Germany. Although experience was found not to be as well rewarded in Denmark as in Germany, an initial earnings advantage upon arrival was sustained. Human capital acquired in the host country generated an earnings premium in both Denmark and Germany. But education after arrival was not rewarded as much as expected, in particular with respect to vocational training, which was rewarded only modestly in Germany and not at all in Denmark. This may help explain why second generation immigrants in both countries stayed away from vocational training. After the inclusion of individual characteristics, the differences across the nationalities disappeared among the Danish immigrants. They remained, however, among the German immigrants: compared to Turks, all groups earned more except the Lebanese, who earned less on average, though few of them worked.

The econometric models were further used to undertake a counterfactual analysis, where German immigrants were moved to Denmark and Danish immigrants were assumed to be in Germany. Such experiments showed that Danish immigrants in Denmark fared better than German immigrants in Germany, better than German immigrants in Denmark, and better than Danish immigrants in Germany for both the age and experience profiles at all levels. If employed Danish immigrants were to have moved to Germany, they would have suffered an earnings loss. German immigrants in Germany fared worse than Danish immigrants in Denmark, worse than the Danish immigrants in Germany, and worse than the German immigrants in Denmark. Based on their earnings-experience profile, if German immigrants were to have moved to Denmark they would have experienced an improvement in their earnings compared to their earnings in Germany. This earnings advantage was especially large at the beginning of their careers, and lasted for 20 years. This suggested that the Danish labour market could offer an earnings-experience advantage to any immigrant in paid employment. Denmark seemed to be more effective in enhancing the employed immigrants' capacities to succeed in the labour market. For the many immigrants in Denmark without a job, the high immigrant wages might have represented a barrier to entry.

9.6. Immigrant self-employment

The project also used the *Rockwool Foundation Migration Survey* to examine a special group of immigrant workers in both countries: the self-employed. The issues investigated were the decision to take up the self-employment route as opposed to the paid-employment option, and the determinants of the earnings of the self-employed. At first sight, both countries seemed to attract immigrants with similar levels of entrepreneurial spirit: 9% of the German and 10% of the Danish immigrants in the samples were self-employed. Among all ethnic groups in Denmark and Germany, the Iranians stood out as being the most entrepreneurial. It is also important to note that the majority of the self-employed immigrants in both counties had had refugee status.

Nevertheless, there were distinct differences between the self-employed immigrants in both countries and between the self-employed and the salaried workers within the countries. Among these differences were the following. Self-employed immigrants in Germany were clearly self-selected with respect to human capital, age, years since migration, and family background characteristics. A larger proportion of the self-employed were home-owners, and a smaller proportion lived in ethnic neighbourhoods, in comparison with those immigrants who were not self-employed. The self-selection of the self-employed Danish immigrants was much less marked, especially with respect to human capital. Self-employed immigrants in Germany earned twice as much as their salaried counterparts in the labour force. However, this was not true for the Danish self-employed immigrants, who earned slightly less than the salaried group. On average, self-employed immigrants in Germany earned much more than in Denmark.

With respect to the self-employment choice, the only similarities between the two countries were the following. Male immigrants were about 2.5 times more likely to be self-employed than females. Iranians appeared to have an entrepreneurial spirit, and were more likely to be self-employed than all other ethnic groups. However, individuals in poor health were less likely to be self-employed in Germany, and more likely to be self-employed in Denmark. A further major difference was that the self-employment choice in Denmark did not depend on other individual characteristics, such as age, time spent in the host country, education, economic conditions and the like, while the reverse was the case in Germany. Education, age, years since migration, father being self-employed, and home ownership all exhibited a positive impact on the self-employment choice, while living in an ethnic enclave had a negative impact on being self-employed in Germany. Hence, self-employment was found to be a selective process in Germany, while it seemed more random in Denmark.

Danish self-employed immigrants were, on average, a group with lower quality characteristics. This is consistent with the fact that they had lower earnings when compared to immigrant entrepreneurs in Germany and other immigrants in the Danish labour force. Consequently, the earnings of the Danish self-employed immigrants were hardly affected by measurable individual characteristics. An exception was poor health, which depressed earnings. However, in Germany, immigrant entrepreneurs of younger age and with larger firms, more business experience and a home outside ethnic enclaves had higher earnings.

In a counterfactual simulation analysis, the investigation also compared the earnings potentials that both the Danish and German migrant entrepreneurial groups had in both countries, using the estimated earnings regressions. The reference case was the observation in the two samples that self-employed immigrants in Germany had higher earnings across all ages if compared with self-employed immigrants in Denmark. According to the simulations, the self-employed Danish immigrants would have fared better in Germany than the self-employed German immigrants in Denmark, and much better than if they had stayed in Denmark. Immigrants to Germany would not really have gained by moving to Denmark.

While these hypothetical computations suggest that Germany provided a somewhat better environment for entrepreneurial activities, the analyses gave no clear-cut evidence that the immigrants attracted to self-employment in Germany were actually a higher quality group than the equivalent group of immigrant entrepreneurs in Denmark. While German immigrants would have done better as entrepreneurs in Denmark than the actual Danish immigrants, Danish immigrants would have done better in Germany than the actual German immigrants. This suggests that a reallocation of the migrants would have created an overall welfare improvement, because it would have maintained the income status of the German immigrants, increased the income of the Danish immigrants, and left both countries with higher total earnings.

9.7. Welfare take-up

It is frequently hypothesized that immigrants make heavy use of the welfare system. The study described the access to the social security systems in Denmark and Germany, and their use by immigrants. The determinants of their take-up decisions were also studied. A first investigation outlined in detail the formal rules of access to the social security systems in both countries, including the rules for unemployment insurance, social assistance, old-age pension, disability pension, housing benefits and child benefits. In general, eligibility rules for foreigners are the same as for nationals, while they are typically easier for refugees. The German benefit system typically relates benefits to work and income, and the replacement rate is constant over a relatively wide income span. The Danish benefits are primarily residence-based, and the benefits provided follow more of a flat rate. This means that low income groups are better compensated in Denmark than in Germany.

With respect to the take-up data, it was found that the proportion of immigrants over the official retirement age who received pensions was about 80% in both countries. In Denmark, however, immigrants received social security benefits more often than in Germany. Social security benefits and the take-up of unemployment benefits interacted in complex ways that were different in the two countries. There were also clear-cut gender differences within and across the countries. In Germany, 15% of immigrant men and 7% of immigrant women received unemployment pay, while the corresponding figures for Denmark were 11% and 9%. In Denmark, 15% of male immigrants and 20% of female immigrants received social security benefits, while in Germany the figures were 10% for males and 9% for females. For men, the differences in both countries could be explained by the fact that unemployment insurance in Denmark is voluntary, and many low-wage workers find themselves better off not being insured in order to receive social security benefits. More female migrants in Germany reported themselves as housewives than in Denmark, and were therefore supported by their husbands, which may explain why their level of take-up for social security benefits was much lower in Germany than in Denmark.

An econometric analysis investigating the determinants of welfare take-up completed the study. A core issue was social security benefits: it was found that good labour market performance, language skills and home-ownership considerably reduced the probability of receiving social security benefits in both countries. But there were also cross-country differences: the analysis for Germany showed that when labour market status was accounted for, women actually had a lower probability of receiving social security benefit, while in Denmark, gender played no particular role. In addition, refugees in Germany had a greater probability of receiving social security benefits compared to other foreigners, while this was not the case in Denmark. A possible explanation suggested was that it was easier for refugees in Denmark to access the labour market than for refugees in Germany, who had significantly lower chances of being in employment than non-refugee immigrants. There were also significant human capital differences between refugees in the two countries. It should be noted, though, that asylum seekers were not included in the Danish sample, whereas they were in the German sample.

9.8. Crime

It is often suggested that immigrant populations exhibit higher crime rates than native populations, but reliable data sources on the issue are scarce. International comparisons, in particular, are very difficult, because definitions and counting rules differ between countries. This is also the case for statistics from Denmark and Germany. Nevertheless, the study of joint similarities and differences in immigrant crime rates between the two countries has opened new horizons for future research into the link between immigration and crime.

All in all, many more similarities than differences were found for Denmark and Germany. Although no sophisticated econometric analyses could be undertaken, the results confirmed the importance of accounting for differences in the age and gender distributions. However, even when such differences were taken into account, citizens with a foreign background were still over-represented in the crime statistics. Evidence available only from the Danish register data showed that the crime rates of immigrants from non-Western countries remained relatively high even when education was taken into account in the analysis.

The results showed that research is still at the beginning of understanding statistical differences based on national origins. Potentially relevant issues that are worth more detailed consideration in future research include the multiple risk factors related to immigrants, such as crime-prone neighbourhoods, lack of knowledge of the national languages, lack of education, and lack of socio-economic integration, all of which might interact in a potentially hazardous way. As a word of caution, it should be noted that greater attention paid to foreign-looking people and more frequent police checks might cause higher clear-up rates among immigrants from non-Western countries than among national citizens and immigrants of European origin, thus distorting the crime figures for the different groups.

9.9. The public exchequer

The consequences of immigration for the public finances were also studied. Ideally, one would wish to study this issue in a life-cycle framework, which would require the availability of longitudinal data. Due to the lack of such data, the analysis was based on cross-sectional data, and was able to make use of more detailed information for Denmark than for Germany. For Denmark, a series of cross-sectional datasets from the 1990s were used, while for Germany only one cross-sectional dataset from 2002 was used.

The evidence found for Denmark was that the net transfers went from Western immigrants to the public sector, and from the public sector to immigrants from non-Western countries. This means that immigrants from Western countries produced a net surplus, while immigrants from non-Western countries represented a net deficit, which was found to be of considerable size. The size of the net transfer per person varied across the business cycle and with the employment rate, and the total amount of the net transfer was found to vary also with the size of the immigrant population. It is a little surprising that the reduction in the net transfer amounts which took place between 1996 and 1998, for both individuals and in total, did not continue in the 1998-2000 period despite an improvement in labour market conditions. In Germany, a net transfer from the public sector to the non-Western immigrants was also observed. As expected given the differences in employment and in the levels of social benefits, the net transfers per person were smaller on average in Germany than in Denmark, and varied considerably among different non-Western immigrant groups. Due to lack of data, the net transfer from Western immigrants in Germany was not calculated.

For both countries, it was also investigated how the individual net transfers to the public sector varied when the econometric analysis controlled for differences in individual characteristics, personal employment situation, and labour income. The individual characteristics were less relevant when work-related variables were taken into account. The employment and labour income variables exhibited very strong effects, although stronger in Denmark than in Germany. These differences may be explained by differences in the tax and transfer systems and in the public sector expenditures. In the German set-up, with more weight placed on experience-related social benefits and with fewer tax-financed public services, the employment rate of a population group seemed to impact less on the public purse: you cannot receive before you have paid in, and therefore the German system seems more self-regulating.

9.10. Socio-economic consequences

The findings pointed to the crucial importance of employment and labour income of immigrants for the size and the direction of the net transfer to the public sector. The analysis investigated in more detail what determines wages and employment across immigrant groups, and compared the results with those for the native populations. The first part of the analysis dealt with the determination of wages; differences between Danes, immigrants from Western countries and immigrants from non-Western countries were studied, with controls for a large number of individual characteristics such as education, training, family characteristics, age and country of origin. It was found that the immigrants born in non-Western countries had significantly lower wages than Danes, though females did somewhat better than males in this comparison. Foreign-born men had 13% lower wages than male Danes, while foreign-born females had only 7% lower wages than female Danes. Immigrants born in a Western country did better, though whereas females were not different from their Danish counterparts, males still experienced a small wage disadvantage of 3%. These differences could not be explained by the differences in individual characteristics measured in the data.

The second part of the analysis dealt with the effects of immigration on the wages and unemployment of Danes. The results indicated that the existence of a larger proportion of immigrants in the population of a municipality had only a marginal effect on the wages of Danes and that it did not increase their unemployment rates. In fact, a larger presence of immigrants in the local labour market was associated with lower unemployment and higher wages among Danes. These results are consistent with the findings in other European countries (including Germany) and suggest that immigrants are complements to natives in the production process. A larger presence of immigrants born in non-Western countries was associated with lower unemployment rates among Danes, while immigrants from Western countries had no significant effect.

The final analysis was an attempt to investigate the amount and direction of redistribution and the degree of inequality among immigrants. For this purpose the disposable incomes of immigrants and Germans/Danes were studied. In comparison to the income of Danes, the average disposable income of Western immigrants to Denmark was about the same, that of Danish non-Western immigrants was at a level of 80%, and that of non-Western immigrants to Germany was 57%. Obviously, immigrants to Denmark did much better than immigrants to Germany, in net terms as well, which was consistent with the investigations in the earlier parts of the book. Danes had a slightly more equal income distribution than the total population in Denmark. Immigrants from non-Western countries had almost the same distribution as the Danes. Many of the non-Western immigrants had no income from employment, but the welfare state works towards an equalized income structure after taxes and transfers. In comparison, non-Western immigrants in Germany exhibited a much more unequal distribution of disposable income.

9.11. Summary

The study described in the book *Migrants, Work, and the Welfare State* was largely based on a rich representative dataset collected specifically for the purpose, the *Rockwool Foundation Migration Survey,* which relates to the same groups of immigrants (Turks, people from the former Yugoslavia, Poles, Iranians, and Lebanese) in Denmark and Germany. Most chapters of the book make intensive use of this data source, while some also add knowledge from other datasets. The analyses are based on descriptive statistics and in-depth econometric investigations used to generate reliable scientific conclusions. The project provided innovative and coherent findings on an important area of social and economic life in both societies that had not been sufficiently studied before.

Both Denmark and Germany shared a similar history of immigration and migration policies in the period analyzed. They were fairly similar in legislation regulating the entry into the countries and access to the respective labour markets. Denmark has followed a more liberal immigration policy towards the Nordic countries and has done so towards asylum seekers in the past, while Germany has always received much higher numbers of migrants, who consequently make up a much larger proportion of its population. Both countries had guest worker programmes which were largely stopped after 1973, as in many other Western European countries.

The project showed that at the time the data were collected, there were greater ethnic differences in Germany than in Denmark with respect to both educational attainment and vocational training. Immigrants in Denmark were found to be less well educated upon arrival, but they acquired more schooling once they were in the country than immigrants in Germany. Apart from the early differentiation in the German school system, education and training systems are similar in the two countries, but the Danish system did not encourage those with low skills to acquire further education during the period analyzed. In comparison to Danes/Germans, at the time of the study there was severe under-employment of immigrants in both countries. The employment rate was lower for non-Western immigrants in Denmark than it was in Germany, although Danes were more attached to the labour force in Denmark than Germans in Germany. Immigrants had a larger presence on the German labour market than in Denmark. Probable reasons suggested for this difference were that immigrants in Denmark were found to be less educated upon arrival, and that financial incentives to take up work were low in Denmark, primarily because the unemployment benefit system paid a higher replacement rate to the low-paid income groups. Education and vocational attainment were found to be powerful determinants of labour market attachment in both countries.

Whereas immigrants in Denmark were less financially motivated to seek employment than their counterparts in Germany, once at work, they earned more throughout their working lives than comparable immigrants in Germany. Although experience was not as well rewarded in Denmark, an initial earnings advantage upon arrival was sustained. Human capital acquired in the host country generated an earnings premium in both Denmark and Germany. If Danish immigrant workers were to move to Germany, they would have suffered a financial loss. However, if German immigrant workers were to move to Denmark they would have experienced an improvement in their earnings compared to their earnings in Germany.

While Denmark seemed to be a more attractive country for employed immigrant workers, Germany was found to offer better opportunities for entrepreneurs. Although the self-employment rates were similar, self-employed immigrants in Germany were clearly positively self-selected, while those in Denmark seemed to be more randomly allocated. Consequently, self-employed immigrants earned much more in Germany than in Denmark, and also more than regular migrant workers in Germany. The Danish self-employed immigrants earned less than the salaried group. The analysis demonstrated that self-employed immigrants from Germany would not really gain by moving to Denmark, while the self-employed immigrants from Denmark would do much better in Germany than in their actual host country.

The last part of the study deals with the alleged idleness of immigrants, the common belief that they are over-represented in welfare take-up and crime, and the direction of the redistribution of public finances. While a sizable level of welfare take-up by immigrants was documented, especially in Denmark, it was also found that good labour market performance, language skills, and home ownership considerably reduced the probability of receiving social security benefits in both countries. The analysis of crime rates showed that even when differences in age, gender, and educational distributions were controlled for, individuals with foreign backgrounds exhibited a greater presence in the crime statistics. Immigrants induced a redistribution through public finances whereby the net transfers in public contributions went from Western immigrants to the public sector, and from the public sector to immigrants from non-Western countries. These redistribution effects brought the average disposable income of Danish non-Western immigrants much closer to the disposable income of Danes, which was much higher than that of German non-Western immigrants. The Danish non-Western immigrants had almost the same distribution as Danes, while the various migrant groups exhibited a much more unequal distribution of disposable income in Germany.

It was concluded that Germany was able to attract more able immigrants, get them into employment, and offer more to people with entrepreneurial talents. Denmark kept more immigrants in the welfare system, but offered better remuneration to regular workers and some incentives for immigrants to educate themselves to higher levels – though not to undertake vocational training.

References

Trانæs, Torben and Klaus Zimmermann. 2004. *Migrants, Work, and the Welfare State*. Odense: University Press of Southern Denmark.

10. The attitudes of the Danish population to the admission of refugees to Denmark

10.1. Introduction

Measurements of the attitudes of the Danish population to immigration problems can be divided into two groups.

The first group covers Danes' views of immigrants once they are *in* the country: as a multicultural element in the population, as a labour force, or as a possible threat to society on the basis of religious beliefs or especially religious fundamentalism. This topic will be covered in Chapter 11, which contains an analysis of foreign views of Danes' current relationships to immigrants. Chapter 12 provides a historical account of the views of foreigners expressed in debates in the Danish newspapers.

The measurements in the other group are concerned solely with viewpoints on the extent of *future* immigration – for example, measurements of whether people feel that there should be relaxation or restriction on the amount of immigration allowed in comparison with the prevailing situation – and this is the topic which will be covered in this chapter, on the basis of Pedersen and Viby Mogensen (2001), Pedersen and Jensen (2002 a, b and c), and Pedersen, Jensen and Viby Mogensen (2002).

There exists an almost completely comparable series of measurements of Danes' attitudes to future immigration for the years from 1985 to 2002. Those from the beginning of the period were compiled by the Department of Political Science at the University of Aarhus. The question that was posed in that instance was formulated with regard to the extent of immigration, and especially the extent of the admission of refugees. However, an analysis by the Research Unit in 2001 on alternative formulations showed that the responses were more or less identical irrespective of whether the questionnaire mentioned "refugees" or "immigrants". The original formulation was therefore retained when the Research Unit continued with the studies in 1999 using the omnibus surveys mentioned in Chapter 2.

The measurement of attitudes to immigration is often confused with the measurement of attitudes to immigrants – for example, when a wish to place some limits on the overall amount of immigration is taken as an expression of distance to the people concerned, perhaps as a form of religious intolerance, xenophobia or even racism. These factors may indeed be present, but this is not necessarily the case.

A given group of people – such as people with right of residence in Denmark – can certainly feel that the limit of what can be tolerated is close, and thus wish for a restriction, without this meaning that they have any personal dislike of the characteristics of the people who might arrive.

This type of situation can be seen very clearly, for example, from the main survey in 1999, when the proportion of the Danish population who felt that the country should accept fewer refugees in the future was measured as being 55%; the proportion of Pakistani immigrants who also held that opinion was precisely the same. Among immigrants with a Turkish background the proportion with that opinion was 68%, while the level for all non-Western immigrants combined was 45%.

10.2. Danes' opinions on the admission of refugees

The opinions of Danes varied somewhat over the period 1985 to 1999. On average, however, 65% of Danes who had an opinion on the matter wanted to see tighter restrictions. This percentage, in other words, excludes "Don't know" responses, or instances where no response was given. This strong popular disapproval of the acceptance of more refugees was at a somewhat lower level in 2000, when only 55% of Danes were in favour of tighter restrictions on the admission of refugees to Denmark.

However, the measurement of February and March 2001 showed that the proportion of Danes who wanted tighter restrictions had again increased, from 55% in 2000 to 60%. Even though the unwillingness to accept refugees was at that point under the average for the previous 15 years (see Figure 10.1), there was nevertheless a considerable majority in favour of tightening up the regulations on admission to Denmark – even for the most needy groups.

The measurement in September 2001 showed that the proportion who wished for tighter restrictions on access to Denmark for refugees had again fallen to 55% (see Figure 10.2). However, this drop was soon cancelled out, with the October measurement showing a significant increase – presumably as a result of the terrorist attack in the USA of September 11 in that year. In October, then, 68% of those respondents who expressed an opinion stated that they wished to see tighter restrictions on entry to Denmark for refugees. This increase was seen across broadly all types of respondents regardless of sex, age, occupation or education.

Less than six months later, in January and February 2002, the proportion of the population in favour of more restrictions had returned to the same level as measured in September 2001 (the great majority of the interviews for that measurement were conducted before 11 September). By August 2002 the proportion of adult Danes who wanted tighter restrictions had fallen to 44%, far below the average level for the 15-year period. This development can probably be attributed to the tightened restrictions on the entry of refugees which the government had implemented and which came into force on 1 July 2002. After August 2002 the proportion of Danes wanting greater restrictions increased a little once more, rising to 48% in October before falling back slightly to 47% in November.

Figure 10.1. Proportions of Danes who thought that there should be more restrictions on the admission of refugees to Denmark than was the case at the time. Percent.

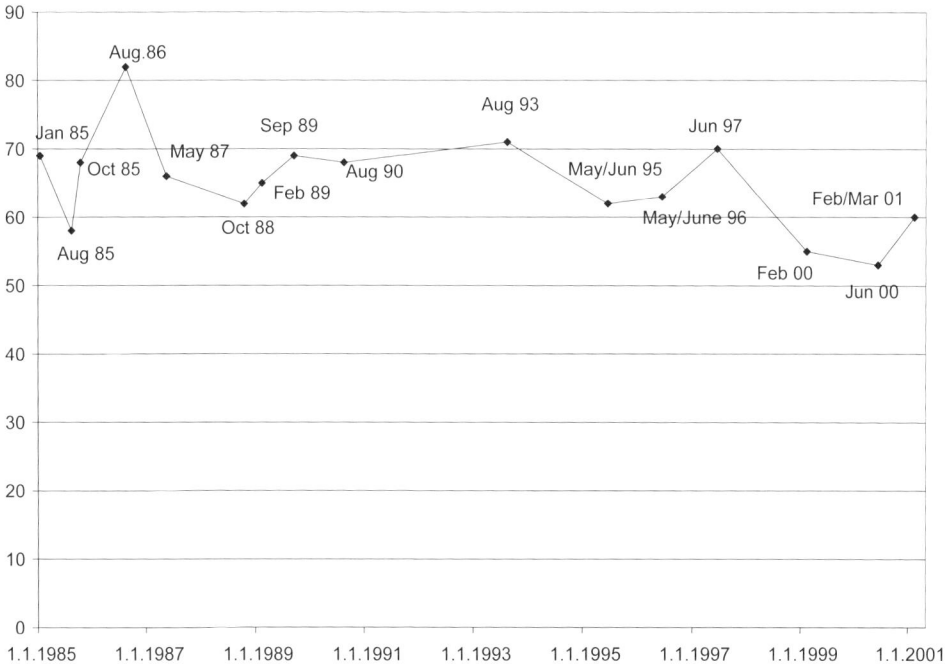

Note: "Don't know" responses and respondents who declined to answer were excluded from the calculations.
Source: *Nyt fra Rockwool Fondens Forskningsenhed*, June 2001.

As Figure 10.2 shows, the proportion of Danes who wanted to *reduce* the restrictions on access to Denmark for refugees was in the months of October and November 2002 slightly below the level for August, but higher than it had been in September 2001. The proportion of Danes who wished the regulations regarding admission of refugees to remain unaltered was at around 38-39% in all the three surveys conducted in the summer and autumn of 2002, which was a rather higher proportion than in January and February, when the corresponding level was 34%.

Overall, then, around half the Danish population wanted to see continued limitations on the number of refugees admitted to the country. However, this did not strongly differentiate Denmark from other Northern European countries such as Sweden, Germany and the United Kingdom.

Figure 10.2. The opinions of Danish adults (ages 16-74) on admission of refugees to Denmark measured in September and October 2001 and in January, February, August, October and November 2002.

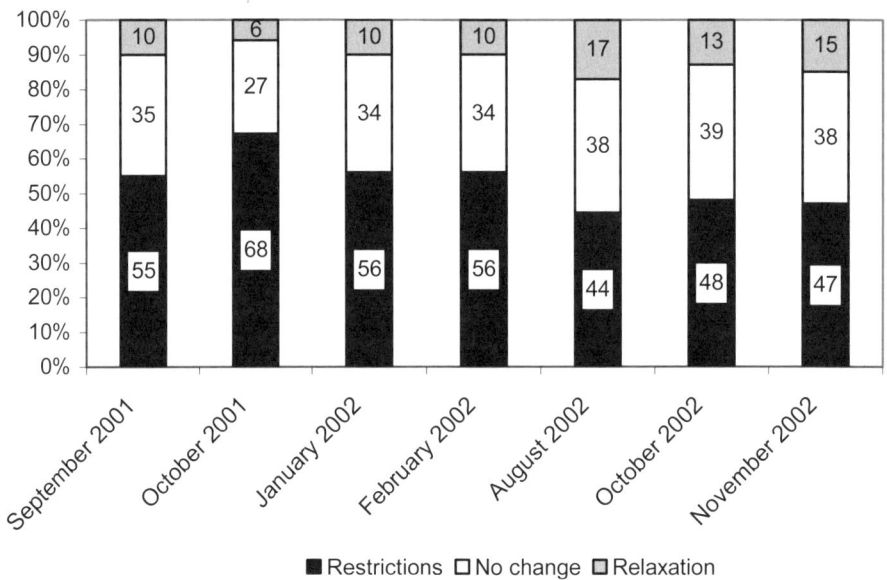

Note: "Don't know" responses and respondents who declined to answer were excluded from the calculations. Source: *Nyt fra Rockwool Fondens Forskningsenhed*, December 2002.

10.3. The opinions of Danes and the populations of neighbouring countries on the admission of refugees

Data were collected in Sweden on 4 and 5 June 2002 by SIFO Research International; also in June of that year, data were collected for the UK by the Social Survey Division of the Office of National Statistics in London; and in April 2002, German data were collected by Infratest Sozialforschung in Munich. The results of these surveys are shown in Figure 10.3. The Danish measurement shown in the figure is that of November 2002.

As the figure shows, one common trait for all four European countries was that only small proportions of the population – generally around 10-15% – wanted a relaxation of the restrictions on the admission of refugees to their respective countries.

There were significant proportions of the populations in all these four countries – never less than 15%, and in most cases more – who were satisfied with their country's policy on refugees at the time of the interview.

Figure 10.3. Opinions regarding the admission of refugees to the country held in 2002 by the populations of Sweden, Denmark (November), Germany and the United Kingdom.

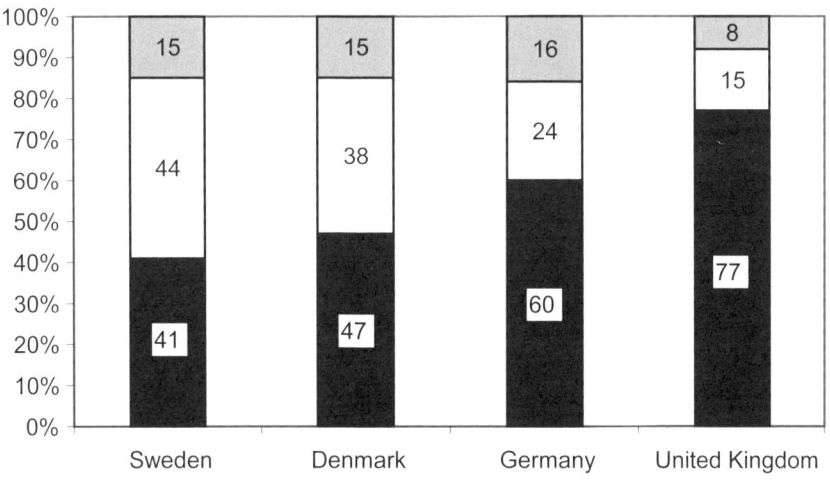

Note: "Don't know" responses and respondents who declined to answer were excluded from the calculations.
Source: *Nyt fra Rockwool Fondens Forskningsenhed*, December 2002.

However, the figure clearly shows that the proportions who wanted to see a tightening of restrictions were relatively low in Denmark and Sweden, with the proportion in Sweden being even smaller than in Denmark. In the two non-Scandinavian countries there were significantly larger proportions who considered their countries' refugee policies to be too relaxed, i.e. 60% in Germany and 77% in the UK.

With respect to the demographic characteristics of those who wanted greater restrictions on the entry of refugees, Table 10.1 shows that there was generally little, if any, difference between the opinions of men and women in any of the countries surveyed. It is very clear, though, that the proportion who wanted greater restrictions increased with age; this tendency was most marked in Denmark, Sweden and Germany.

In order to make comparisons possible between the various countries, education completed is divided into three levels: lower secondary school level (compulsory schooling) plus vocational training; upper secondary school level; and further/higher education, whether on short, medium or long courses. In Denmark there was a considerably greater proportion of people with lower secondary school education/vocational training who wanted greater restrictions (63%) than the proportions in the other two groups (41% and 40% respectively).

Table 10.1. Proportions of adults aged 16 to 74 who wanted greater restrictions on admission of refugees to their countries in 2002 in Denmark, Sweden, Germany and the United Kingdom, shown by gender, age, occupation and level of education. Percent.

	Denmark	Sweden	Germany	United Kingdom
Men	57	41	58	78
Women	55	41	62	77
Age 16-19	48	(19)	42	70
Age 20-29	49	28	48	74
Age 30-39	55	36	59	77
Age 40-49	52	40	65	77
Age 50-59	59	49	62	78
Age 60-69	68	49	66	83
Age 70-74	65	57	69	80
Students/school students	38	(19)	35	(59)
Unemployed	46	(47)	62	74
Pensioners	65	54	69	80
Salaried/waged employees	56	39	59	76
Own business	67	42	60	86
Others	62	(51)	64	79
Education to lower secondary school and vocational training	63	56	71	82
Education to upper secondary school	41	46	64	74
Higher education	40	20	44	66
Total	56	41	60	77
Number of individuals	1,853	832	1,642	1,603

Note: Figures in parentheses indicate greater statistical uncertainty than normally acceptable, because of the low number of observations (under 20). "Don't know" responses and respondents who declined to answer were excluded from the calculations.
Source: *Nyt fra Rockwool Fondens Forskningsenhed*, October 2002.

The same pattern was found in the other countries. Thus, in Sweden 56% of those with lower secondary schooling wanted greater restrictions, while the proportion fell to 46% among those with upper secondary schooling. The figure for Swedes who had taken courses of further/higher education who wanted greater restrictions was only 20% – the lowest level found in any of the countries surveyed.

In Germany and the UK, 71% and 82% respectively of people with lower secondary schooling wanted increased restrictions, while the proportions were 44% and 66% respectively for groups with further education. The latter figure for Germany was around the same as the corresponding figure for Denmark, while the United Kingdom had a level appreciably above that of the other countries.

The relationship between occupation and attitude to the admission of refugees reflects the significance of both age and education level. Thus, in almost all countries, the largest proportions who wanted more restrictions were found among retired people, while the proportions were lowest among students.

International research covering North America generally shows that in the USA, the proportion of the resident population who are negative in their attitude towards future immigration has for many years been at about the same high level as in the UK and in Germany, e.g. 66-68% in the mid-1990s. In contrast, the corresponding proportion in Canada was at a level of around just 40%, this may be because immigrants to Canada are in principle selected on the basis of the likelihood that they will be able to support themselves (Viby Mogensen, 2006).

10.4. Immigrants' opinions on admission of refugees

As mentioned previously, a question was asked in the main survey in 1999 to people in each of the eight major immigrant groups concerning their opinions on the admission of refugees to Denmark. As Table 10.2 shows, there were significant differences between the groups in terms of the responses given (Nielsen, 2000).

Immigrants were not united in supporting a liberal refugee policy. It is true that only 45% of the combined total of immigrants from all groups wanted tighter restrictions, as opposed to 55% of Danes; but 45% is a substantial minority, and the difference in relation to Danes is fairly modest. There were also distinct differences between the various immigrant groups. On the one hand, even more Turks and Poles than Danes were in favour of a restrictive refugee policy, while in contrast those from the former Yugoslavia and from Somalia took a significantly more liberal view than Danes. Thus, it would *not* be true to say that in general, the views of Danes and immigrants are diametrically opposed.

There is a striking pattern in the opinions of the various immigrant groups, in that the differences in opinion coincide very clearly with the number of people from the different countries who arrive as refugees: those groups which number few refugees amongst them take a more restrictive line, while those groups with many refugees are more liberal in their attitudes. However, this difference is not necessarily connected to the situation of the individual immigrant. A closer analysis shows that those who arrived as refugees are indeed more liberal in their attitudes than those who did not, but there are nevertheless still significant differences between the opinions of nationalities among both refugees and other immigrants from the same countries.

Table 10.2. The opinions of immigrants and Danes on refugee policy in 1999. The various national groups are sequenced from the most negative to the most positive in terms of their opinions on admission to Denmark for refugees.

Respondents' home countries	There should be tighter limits on the access to Denmark granted to refugees (percentage agreeing)	Percentage who arrived as refugees themselves (primary basis for grant of residence permit)
Turkey	68	2
Poland	61	18
Denmark	55	•
Pakistan	55	1
Lebanon	32	62
Iran	32	80
Vietnam	28	61
Former Yugoslavia	27	66
Somalia	14	61
All immigrants	45	42

Note: In the calculation of the averages for all immigrants, each national group is weighted in accordance with its representation among refugees and immigrants. • Figures not available.
Source: Main survey for the opinions of immigrants, and omnibus survey for those of Danes.

10.5. Summary

For Denmark, there is an almost completely comparable series of measurements of the opinions of the population on admission of refugees to the country available for the period from 1985 to 2002. The measurements at the beginning of this period were made by the Political Science Institute at the University of Aarhus, and the later ones through the omnibus surveys described in Chapter 2.

During the period 1985 to 1999, an average of 65% of adult Danes who expressed an opinion on the subject wanted to see tighter restrictions on the number of refugees admitted to the country. In 1999, 45% of all immigrants from the eight national groups included in the survey also wanted tighter restrictions, and 68% of immigrants from Turkey were of this opinion. The desire for restrictions expressed by Danes cannot then be assumed without further evidence to be an expression of, for example, xenophobia.

The number of Danes who wanted tighter restrictions increased to 68% in the immediate aftermath of the terrorist attack in America of 11 September 2001. This increase was seen across broadly all types of respondents regardless of sex, age, occupation or education. However, by the beginning of 2002 the proportion of those wanting tighter restrictions had already fallen back to the level measured prior to the attack. After the Danish government did actually tighten up the restrictions there was a further fall in the proportion of the population who felt that admission to the country should be even more limited.

After these restrictions had been put into place, the opinion of Danes on the admission of refugees did not differ markedly from that of the Swedes, even though the proportion of Danes in favour of further restrictions did remain slightly higher. In comparison with the differences between the proportion in Denmark wanting greater restrictions and the proportions in Germany and the UK, however, the difference between Denmark and Sweden was modest.

In all four countries studied – Denmark, Sweden, Germany and the UK – the largest proportions of the population who wanted greater restrictions on the entry of refugees to the country concerned were to be found among those with the lowest levels of education.

Immigrants were not found to be united in supporting a liberal refugee policy. It is true that only 45% of people in the eight nationality groups of non-Western immigrants in the 1999 survey wanted tighter restrictions, as opposed to 55% of Danes; but 45% is a substantial minority, and the difference in relation to Danes was fairly modest. There were also distinct differences between the opinions expressed by the various immigrant groups. On the one hand, even more Turks and Poles than Danes were in favour of a restrictive refugee policy, while in contrast those from the former Yugoslavia and from Somalia were significantly more liberal than Danes. Differences in opinion between the various immigrant groups were closely related to the number of immigrants from each country who had entered Denmark as refugees: a more restrictive attitude was prevalent in groups that contained few refugees, while groups with a high proportion of refugees were more liberal in their opinions.

References

Nielsen, Hans Jørgen. 2000. "Forholdet mellem etniske grupper", in Gunnar Viby Mogensen and Poul Chr. Matthiessen (eds), 2000. *Integration i Danmark omkring årtusindeskiftet*. Aarhus: Aarhus University Press, 409-433.

Pedersen, Søren and Gunnar Viby Mogensen. 2001. "Befolkningens holdning til antallet af flygtninge", *Nyt fra Rockwool Fondens Forskningsenhed,* June 2001.

Pedersen, Søren and Helle Cwarzko Jensen. 2002 a. "Befolkningens holdning til antallet af flygtninge: Tendens til fald i uviljen i det sidste tiår, men ny kraftig stigning efter terrorangrebene i USA", *Nyt fra Rockwool Fondens Forskningsenhed*, February 2002.

Pedersen, Søren and Helle Cwarzko Jensen. 2002 b. "Befolkningens holdning til at indføre begrænsninger i antallet af flygtninge er tilbage på niveauet før terrorangrebet den 11. september i USA: 56 pct. ønsker stramninger, 10 lettelser", *Nyt fra Rockwool Fondens Forskningsenhed,* June 2002.

Pedersen, Søren and Helle Cwarzko Jensen. 2002 c. "Befolkningens holdning til at indføre begrænsninger i antallet af flygtninge til Danmark", *Nyt fra Rockwool Fondens Forskningsenhed*, December 2002.

Pedersen, Søren, Helle Cwarzko Jensen and Gunnar Viby Mogensen. 2002."Befolkningens holdning til at indføre begrænsninger i antallet af flygtninge i Danmark, Sverige, Tyskland og Storbritannien", *Nyt fra Rockwool Fondens Forskningsenhed,* October 2002.

Viby Mogensen, Gunnar. 2006. *Folkevandringen til de rige lande. Nordamerikanske erfaringer*. Odense: University Press of Southern Denmark.

11. Are Danes hostile towards immigrants? Foreign media images of Denmark

11.1. Introduction

The following is based on Nielsen (2004) and aims at providing an overview of the extensive research project conducted on behalf of the Rockwool Foundation Research Unit concerning foreign perceptions of Danish attitudes towards immigrants.

The source material was primarily the content of printed reports and material from the mass media found via the Internet, and the analysis was further refined through in-depth conversations with foreign journalists and politicians.

The validity of the various reports about Denmark was assessed by:

- comparisons with the actual situation in Denmark as revealed through available statistics, journalistic and historical accounts, election studies, opinion polls, etc;

- an examination of international studies of attitudes towards immigrants to establish whether Danish attitudes were different from those in other countries;

- comparison of the Danish debate about immigrants with similar debates in neighbouring countries to see whether the debate in Denmark was "harsher" or "gentler" than that in other countries.

The foreign countries focused on in the study were primarily Denmark's neighbours and not, for example, the USA, Japan or Italy.

The study distinguished between three different periods (see Box 1):

- from the beginning of 2000 to the election of November 2001

- the 2001 election itself.

- the period under the new right-of-centre Liberal-Conservative government up to the end of 2002.

Figure 11.1 provides the basis for the broader discussion. The figure shows how the real situation in Denmark gave rise to various accounts of that situation, and

Figure 11.1. Factors influencing opinion formation.

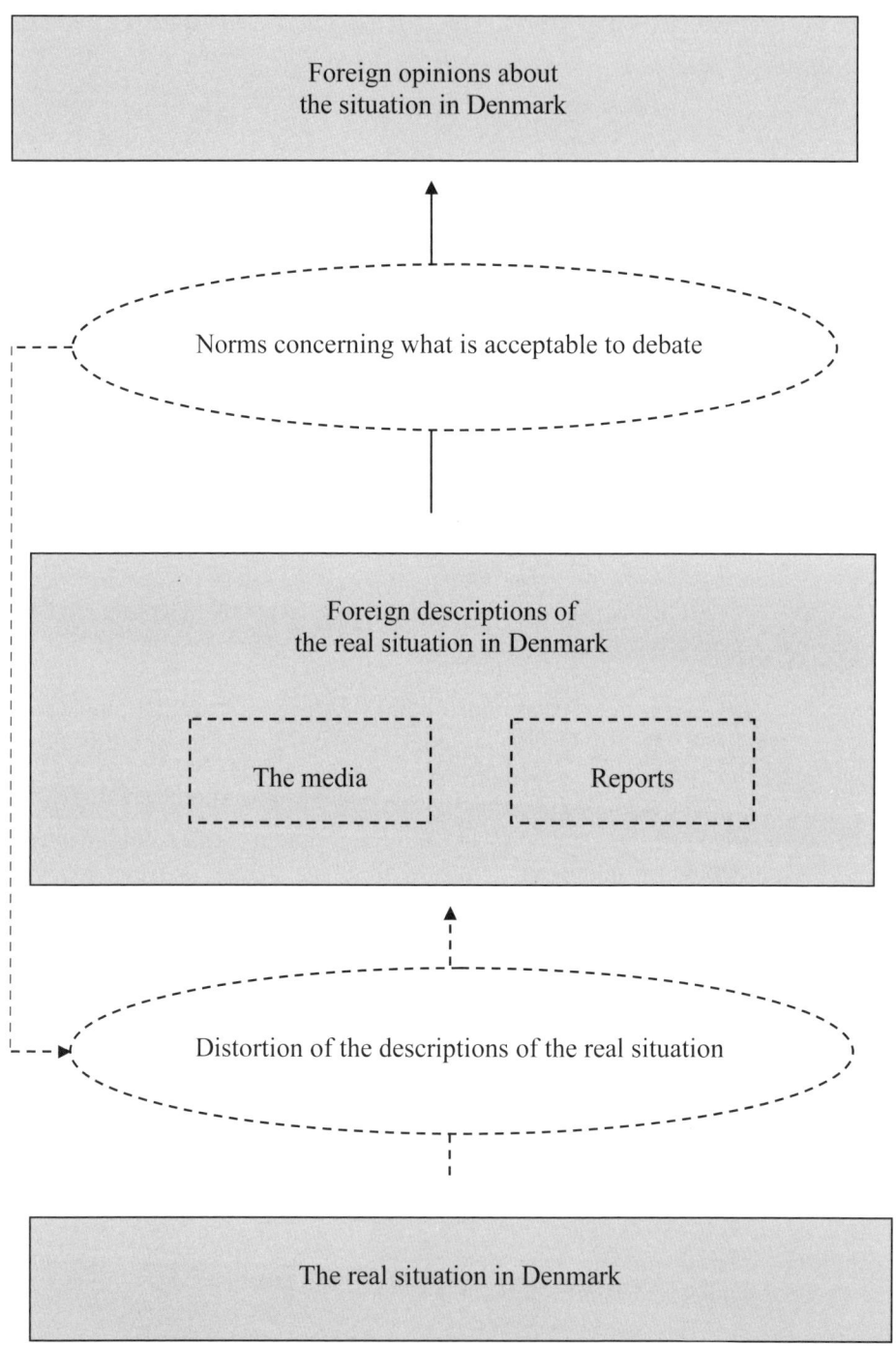

how these in turn created various positive or negative views of the circumstances in Denmark (the rectangular box in the figure).

The figure also reflects the fact that accepted norms play a part in creating images. In the field of "immigrants and refugees" very strong opinions exist as to what it is permissible to write about, and how the subjects may be tackled; such views can very easily influence the nature of the descriptions written. Further, people's opinions about Denmark depend on their own preconceived values and views, for example in terms of their differing perceptions of what might constitute a reasonable immigration policy, or their opinions on how to conduct a decent debate on the topic. One could certainly not expect that there would be a broad acceptance in other countries of Danish attitudes towards immigrants. However, if the descriptions are distorted or misleading, then it is not simply a question of subjective norms playing a role in the creation of opinions, as opinions about Denmark will also be coloured by the fact that opinions to a greater or lesser extent are reactions to a distorted image of the country.

11.2. Scanning the press

In practice, the analysis focused on the "near neighbours", i.e. Norway, Sweden, Germany and Great Britain, via a systematic scanning of the media, and through further interviews, especially in Norway and Sweden.

A two-step procedure was applied in scanning the press by using the Internet.

- *For a central period from January 2001 to the middle of 2002*, the search was very "deep", using many different keywords and looking at many events using one or two newspapers in each country (*The Independent* in Great Britain, *Dagens Nyheter* and *Sydsvenska Dagbladet* in Sweden, *Aftenposten* in Norway and *Die Welt* in Germany). It was recognised in advance that one or two newspapers could not cover the entire press in each country, but the range of papers selected meant that there was variation across countries, as the first three publications can be described as "quality newspapers" which take a liberal stance on the issue of immigration, while the last two are more conventional "general newspapers" taking a more neutral position. The normal right-left division plays a fairly limited role in the area of immigration, as in several countries it is the conservative parties and media who support the idea of immigration of labour.

Box 1. Political attitudes

	Proportion of votes		Parliamentary position		Policy on asylum and family reunification	Party leaders named in texts
	1998	2001	1998-2001	2001-		
The left wing	**10.3**	**8.8**				
The Red-Green Alliance	2.7	2.4	Govt. supporting party		Liberal	
Socialist People's Party	7.6	6.4	Govt. supporting party		Liberal	
Social Democrats	**35.9**	**29.1**	Government coalition partner		Restrictions, but party split	Poul Nyrup Rasmussen, Prime Minister 1993-2001
Centre Parties	**10.7**	**9.3**				
Social-Liberals	3.9	5.2	Government coalition partner			Marianne Jelved, Deputy Prime Minister, 1993-2001
Centre Democrats	4.3	1.8		*		
Christian People's Party	2.5	2.3				
Conservative parties	**32.9**	**40.3**				
Liberal	24.0	31.3		Government coalition partner		Anders Fogh Rasmussen, Prime Minister 2001
Conservative	8.9	9.1		Government coalition partner		
The new right	**9.8**	**12.6**				
Danish People's Party	7.4	12.0		Govt. supporting party[1]		Pia Kjærsgaard
The Progress Party	2.4	0.6		*		

* The Centre Democrats and the Progress Party were no longer represented in Parliament after the 2001 elections.

[1] Danish politics are not based on a bilateral division between the government and the opposition, but on a tripartite system. The category "Government supporting party" means a party that has an interest in keeping the government in power by voting with it, but on which the government cannot depend in advance for their support on every issue. In the 1980s the Social-Liberals were a supporting party for the minority Conservative government, and supported them in their economic policies, but pushed the government into a minority over issues such as the environment, the EU and NATO.

- *For the whole of the period from the start of 2000 to the end of 2002,* the results of the deep search were used to search more widely – ideally across the whole spectrum of the press – using search words which had given a particularly large number of results in the previously mentioned central period, chiefly using general search engines. One of the results of this was that *Expressen* in Sweden and *The Financial Times* in Britain frequently came strongly into the picture.

The statements made below are thus linked to the material found, with the built-in proviso that the use of different media might have resulted in a different picture being created.

11.3. The image of the Danes as xenophobic

The examination of the material quickly produced a significant conclusion, namely that the media in the neighbouring countries wrote extensively about Danish attitudes towards immigrants. It also became apparent rather quickly that there were many strong opinions abroad about the Danes' attitudes to immigrants. In many of the media, the descriptions of the situation in Denmark had a marked critical tendency.

- There were many reports that portrayed the Danes as having a negative attitude to immigrants.

- There were also some neutral reports.

- There were only very few reports which portrayed the Danes as being welcoming towards immigrants.

In addition, various strong expressions were used: the Danes were described as "xenophobes" or directly as "racists".

This image was not of recent origin, nor was it created during the election of November 2001. As early as February 2000, in relation to the sanctions against Austria, the respected German newspaper *Frankfurter Allgemeine Zeitung* published an article by Jasper von Altenbochum under a headline referring to Jörg Haider, the leader of the Austrian Freedom Party, whose participation in the government triggered the European sanctions. Jasper von Altenbochum felt able to state that Haider's ideas were already government policy in Denmark. The Swedish tabloid *Expressen* took the same line, also in February 2000. The paper's Copenhagen correspondent, Lars Klint, found it misleading that the Danish Tourist Board wanted to market the country on the basis of the keywords *"hygge,* design, oasis, unpretentious, talented, free". Lars Klint went on to expand on the meaning of *hygge* – a special Danish quality of well-being, cosiness and comfort – as follows:

> "The mentality, the national character, the Danish sense of community. That which excludes immigrants and creates racial conflicts and xenophobia on a par with that in Austria".

It was also striking that Lars Klint wrote directly of "the national character", not just of a particular government initiative. This was more than just a vague hint and very clearly showed that Lars Klint found something fundamentally wrong with the Danes.

Around the same time, even more directly, Lasse Dude wrote in the German *Die Woche* about the Danes:

> "Within Scandinavia, the Nordic "southerners", i.e. the Danes, with their "Die Fahne hoch" mentality and their underlying "we can manage things ourselves" attitude, have always been regarded as somewhat special".

Here the parallels to the racism in the southern states of the USA and to German Nazism were evident. Referring to an unnamed source at the Swedish newspaper *Aftonbladet*, Lasse Dude explained to his German readership that linguistically the Danes were the Saxons of Scandinavia, and politically they were the Bavarians. The Saxons are renowned for speaking dreadful German, and the Bavarians for being reactionary, and so Lasse Dude was illustrating both a Swedish phobia of their neighbours and German prejudices.

During the election campaign of 2001 this perspective was even more clearly expressed in the foreign media. *Deutsche Presse Agentur* wrote that the description "brutal" could never have been more appropriately applied to any election campaign than to the current one in the otherwise apparently peaceful Denmark, and also described the electoral campaign as an "unprecedented" battle for votes on the basis of the immigration issue. *Dagsavisen* in Oslo illustrated the Danish election campaign with a picture of a Norwegian Neo-Nazi outside a Danish law court, and drew the connection with the caption:

> "Xenophobia and immigration have been a key theme in the Danish election".

After the 2001 election, the Swedish tabloid *Aftonbladet* – the biggest daily paper in the Nordic countries – published an offensive article in which the Danes were called "Danish Devils" and which said that the "obviously obnoxious" Anders Fogh Rasmussen had won on a racist ticket.

The criticism continued for months. In June 2002, Stephen Castle wrote in *The Guardian*:

> "Over the past year, the unheralded swing to the right in Danish politics has made the gradual increase in the Germans' vote for the Nazis look slow".

Even later – in fact after the period of this research – the second biggest paper in Sweden, *Dagens Nyheter*, made a direct comparison to Nazism:

> "The Danish law on family reunification has a concrete parallel. The Nazi policy of extermination began in 1935 with the Nuremberg Laws, which included a ban on family relations between Jews and Aryans. These laws started a downward path which ended in the gas chambers ... Those who do not protest against the Danish policy have failed to understand its downward direction and the historical parallel".

Some of the criticism can be taken relatively lightly. Today "racist" is a term used fairly widely. For example, the Danish Supreme Court ruled to acquit in a case brought by the leader of the Danish People's Party, Pia Kjærsgaard, against a political opponent who had accused her of racism. The judges placed importance on the fact that the allegation against Pia Kjærsgaard had been made in a highly politicised context, but also stressed that today the term "racism" can even be used to describe the feelings of ill-will directed towards groups of people who are members of one's own race. If that is indeed the case, not much is needed, at least not in a political context, to call others "racists".

It is, however, more serious when Denmark and the Danish election campaign are depicted as being comparable to Nazism and the racial attitudes in the American Southern States, whether by insinuation, pictures, or directly. This is what happened in the Norwegian, German, Swedish and British press. In such cases the highly negative view of Denmark was beyond doubt. And there is a diffcrence between criticising specific government proposals and specific laws, and criticising the general characteristics of the whole nation, as was done in *Expressen* and *Die Woche*.

The examples quoted represent a selection of the strongest opinions about Denmark and the Danes' attitudes to immigrants, and there were many other statements of a similar nature. However, there were also some more neutral accounts. Generalisations can be dangerous here, as the particular selection of media can distort the picture, but it seems that:

- The critical viewpoints *in the first period* (up to the election in 2001) were expressed especially in the Swedish and German media. During this period, the English language press wrote virtually nothing about Dane's attitudes to immigrants. Those Norwegian reports which were found were generally neutral.

- *During and after the election campaign of November 2001* critical accounts appeared everywhere.

11.4. Selectivity in the description

The existence of critical opinions in the foreign media regarding the Danes' attitudes to immigrants can be taken as a given fact. Much less clear, however, is whether these descriptions conveyed a true picture of the real situation in Denmark. Here it seems that there was a marked selectivity as to which parts of the Danish situation the foreign media chose to highlight. For the sake of clarity the analysis of this point can be concentrated on the first period, up to the change of government in 2001. There were two notable features of this period:

- In the Danish public debate there was much talk of the tightening of the regulations concerning family reunification, fighting crime amongst asylum seekers, rejection of the repression of women in immigrant communities, etc., and indeed the regulations actually were made stricter.

- At the same time, in relation to the size of its population, Denmark, like Norway, gave asylum to more applicants than Sweden, and to many more than Germany and Great Britain. The number of family reunifications increased by 25 percent from 1999 to 2001, despite the tightening up of the regulations, and the new arrivals were entitled to some of the highest levels of social services in the Western world, if not actually the highest.

The foreign press only mentioned the restrictions and proposals for further restrictions, rather than what Denmark actually offered the immigrants in public welfare, as shown by the quotation above from *Frankfurter Allgemeine Zeitung* in February 2000 which claimed that Haider's ideas were already government policy in Denmark. This distortion meant that Denmark almost automatically came to be seen as a nation of hardliners.

At the same time, the fact that there might be problems in immigrant communities was played down. When the Social Democratic Minister of the Interior, Karen Jespersen, in August 2000 spoke about isolating criminal asylum seekers in some isolated place, even on a desert island, Lars Klint wrote that the proposal was bound to flop, as, according to *Ekstra Bladet*, no such islands were available. He continued:

> "So now she may well speculate about new ideas to speed up the processing of asylum seekers and how the true Danish people can be saved from too close and risky contact with people from other nations".

Deutsche Presse Agentur reported that according to the police, 100 criminal asylum seekers were arriving every month to Denmark. The journalist added that by international standards this was nothing unusual. What *Deutsche Presse Agentur* failed to mention was that the criminal asylum seekers, primarily from the former Soviet Union, were causing real problems in the vicinity of the asylum centres.

Another German journalist, Hannes Gamillscheg, told the Danish newspaper *Politiken* that his editor's ears pricked up when he found he could write about a Danish Social Democrat who expressed herself in a way that – according to Hannes Gamillscheg – no German Social Democrat ever would do.

A week later two virtually identical articles by Hannes Gamillscheg appeared, one in Vienna and one in Frakfurt am Main, with a portrait of Karen Jespersen with the headline "Disgusting tones in Denmark". These reported Karen Jespersen as saying that she did not wish to live in a multi-cultural society, as she held values such as human rights and equality too sacrosanct. This was tersely dismissed with the exclamation: "As if there were any contradiction!" With regard to the proposal to isolate criminal asylum seekers, it was stated:

- that Denmark would never put mass murderers and child molesters on a desert island, and

- that it should be possible to deal quite easily with a couple of dozen gangsters using the ordinary criminal law.

The first was pure invention. Karen Jespersen had suggested Middelgrundsfortet at the entrance to Copenhagen Harbour as an example of an isolated spot, and in fact this fort had been used as an asylum centre for a short time in the 1980s. The island of Livø in the Limfjorden was used as an asylum centre for a somewhat longer period. For decades the island had been used as a place of gentle custody for mentally retarded criminals, and later – in the 1970s and 1980s – it was used as an asylum centre. It is also unclear how the 100 criminals a month, which the first journalist wrote about, had shrunk to "a couple of dozen gangsters". However, common to both reports was the belittling of the problem.

When the criminal asylum seekers actually were isolated – not on a deserted island, but in the Sandholmlejr asylum centre – the stack of asylum applications from the Commonwealth of Independent States fell from 1,100 to 650, and at the same time the number of criminal charges against asylum seekers declined from 1,403 per quarter to 632.

The way in which the foreign media played down the potential problems with certain immigrant communities had the side effect that the Danish proposals to tighten up the regulations came to appear to be clearly unjustified. Instead, the foreign press offered an alternative explanation as to why the politicians had come up with such proposals: namely, a populist battle for votes with the strongly anti-immigration Danish People's Party. In the article in *Frankfurter Allgemeine Zeitung* in February 2000, Jasper von Altenbochum wrote that the Social Democrats were under pressure from the Danish People's Party, and that the government wanted an "immigration package" to dampen the hysteria about being swamped by immigrants, which had lasted for months.

Similarly, in February 2000, Lasse Dude pointed out that the Social Democrats were under pressure from the Danish People's Party, and wrote that the Prime Minister, Poul Nyrup Rasmussen had responded to this competition by appealing to the xenophobic instincts of his fellow countrymen. In his New Year Speech of 2000, the Prime Minister had rejected the idea that Denmark was a multi-cultural society, and then in February the government tightened the rules for family reunification.

The European Commission against Racism and Intolerance (ECRI) also referred to the competition from the Danish People's Party. An ECRI report from spring 2001 included the following:

> "extreme right political parties, such as the far-right Danish People's Party ... have become increasingly prominent on the Danish political scene, promoting racist and xenophobic ideas" (paragraph 38 of the report).

Once again, the very strong terms "racist" and "xenophobic" are used. The criticism was extended to "the centre political parties":

> "For fear of losing electoral support from segments of the population supposed to be hostile to foreigners, the latter parties tend to adopt a rhetoric portraying non-Danes as a problem within Danish society, thus contributing to a climate of xenophobia and intolerance" (paragraph 39 of the report).

Once again there is a generalisation in the use of the expression "a climate of xenophobia and intolerance".

The foreign media failed to mention that the difficulties the Social Democrats were undoubtedly experiencing from the electoral competition of the Danish People's Party could only partly explain the government's proposals – for example, to tighten the rules for family reunification – as the Social Democrats did not, after all, form a one-party government. The government was a coalition between the Social Democrats and the Social Liberals, and even though the government could win support from the Liberals and the Conservatives over the immigration restrictions, the further survival of the government required support from the left wing. Both the left wing and the Social Liberals supported a liberal immigration policy.

There are more concrete reasons why it was problematic to refer solely to the problems faced by the Social Democrats. In his New Year Speech on 1st January 2000, Prime Minister Poul Nyrup Rasmussen did indeed talk about Danes feeling like foreigners in their own country, but as early as 9th January Marianne Jelved stated that the Social Liberals were ready to consider further restrictions to prevent arranged marriages, both by setting an age limit for family reunification and by requiring that immigrants should have an independent place of abode before they could bring their spouses into Denmark. This was long before a proposal for a revised immigration policy was presented, and there was a very great chance that Marianne Jelved meant what she said. A substantial part of the background to the policy was therefore ignored in the foreign coverage.

In actual fact, events in the period up to the election in 2001 could actually have provided the basis for underlining how positive Denmark's stance towards immigrants was. But the picture presented by foreign media in our material was negative, as it did not mention that:

- Denmark granted asylum to a very large number of applicants

- family reunification was increasing rapidly

- new arrivals were offered very high levels of social services.

At the same time, the following problems were minimised:

- the position of women in immigrant communities and problems relating to arranged marriages

- asylum seekers with criminal intentions.

This meant that the proposals for tightening up immigration policy appeared to be either unjustified or based on populist vote-catching. There was frequently an emphasis on the general climate of xenophobia and intolerance. Overall, it seems that the descriptions only covered part of the real situation in Denmark, namely that part which could be used to present an image of the Danes as "xenophobic".

11.5. The attitudes of the Danish people, according to the foreign media

So far, the Danes themselves had only had a walk-on role in the foreign discussions of Denmark, insofar as the politicians' initiatives were explained by the supposed xenophobia of part of the population. But there were also more direct discussions about the attitudes of the population.

In some cases, the discussion actually presented a positive picture. In Sweden, *Expressen* carried a report which suggested that the attitude of Danes to refugees was much more sophisticated than would appear from the political debate. A new opinion survey showed that two out of three Danes thought that immigrants enriched Danish culture, and the number of Danes who saw immigrants as a serious threat to Danish culture had fallen from 41% in 1991 to 30% in 2000.

In the Norwegian newspaper *Aftenposten* of 10th February 2001, the Copenhagen correspondent Ole Martin Larsen reported on a survey, and he focused on the tolerance of the Danes. However, he added that many restrictions were being introduced to the immigration laws and that immigrants found it difficult to find employment. A week later, *Aftenposten* reported that a survey carried out in Norway showed that Norwegians had become more positive towards people with different cultural backgrounds, and added that the same questions had been asked in Denmark, with results that were very close to those in Norway.

Nonetheless, there were also a number of reports displaying the opposite tendency. On 20th December 2000, the Swedish newspaper *Sydsvenska Dagbladet* published a press release from the European Union Monitoring Centre of Racism and Xenophobia (EUMC), according to which Denmark was the country in the EU where most people felt disturbed by people with other religions. The headline was: "Danish EU record in religious intolerance". In a leader in *Expressen*, Jan-Olof Bengtsson combined this with another Danish opinion survey that showed that 45% felt that immigration and integration were the most important political issues, and Jan-Olof Bengtsson added:

> "Danishness and the established order are now very much in fashion, as opposed to globalisation and tolerance."

According to Bengtsson, fears of perceived loss of identity and of an over-relaxed immigration policy could also be found in Sweden. But in Denmark, Pia Kjærsgaard (The Danish People's Party) – along with her political colleagues, who were in shock following poor opinion polls – had made the themes fully legitimate.

Ewa Svensson, the Copenhagen correspondent for *Dagens Nyheter* in Stockholm, also took up the possible difference between Denmark and Sweden. In spring 2001 she presented an overall picture of Denmark under the headline "racism has been house-trained". A number of reports followed. The OECD was quoted as saying that Denmark was in last place when it came to finding work for immigrants It was also said that the European Commission had described Denmark as an intolerant and xenophobic country, and that the reaction to this amongst the media and politicians was a sense of injustice. Finally, Ewa Svensson reported that a new EU study showed that in Denmark 20% of the population were intolerant towards immigrants and refugees, as against only 9% in Sweden.

On the other hand, Ewa Svensson failed to mention that according to the EU study the number of what they called the "actively tolerant" considerably exceeded the number of intolerant people, even in Denmark. According to the study, there were 33% of the intolerant type of people in both Sweden and Denmark. But this information could have ruined the headline about house-trained racism. Ewa Svensson felt that the Danish politicians were responsible for the ongoing debate on immigration, and that they had to a great extent focussed only on the problem.

11.6. Generalisations

The coverage of the election itself points to a further question, namely the degree of differentiation between Danish political parties and between Danes with different attitudes.

During the election campaign, there were more analyses that differentiated between the parties. In Norway, Erik Sagflaat writing in *Dagsavisen*, identified disagreements both between the parties and internally amongst the Social Democrats. Prime Minister Poul Nyrup Rasmussen had calculated on achieving a high profile as an experienced statesman in the aftermath of the terrorist attacks in New York on September 11th, but now immigration policy had become the number one issue. On this issue, as Erik Sagflaat saw it, the Social Democrats could lose votes, as the large non-socialist parties wanted to insist on tightening up regulations but the Social Democrats could not follow suit, as the party was split. Many voters wanted stricter rules, but a part of the Social Democrat electorate considered family reunification a human right. Whereas the Social Democrat Minister of the Interior, Karen Jespersen, wanted tighter restrictions, the Minister of the Environment, Svend Auken, also a Social Democrat, could not see the need.

Similarly, Matilda Hansson, writing in the Swedish *Sydsvenska Dagbladet* just before Election Day in November, distinguished between the views on immigration of the various Danish parties. The Danish People's Party would prefer to stop immigration; the non-socialist parties wanted to limit immigration and punish crime more harshly, but also to find work for immigrants already in the country; while the Social Democrats and other parties on the left talked mainly about integration.

What is important is not whether these analyses were – or were not – completely or partly correct, but that they represented an attempt to make distinctions. This was something that many others did not do.

On 16th November 2001, the columnist Hanne Kjöller wrote in the Swedish newspaper *Dagens Nyheter* that the two Danish candidates for Prime Minister, Poul Nyrup Rasmussen and Anders Fogh Rasmussen, were trying to out-do each other in terms of who could go furthest in regard to immigration policy. She went on to ask what it must be like to be an immigrant or a refugee in a country where virtually all the parties agreed that non-Nordic citizens were undesirable. She found the difference between Poul Nyrup Rasmussen and Anders Fogh Rasmussen, the challenger, to be microscopic.

On the day of the election, the Norwegian *Bergens Tidende* commented:

> "Politicians in most parties – from the Social Democrats to the Progress Party – have played on xenophobia in a deluge of rather less than pleasant ploys. The gentle, sweet Danes have simply become the hard, inflexible neighbours".

In Sweden, Mauricio Rojas, MP, elected in affiliation with the Liberals and himself a refugee from Chile, was even more critical. In an interview as part of this project, he was asked about his view of the Danish election campaign, and he answered:

> "I found it completely disgusting ... A party like the Danish People's Party. This party dominated the debate about integration and immigrants. ... The entire political establishment, and the press, and all the other parties tried to adapt to this most disgusting political discourse."

11.7. Norms for what may be written and for how it is written

It would probably be too much to expect broad media coverage of Danish politics in Germany, Sweden or Norway because Denmark is a small country, and perhaps not of particular interest to everyone abroad. The German journalist Hannes Gamillscheg, mentioned earlier, remarked that his editor's ears had pricked up when Gamillscheg stated that he could write about a Danish Social Democrat (the Minister of the Interior Karen Jespersen) who had expressed herself in a way that no German Social Democrat ever would. About the coverage of the election contest he said:

> "So you find out that the immigration debate has the highest interest, and then you write about it without mentioning that 90 percent of the Danish election campaign was conducted on the basis of other issues, but that is the way it is ... You cannot cover a Danish election campaign or debate as though that in itself was what interested foreigners most."

Talking about the election, Julian Isherwood of the *Daily Telegraph* and "Copenhagen Calling" (BBC and NPR) said that the foreign press was largely uninterested in the EU question, the Danish economy or the welfare state:

> "It was the whole right wing movement in Europe which was of interest. That was because of the Haider case in Austria, for one thing. There was an impression that the Liberals were close to the Danish People's Party, and that was interesting. That was definitely number one. The headlines were mainly that there was a right-wing party that wanted to take power in Denmark. Immigration was by far the biggest thing."

In Oslo, a third veteran reporter on Danish politics, Erik Sagflaat of *Dagsavisen*, took the same line.

Immigration topics are, at least in certain periods, "good copy" abroad. At the same time, this is an area with strongly established norms. This also applies here in Denmark: as recently as spring 2002, *Jyllands-Posten* received a complaint from the Press Council for mentioning the ethnic origins of the defendants in reporting a criminal case. This is also the case in an international context. In their annual report for 2000 (published in 2001), the EUMC pointed out that "racism" is no longer based upon crude stereotypes. According to the EUMC, arguments other than "race" may be used. The EUMC talks of "subtle racism", and offers examples of contributions to the debate referring to:

> "financial requirements, cultural differences, safety and medical threats, which are defined in contrast to the supposedly culturally homogeneous 'host population'".

Simple reporting of "racist ideas" without expressing opposition to them can similarly be seen as approbation of those ideas. The EUMC annual report states that racism in the media can occur through the presentation of opinions as if they were facts, if this is done without any "refutation of or challenge to racist ideas".

Caution in criticism of immigrants is widespread and has existed for a long time. A Norwegian journalist was thus able to recount a story from the 1970s when he and his colleagues found out that the Gypsy Office of the Municipality of Oslo had more employees than there were gypsies in Oslo. This could have been a good example of bloated bureaucracy. Yet the editor rejected the story, as it could have been interpreted as being hostile to gypsies.

It is perhaps these considerations which can offer some explanation for the critical angle of the reports about Denmark:

- immigration is "good copy"

- the Danish debate was both "bad" and perhaps displayed "subtle racism" in its identification of the problems with immigration.

This is perhaps also an explanation for the minimalisation of the Danish politicians' concerns about the problems caused by criminality or the repression of women in the immigrant communities. It is simply not acceptable to report such arguments.

11.8. Are the Danes more "xenophobic" than anyone else?

The foreign reports in the material were not identical, but taken as a whole it would not be very surprising if foreigners got the impression that Danes were especially opposed to refugees and immigrants, and that the Danish debate was characterised by a particular dislike of minorities.

The question of the attitudes of the Danes to minorities was discussed in the Rockwool Foundation Research Unit's newsletter (March 2002) on the basis of an extensive study carried out by the EUMC in all EU countries in spring 2000. There were two main points in this newsletter article.

- Whether or not Danes were more open or, conversely, more xenophobic than other nations depended entirely on the subject under discussion:
    - Danes felt much more disturbed than other nationalities by the presence of people of a different religion.
    - Danes were on the other hand far above the European average when it came to willingness to accept refugees from countries with internal conflicts, and more willing than others to involve immigrants in politics.
- On average, across various topics, Danes were rather in the middle in terms of openness to ethnic minorities. More specifically, Danes were less welcoming to minorities than Swedes, but on the other hand, more welcoming than the Germans or the Austrians.

This information can be supplemented with examples from a further analysis of the material from the EUMC. First and foremost, Danes are the national group whose ranking varies most from subject to subject. If Danes are to be called especially "xenophobic", then a strong selectivity has to be exercised to focus on precisely the issues where the Danes are most xenophobic, and to ignore the other topics.

The European Values Study (EVS) in 1999 presented a picture of the Danes as very welcoming to minorities. While the EUMC study asked generally about feeling disturbed by the presence of people of a different religion – and correspondingly by people of a different race or nationality – the EVS in 1999 asked, more precisely, how respondents would feel about having a neighbour from certain specific groups: Gypsies, Jews, immigrants, Muslims and people of a different race. Amongst 31 European nations, the Danes came in 25th, with the 31st place being the most tolerant.

Similarly, in a situation of unemployment, the Danes, Swedes and the Dutch would not give preference to a fellow countryman when taking on a new employee. The other 28 nations would.

Thus far, EVS 1999 placed Danes amongst the most open of peoples in Europe. However, this was not true across the board. Danes were middle-ranked when it came to the immigration of labour from developing countries, and were also one of the nations who placed the greatest importance on immigrants adapting to the culture of the host country.

Once again, Denmark's position varied from topic to topic, but on average across the topics, the Danes were very clearly one of the most welcoming nations. Once again, the Swedes were even more welcoming, while the British and the Germans were about the same as the Danes. Unfortunately, Norway was not included in the survey.

The results are not identical from study to study at a detailed level, but taking the surveys as a whole, the conclusions would seem to be:

- Danes are not as welcoming to minorities as Swedes are

- but in the various comparisons (amongst 15 EU, or 31 European nations) they are nonetheless amongst the more welcoming, while

- their place in relation to the neighbouring countries (Germany and Britain) varies.

The main survey in the research project on the living conditions of non-Western immigrants in Denmark (1999) included a question regarding attitudes towards marriage to a person from another ethnic group (Nielsen 2000). Responses to this question are often interpreted as indicators of attitudes towards other ethnic groups. The results shown in Table 11.1 are perhaps unexpected, in that the non-Danes displayed at least as much negativity towards other foreigners as the Danes did. Danes were asked the question about marriage to people from other ethnic groups in the special omnibus survey, and a comparison of the responses placed them at the more open-minded end of the scale in terms of their relatively limited negativity towards foreigners; their attitudes were approximately on a par with those of immigrants from the former Yugoslavia, Iran and Somalia.

Chapter 1 of this book also shows that immigrants largely marry within their own national groups.

The results shown in the table thus suggest that there is no great division between Danes and immigrants on this issue.

Table 11.1. Opposition to marriage. The various nationalities are arranged in order from the most negative to the most positive in their attitudes towards marriage to foreigners. 1999.

Respondents' home countries	Percentage opposed to marriage to a young person from an ethnic group other than their own (average)
Turkey	77
Pakistan	72
Lebanon	66
Vietnam	58
Poland	53
Somalia	48
Denmark	48
Iran	42
Former Yugoslavia	39

Source: Main survey, and the omnibus survey of Danes for 1999. Only those who expressed an attitude towards *all* groups are included in the statistics.

11.9. Is the Danish debate more "xenophobic" than that in other countries?

The foreign coverage might have given the impression not only that Danes were "xenophobic", but also that the Danish debate itself expressed unanimous negativity towards foreigners. In Sweden, *Expressen* wrote that the Red/Green Alliance was the only decent party in Denmark; Hanne Kjöller expressed her view in *Dagens Nyheter* that pretty much all the parties found non-Nordic citizens "undesirable"; and the Swedish MP Mauricio Rojas found the Danish debate detestable, as it was completely dominated by the Danish People's Party. Other foreign newspapers were, however, aware of the disagreements over the issue of immigration, and as a Dane it is difficult – with any sense of reality – to consider the Social Liberal Party or the Socialist People's Party clones of the Danish People's Party.

As far as the Danish press is concerned, a study by the Institute of Journalism at the University of Southern Denmark indicates that the debate was also varied. The Institute conducted a study in 1999 on behalf of the Commission for Ethnic Equality, which examined the press coverage of the immigration issue in week

46. As the study was repeated in 2001, week 46 actually fell during the election campaign. It turned out that 30% of the news items in the newspapers were positive towards immigrants, as against 22% that were negative. The remainder were neutral. Amongst opinion pieces, 38% were positive and 37% negative. Once again, the rest were neutral.

On this basis, the Danish debate cannot be described as either positive or negative towards immigrants and immigration, as it had elements of both sides.

Less clear is the comparison with other countries. In Sweden there is clearly an element of "political correctness". The Editor-in-Chief of *Dagens Nyheter*, Hans Bergström, pointed out in an interview with the Danish newspaper *Berlingske Tidende* that his paper did not want to turn immigrants into a special problem, and also that the debate about the honour-killing of a Kurdish woman in Sweden had ended up as a general discussion of the conditions of women. This was apparently not a self-criticism – rather quite the opposite.

On the Swedish TV programme "Agenda" the Political Editor of *Dagens Nyheter*, Niklas Ekdal, expressed a wish for more debate about immigration, but not like that in Denmark, where, in his opinion, the immigrants were being blamed for the problems of the country. For him, the issue was actually different, namely how to live together with foreigners, and in this respect he felt that people had performed badly. Thus Niklas Ekdal located the problem with the Swedes, but still he wanted a debate. On the other hand, the Chief Political Editor of *Aftonbladet*, Helle Klein, did not really want such a debate:

> "If the debate is going to be about whether there is a problem with refugees and immigrants, then we do not want it, as we want a debate to be conducted on the premises of democracy".

However, not all of Helle Klein's staff agreed with her. In *Aftonbladet*, Yrsa Stenius wrote about an ethnically Swedish youth who felt under threat from groups of immigrant boys who demanded his respect:

> "The lad must be allowed to say what he experienced without us coming up like opinion-police saying, 'no, no, it isn't the immigrants that are the problem, it is us who do not treat them properly'".

There was also disagreement regarding crime amongst immigrants. The Swedish Crime Prevention Council (Brå) wanted to publish crime statistics divided up according to ethnic criteria. This produced the following reaction in *Aftonbladet*:

> "If Brå makes a distinction in crime statistics between 'Swedes' and 'Immigrants', then the authorities are actually saying that ethnicity can

cause crime. ... The debate must be conducted seriously. Not by using crime statistics that just by their existence confirm racial prejudice."

Similarly, Cecilia Magnusson of the Swedish Conservative Party said in a radio debate that people could not just close their eyes to juvenile crime amongst immigrants: crime might be a way to gain respect for people who are otherwise outsiders. Mona Sahlin, Minister for Integration, reacted very negatively – again by refusing to take up the debate:

> "I think it is terrible what Cecilia says. Ethnicity and crime is a discussion we do not want. On the other hand, class poverty and crime, that is something quite different, Cecilia!"

So far, a picture emerges not only of politicians and journalists who do not want a debate, but also of important public actors who do not only reject certain views, but also refuse a debate in which immigrant background is directly introduced as an explanatory factor. This means that the Danish debate appeared negative according to many Swedish norms. A similar picture emerges from the material from Germany. Therefore, from German viewpoint the Danish debate could be seen as negative towards immigrants.

What is much more difficult is to see any great difference between Denmark and Norway in the material examined. The Editor-in-chief of *Dagsavisen*, Hilde Haugsgjerd, suggested that the debate in Norway lay somewhere between the Swedish rejection of discussion and the Danish openness. Looking back, the MP Ranveig Frøiland of the Workers' Party stated in 2002:

> "The distance between the press and the people is just as great as that between the politicians and the people. I think we shared the fear that once you start talking about immigration, an equals sign appears between immigrants and racism. We as politicians do not wish to be racist, and I do not think that the newspapers do either. And so, we avoid addressing the issue, but clearly this is very stupid".

The Norwegian debate was especially marked by a great awareness of the position of women in immigrant communities. Thus, the Norwegian-Pakistani commentator, Shabana Rehmann, wrote in 2000:

> "While the strong women struggle for good salaries and top jobs, other women in Norway are running the risk of being murdered. Murdered, if they demand the same rights that Norwegian women have already won. This is happening in Norway today".

This is in strong contrast to the view of the Editor-in-Chief of *Dagens Nyheter*, Hans Bergström, who suggested that the debate about the honour killing of a young Kurdish woman had been transformed into a general discussion about "the position of women".

Similarly, the Norwegian Professor of Anthropology Unna Wikan claimed that society was betraying young immigrant girls for fear of interfering in their "culture". She made a demand for openness. This is what she said to *Aftensposten:*

> "The authorities treat information about immigrants and their living conditions as dangerous. They are afraid that if the facts come into the open about how the policy of integration has failed, this will fuel increased racism amongst the Norwegian population. This is a case of evil being done in the name of good".

Once again there is a contrast to Sweden, as seen, for example, in Aftonbladet's opposition to debate and to publishing statistics.

In summer 2000, Norway had appeared to be engaged in the same debate as Denmark about criminal asylum seekers who used the asylum centres as their bases. The biggest difference from Denmark, however, seems to be a less sharply drawn division, where the Norwegian Progress Party advocated a milder line than the Danish People's Party, while, conversely, the parties who were normally the most liberal on issues of refugees and asylum policy were also saying that enough was enough, and calling for "putting our foot down". Otherwise it is fairly difficult to see any great differences in the scope and content of the debate. In our material, it is pretty much the same themes which come up.

11.10. A reality created by opinions?

This overview raises a fundamental question:

- Are opinions determined by "facts" or are "facts" determined by opinions?

Figure 11.1 took its starting point in "the real situation in Denmark". There were normative filters, but the arrows leading from "the real situation in Denmark" ended up as the basis for "opinions about Denmark".

However, the analysis suggests that this is to underestimate the importance of norms:

- when it is "subtle racism" (EUMC) to suggest that immigration can, for example, be an economic burden on the host country,

- when no one wants to allow a debate about problems with immigration and refugees (Helle Klein),

- and when it is "terrible" to discuss criminality amongst immigrants (Mona Sahlin and *Aftonbladet*),

it does not just mean that the media offers "nice opinions" on immigrants. It also means that only one aspect of the real situation is presented – when in fact it would not always be so terrible if the "decent attitude" also had to consider the other side of the coin. The case of the criminal asylum seekers concerned a small hard core from Eastern Europe, who were quite different from normal asylum seekers.

The desire to present only "nice opinions" is probably unsustainable, because it is unrealistic to want to integrate large groups without any problems arising – on both sides, and not just on one. The reluctance to talk about problems regarding "the position of women in immigrant communities" cannot continue. So with respect to "the position of women in immigrant communities" the refusal to discuss the problem has broken down. When Karen Jespersen pointed out the problems in the late summer of 2000, a German newspaper dismissed her words with an exclamation mark. Yet, in the early summer of 2001, Mona Sahlin stated that this was an issue about Swedish values, which had to be imposed. In the first half of 2002, the Socialist Left Party in Norway spoke out with "The tolerance we show should be reciprocated".

And so there is a problem for the democratic debate: the best possible way to maintain a "nice attitude" is to keep quiet. But naive silence destroys any possibility of a proper debate about the problems, which will certainly arise. And so it means that those who refuse to be naively accommodating will be criticised.

First and foremost, norms either written or spoken, as well as norms about what should be silence, can result in a distorted view of reality, and this hurts the descriptions of the Danish reality, as the Danish discourse does not stick to such norms.

It is still a question of balance. This chapter has presented a number of examples of extreme characterisations of the Danes and the Danish political debate as being "xenophobic", alongside examples of more neutral articles and some which draw attention to splits amongst the Danes. The actual results of the survey depend upon the weight given to the different types of description.

This is not a simple numerical criterion, as a single harsh article can have a much greater impact than ten neutral ones. On the basis of the material collected, however, there seem to be differences between time periods and between countries. Up until the election campaign, the media seem to have presented an image of the Danes and the Danish debate as being "xenophobic" to (sections) of the Swedish and German public, but not to "people abroad" in general. During and after the electoral campaign in 2001, such images became so widespread and often aggressive in their formulations that the foreign press clearly must have been a factor in causing Danes to be identified as xenophobic. Whatever the period in which they were published, many of the descriptions refer to the conditions in Denmark. But which conditions? In any country, examples can be found of more or less anything, but here there was a very clear selectivity in what was presented, and often a lack of differentiation, with the result that the media actually played an independent role in opinion-forming, which cannot be simply described as writing about "the real situation in Denmark". Perhaps this is what they did in some ways, but they did not write about the real situation in its entirety.

11.11. Summary

This chapter discussed a large-scale study by the Rockwool Foundation Research Unit of foreign views of Danes' attitudes to immigrants. The study covered both international organisations and foreign media and politicians. The source material was primarily published reports and material from the mass media found on the Internet, and the analysis was further expanded through in-depth conversations with foreign journalists and politicians. The foreign countries involved were primarily Sweden, Norway, Germany and the United Kingdom. The study covered a period which saw a relatively dramatic revision of Danish immigration policy, namely from the beginning of the year 2000 to the end of 2002, taking in the election of the autumn of 2001 and a period under the new right-of-centre Liberal-Conservative coalition government which took office afterwards.

The material collected showed that there were many accounts that stressed negative attitudes among Danes towards immigrants and few that suggested that Danes were welcoming to them. The negative accounts described Danes as "anti-foreigner", or even explicitly as "racists". The critical viewpoints in the first period (up to the election in 2001) were expressed especially in Swedish and German media. During this period, the Anglophone press wrote virtually nothing about Danes' attitudes to immigrants. The Norwegian reports which were found were generally neutral.

In the Danish debate in the run-up to the election of November 2001 there were calls for stricter regulations for family reunification, for combating crime among asylum-seekers, and for the condemnation of the repression of women in the immigrant communities. A tightening up of the regulations did indeed take place. At the same time, however, Denmark, like Norway, was giving asylum to somewhat more applicants in relation to the size of its population than was

Sweden, and to many more than Germany or the United Kingdom. Furthermore, the number of family reunifications increased by 25 percent from 1999 to 2001, despite the tightening up of the regulations, and the new arrivals were entitled to some of the highest levels of social welfare benefits in the Western world. Nevertheless, the foreign media discussed only the stricter regulations and the proposals for yet more restrictions, making no mention of what Denmark was actually doing for refugees.

There were instances of the foreign media presenting a positive picture of Danes' attitudes to foreigners. For example, *Expressen* in Sweden published the results of a new opinion poll which showed, according to the paper, that the proportion of Danes who saw immigration as a serious threat to Danish culture had decreased from 41% in 1991 to 30% in 2000. But there were also reports presenting the opposite picture. In December 2000 the Swedish newspaper *Sydsvenska Dagbladet* published a press release from the European Union Monitoring Center on Racism and Xenophobia (EUMC), according to which Denmark was the country in the EU where most people felt disturbed by people of other religions. However, no mention was made of the fact that the number of actively tolerant people in Denmark far exceeded the number of intolerant people.

The conclusions of a study by the EUMC in 2000 and of the European Values Survey of 1999 appear to have been that the Danes were not as tolerant of minorities as the Swedes, but that nevertheless the Danes were among the more tolerant of European peoples in different comparisons (among 15 EU peoples and 31 European peoples), and their placement in the rank order for tolerance in relation to the positions of their neighbouring countries (Germany and Sweden) varied.

The widespread discussion and critique of Denmark's handling of immigration issues may be explained in part by the fact that treatment of foreigners makes good news material, and by the fact that the debate in the Danish media on problems connected with immigrants was much more open than in, for example, Sweden and Germany. As Hans Jørgen Nielsen has suggested (Nielsen, 2004, p 217), Danish politicians may have been early in pointing out the existence of problems, and in the terms of various norms it is also possible to hold the opinion that the Danes have made too much of these problems. On the other hand, the foreign press coverage of Denmark in the period 2000-2002 appears today to be rather dated in its failure to recognise the existence of these immigration problems.

References

Nielsen, Hans Jørgen. 2000. "Forholdet mellem etniske grupper", in Gunnar Viby Mogensen and Poul Chr. Matthiessen (eds.), *Integration i Danmark omkring årtusindeskiftet.* Aarhus: Aarhus University Press, 409-433.

Nielsen, Hans Jørgen. 2002 "Are the Danes less tolerant than other people?" in *News from the Rockwool Foundation Research Unit.* March 2002.

Nielsen, Hans Jørgen. 2004. *Er danskerne fremmedfjendske?* Aarhus: Aarhus University Press.

12. Foreigners in the Danish newspaper debate

12.1. Introduction

The present-day debate on refugees and immigrants has deep historical roots. The concepts of "the foreigner" or "the other" are as old as records stretch back into the past. The way the Greeks dismissed all non-Greeks as "Barbarians" is one of the oldest known examples of the systematic rejection by one society of all others. Today, social anthropologists can testify to similar mechanisms at work in "pre-modern" societies.

Even if the propensity to debate foreigners as an issue in one way or another is thus universal in character, the exact content of the debate, its intensity and its idiom are obviously governed by its actual historical setting.

This chapter is based on Bent Jensen's book on the newspaper debate on foreigners in Denmark (2000). The examination of the newspaper debate in that book, which is based on a qualitative analysis of the opinions expressed in the most politically influential papers in Denmark and in two popular papers – *Aftenbladet* and *Ekstra Bladet* – shows that the theme has recurred constantly ever since the establishment of a free press in Denmark in 1849. In fact, the topic has often been the object of particular attention in much of the party political press.

The study also shows that from the outset there were actually two broad themes that recurred frequently, these being presented from different viewpoints in accordance with each paper's political and editorial convictions. One of these themes was the debate on the migration of labour, and the other was the welcome accorded by Denmark to refugees and asylum seekers.

12.2. The migration of labour

12.2.1. The immigration of Swedish labour

The issue of the migration of labour arose as early as 1848 during the Three Years' War over Schleswig-Holstein and again in 1864 in connection with German craftsmen and brick-makers being threatened by enraged Danish craftsmen and labourers during the war against Prussia and Austria. The matter really became a major issue with the long-running debate on Swedish workers in the 1880s.

In the course of the sometimes very pointed exchanges of opinions, the newspapers of the right – *Berlingske Tidende* and *Jyllands-Posten* – insisted that there should be free movement of labour, and that therefore it was wrong for Denmark to place severe limitations on the hiring of Swedes on the labour market. These self-same bourgeois papers, however, were opposed to Swedish workers being able to enjoy the benefits of Danish poor relief in the event of unemployment, illness or old age. For example, in a debate on the right to citizenship in 1893, these papers wanted very strict limitations to be placed on the numbers of Swedish workers who were to be granted Danish citizenship, and who would thus be able to access the new social security systems of the 1890s. And it was these papers that supported the demands of the political right for law and order, advocating strict regulations governing the stay of foreign workers in Denmark to guarantee that they did not pose a threat to the property and security of Danish nationals.

Social-Demokraten found itself in a dilemma of a different nature. The paper and the Social Democrat party were in favour of internationalism on principle, and in theory they should have been able to adopt a well-disposed attitude towards the Swedes when they came to constitute a significant presence on the labour market – provided they were prepared to unionise, naturally. However, in the toughest period of the 1880s, when unemployment was high and the migration of farm-workers to the cities was great, it was difficult to maintain sympathy with these Swedish comrades. It was very clear that the paper felt that it would be better if the Swedish workers stayed at home – or at any rate did not come to Denmark in such large numbers. Public employment should be reserved for Danes, and the import of foreign labour by recruitment agents forbidden. However, it should be noted that the paper seldom expressed directly xenophobic sentiments, and that a comparison with the news coverage in other papers suggests that *Social-Demokraten* chose deliberately to down-tone its reporting of some of the notoriously violent clashes that occurred between Danish and Swedish workers.

Around the mid-1890s, as the employment situation started to improve, it seemed that the paper could take a more relaxed view on the presence of Swedes in Denmark. It became possible to emphasise the importance of international solidarity once more, just as the paper had expressed ideas of solidarity with class comrades from a sister people during the Parliamentary negotiations on the granting of Danish citizenship to impoverished Swedes.

During this period, the Social-Liberal *Politiken* was firmly positioned on the political left, but was also clearly not an organ of the Socialists. The paper thus had no internationalist ideology to defend, and consequently, it could present a more direct and unfiltered account of the violent confrontations between Swedish and Danish workers. At times, it is also possible to detect opinions in the paper that were clearly anti-foreigner. Only when the Swedish issue became caught up in the political debate between Government and Opposition did the paper express strong and undivided sympathy with the Swedish workers.

The press organ of the Liberal Party, *Fyns Tidende,* with affiliation to the farmers, also adopted a type of middle position. The paper saw it as undesirable from the taxpayers' point of view that there should be such a voluminous stream of poor immigrants into the country, and from the point of view of property owners it was seen as important that there should be effective police supervision. On the other hand, the paper defended the legal rights of the foreigners, including their right to protection from arbitrary expulsion.

12.2.2. The Polish workers in Denmark

An examination of the debate on the Polish workers who came to Denmark between 1892 and 1929 reveals many points of similarity with the debate on the immigration of Swedish labour.

The media of the political right generally saw no problem with the use of Polish workers, and *Berlingske Tidende* in particular missed no opportunity to emphasise the necessity for this import of labour for Danish agriculture as a result of work discipline being far too lax among Danish agricultural labourers. When the question arose of passing a protective law to guarantee a number of basic rights for the Polish workers, these papers were consistently positive towards the idea. These opinions should be viewed in the light of increasing demands from the Austro-Hungarian authorities. Poland did not exist as a nation state during the period 1795 to 1918, and many Poles were thus residents of the Austro-Hungarian Empire before the outbreak of the First World War. If the great landed interests in Denmark were to attract and retain the Polish agricultural workers for the coming seasons, a law offering the Poles a certain degree rights on the Danish labour market would appear to be justified. *Fyns Tidende* also considered it reasonable that there should be some legal protection, as did the local bourgeois newspapers on the island of Lolland-Falster, where the Poles were concentrated, working in the fields with sugar beets.

Social-Demokraten gave extensive coverage to the Polish workers. Up until 1914 the paper continued to have a strong internationalist orientation, and this came out in its views on the Poles. Movement of labour should be allowed on condition that there was a law to prevent the abuse of the Polish workers while simultaneously ensuring that Danish labourers were able to compete equally with them. A number of articles described how Social Democrat party officials had sought to assist grossly exploited Polish workers. The paper had a particular liking for recounting episodes where Poles had reacted against their unsatisfactory working conditions. In the political debate, *Social-Demokraten*, as the paper of the workers, made much play – as it had in relation to the Swedish workers – of the way in which the bourgeois papers revealed their lack of patriotism through their whole-hearted endorsement of the unregulated use of foreign labour.

It is, however, also evident from the press coverage that the rank-and-file Danish agricultural workers harboured a deeply felt suspicion, bordering on contempt, for the Poles; this sometimes came out very strongly in the agricultural workers' papers and in the local paper also named *Social-Demokraten* published on the island of Lolland-Falster.

During and after the First World War the Social Democrat party changed its strategy, with the international orientation being toned down considerably. Instead, the party, the unions and their press organs demanded strict limitations on the use of foreign labour. This line of policy reached its fullest expression under a Social Democrat/Social Liberal government, which ceased to permit the import of Polish labour from 1930 onward. Since the number of Polish seasonal workers coming to Denmark in 1928 and 1929 had been very small in any case, this decision must be viewed as having primarily a symbolic value; during the international economic recession from 1929 onward the government and the Agricultural Workers' Union had a need to demonstrate their strong resolve.

Like *Social-Demokraten*, *Politiken* took up the issue of the Polish workers from the time of the first arrivals in 1892. Initially, *Politiken*'s angle was not very different from that of *Social-Demokraten*, in that the paper expressed its indignation over the import of impoverished foreign labourers. Later, however, the view of *Politiken* began to differ from that of the workers' paper, in that it started to emphasise the need for land reform. Such a reform, which was a key element in the programme of the centrist Social Liberal party, would ensure the retention of a Danish labour force in agriculture – and would, coincidentally, help to strengthen the party's electoral base by establishing more smallholdings. When Parliament debated a law protecting foreign workers in 1908, *Politiken* associated itself with the necessity for such a measure, as did the popular paper *Ekstra Bladet*.

Fyns Tidende and the local Liberal paper *Lolland-Falsters Folketidende* also considered the legislation to be justified.

12.2.3. Immigrant labour, 1963-1980

The next time the issue of the international movement of labour was substantially discussed in the Danish press was in the 1960s. A widespread debate sprang up in the summer of 1964 in the wake of a feature article published in the Social Democrat paper *Aktuelt* by the Social Liberal Minister of

Trade at that time, Hilmar Baunsgaard. Without presenting a particularly detailed argumentation, Baunsgaard asserted in the article that the import of foreign workers at a time when there was a pressing shortage of labour could increase prosperity in the country, and this when the spirit of the times was particularly focused upon – as the Social Democrat election slogan had it – "making the good times better".

The idea of using foreign labour was immediately met with a storm of criticism in all the other papers, with the exception of *Jyllands-Posten* and *Politiken*. The absolute opposition of the Trade Union movement to such an idea was very clearly expressed in *Aktuelt*, for example (the paper which had published the article in the first place!), and also in *Berlingske Tidende*, in the politically independent *Information*, and in *Vestkysten* (right-of-centre). The representatives of the trade unions adopted a line of argument that they were to maintain throughout the 1960s. Their view was that it was always preferable to invest in new technology rather than to import Southern European or Turkish workers, whose presence would both contribute to depressing wages through competition for employment and tend to entrench old-fashioned production methods and systems. *Information*, with the support of some economic experts, propounded a similar viewpoint, focusing on the idea that technological upgrading was preferable to the import of unskilled labour. Several newspapers rejected the idea on the practical grounds that it would – in any case – be difficult to attract foreign workers to the country.

In the following year, the right-of-centre papers clarified their views on the issue when a discussion arose of the problems of the meat industry in finding sufficient labour for the abattoirs. All the right-of-centre papers then declared that the use of foreign labour could help to solve problems of production bottlenecks, slow inflation and stimulate a desirable expansion of the Danish export. *Vestkysten* and *Jyllands-Posten* were influenced by the fact that there were considerable agricultural interests involved.

Aktuelt and *Information* remained by and large opposed to the idea, while *Ekstra Bladet* began to lean towards a more Liberal view of the matter.

These views were maintained by the various newspapers more or less unaltered throughout the subsequent years up until 1970, though the ideas of the trade union movement did exhibit certain changes in phase with changes in the business cycle and the level of employment. Thus, in 1967 it was possible to believe that unemployment was a thing of the past, and consequently ever more accommodating views were expressed. But when there was a temporary economic downturn in 1968, while at the same time the immigration of labour increased in scale, the union movement changed its tune again. Towards the end of the 1960s *Aktuelt, Information* and *Politiken* also started to take note of the social problems arising among the foreigners in Denmark, and the three papers began to demand that the right-of-centre government of the time should formulate an immigration policy.

The pressure for such a policy culminated in the autumn of 1970 with the first temporary halt to the issue of work permits to applicants who had not worked in Denmark previously. The debate also showed that a majority of the population were now opposed to a continued influx of immigrants, and that the parties of the centre were in agreement that immigration needed restraining in order to provide a pause for the formulation of policy in the area. Disagreement now centred on the length and stringency of this temporary halt to immigration; the right-of-centre papers argued for a rather flexible halt which would allow for accommodating possible shortages of labour in certain regions or industries.

However, when the oil crisis hit in the autumn of 1973, accompanied by gloomy forecasts in the press of steep rises in unemployment, the differences between the papers began to disappear. The majority of the newspapers were now in agreement that access to the country for immigrant labour should be shut off, and this unanimity persisted right through to the end of the period considered in this section.

During the 1970s the emphasis in the debate shifted once more, this time to the effect of immigrants on the ever problematic balance of payments and to the social problems among the immigrant population. With the change in the 1970s in the nature of immigration away from the import of labour and towards family unification, and the subsequent pressure this placed on the welfare system, the debate also changed in character once more as the end of the decade approached. A contributory factor to this shift was that the gap in the political system for opinions critical of foreigners had now been filled, as a consequence of the founding of the Progress Party.

12.3. Refugees and asylum seekers

12.3.1. Russian Jews and revolutionary refugees, 1905-1920

Refugees were probably discussed in the Danish press from time to time from the beginning of the 19th century onward, for example after the waves of revolutions that took place in Europe in 1830 and 1848, which led to a refugee problem throughout the continent. The Polish uprising of the 1860s similarly led to a wave of refugees from Poland, fleeing from the forces of the Russian Czar.

In the period covered by this analysis, the issue arose for the first time in connection with the impoverished Jews fleeing from the pogroms in Russia and the dreadful economic conditions in Eastern Europe. In 1905 the Jews were joined by Russian socialists and other revolutionaries escaping after the unsuccessful uprising of 1905.

Social-Demokraten took a relatively clear and consistent line on the Russian socialist refugees and the immigrant Jews throughout the years from 1905 until the end of the First World War. Solidarity with the political refugees was both constant and comprehensive, and was expressed in a number of cases where the paper emphasised its role as a part of "the fourth estate" in opposition to a right-wing government which would prefer to see the revolutionary Russians leave the country.

The paper was also prepared to defend the interests of the poverty-stricken Jews even when these conflicted with the interests of the established Jewish communities in Denmark.

However, this was only as long as the presence of the East European Jews did not begin to depress the level of wages. Were they to do so, the paper was prepared to enter into a campaign directed specifically against them. One side-effect of the newspaper's support for the foreign Jews was that, to a certain extent, they in turn showed support for the Danish Social Democrat party and joined the Trade Union movement.

Politiken was also generally sympathetic towards both groups of arrivals, even though the newspaper distanced itself very clearly from refugee conspirators. Shortly before the outbreak of war, however, the influx of East European Jews became so substantial as to give the paper pause for thought. In the disputes between the immigrant Jews and the established Jewish communities, the paper tended to take the side of the existing residents.

Ekstra Bladet also gave indications that the editors were unhappy with the continued immigration, perhaps most clearly in the course of the press debate that arose after a Pole murdered a Danish property owner in Northern Zealand. The subsequent debate expanded into a general discussion of the immigration of impoverished Eastern Europeans to Denmark; the popular paper *Aftenbladet* was of the opinion that the murder should have consequences for Danish immigration policy. *Ekstra Bladet* supported the Russian revolutionaries' right of asylum, and the paper rejected all forms of Danish anti-Semitism in the wake of the formation of the xenophobic "Danish League" in 1917. *Politiken*, too, was opposed to anti-Semitism in Denmark in any shape or form.

Not surprisingly, *Berlingske Tidende* and *Jyllands-Posten* were united in pressing for stricter controls with respect to the Russian immigrants, especially as far as revolutionaries were concerned. These papers warned their right-of-centre readers against the insistence by left-wing circles on granting the right of asylum to the Russian malcontents, but they took a rather different line with respect to the immigration of hard-working Polish labourers. The two papers were also influenced by a fear of the political implications of granting asylum; the Russian Imperial family had close family connections with the Danish royal house, and in addition Russia had supported Denmark against Prussia during the events of 1864.

12.3.2. Prisoners of war, revolutionary agents and White Russian refugees, 1915-1920

The next group of refugees, in the form of fleeing Russian prisoners of war who had been set to work in the agricultural sector in Northern Germany, arrived in Denmark over the period 1915 to 1919. An examination of the newspaper debate reveals a picture of clearly expressed hostility towards the Russians in *Fyns Tidende*, *Jyllands-Posten* and most particularly *Ekstra Bladet*. These newspapers associated the unwanted Russians with a string of unpleasant characteristics; they were accused of being awkward characters, a threat to the established order and potential revolutionaries.

The other papers expressed greater understanding for the refugees. *Social-Demokraten*, for example, invited readers to identify with the Russians by portraying them as fathers who had been cut off from their homes and families for several years. *Politiken* showed them as being driven by a longing for their homes rather than an urge to financially exploit Danish society. *Berlingske Tidende* also displayed understanding for the Russians, in part by toning down any suggestion of a connection with revolutionary activities. According to the paper, they had only a vague idea of recent events in their home country.

For four or five years from 1917 onwards, Denmark also received groups of refugees fleeing from the Russian revolution and the subsequent civil war. The press exhibited strong sympathy for these unfortunate exiles. The descriptions of the refugees and their problems appeared in newspapers from all shades of the political spectrum, from *Social-Demokraten* through *Politiken* to the popular papers and the right-of-centre press. There was general consensus that these people had had every reason to flee their country, since the new regime was, according to the papers, extremely repressive in its stance towards the old ruling class and indeed political opponents of all kinds. However, the arrival of the Dowager Empress of Russia Maria Feodorovna – before her marriage, Princess Dagmar of Denmark – in Copenhagen in 1919 led to a denouncement in *Ekstra Bladet* of the strongly royalist sentiments expressed by *Berlingske Tidende*. According to the popular paper, these were not the times for such royalist obsequiousness. However, the debate was not taken up by the other papers, and *Social-Demokraten* forbore from reporting the former Czarina's arrival at all.

12.3.3. Refugees from Hitler's Germany, 1933-1940

Refugees from Hitler's Germany began to appear from 1933 onwards. All the papers, from all parts of the political spectrum, showed sympathy for these refugees. The papers frequently informed readers of – or actively supported – the private collections that were started to provide these refugees with basic comforts in Denmark.

However, the papers' commitment to the cause never seemed overwhelmingly enthusiastic. This lack of warmth was clearly linked with the refugee policy adopted by the Social Democrat/Social Liberal government, which sought to avoid too intense a public discussion that might seem to offer a challenge to the large and ever more aggressive neighbour to the south, a country which as the decade progressed made less and less effort to conceal its territorial ambitions.

When the Minister of Justice, K.K. Steincke, floated the idea in 1938 of the need for a more restrictive Danish refugee policy, this suggestion was not challenged by any of the major opinion-forming newspapers. The restrictions thus appeared to be an expression of consensus politics covering all the four major Danish parties – The Social Democrats, the Conservative Party, The Social Liberal Party and the Liberal Party (Venstre) – and their adherent media. Regret was expressed over the situation of the German Jews, while at the same time the media were unanimous in their view that Denmark alone could not make any significant contribution to resolving what was known at the time as the "Jewish Question".

12.3.4. German refugees in Denmark, 1945-1949

Apart from some small groups of Spanish and Finnish children who arrived in Denmark in 1938 and 1940, the next group of refugees to enter the country were Germans fleeing from East Prussia in the spring of 1945 to avoid the Red Army. Never before or since has Denmark received so large a group of foreign nationals within such a short space of time (225-250,000). Arriving as they did immediately before and after the liberation of Denmark, it cannot be any surprise that these refugees were the object of strong, almost venomous attacks in the newspapers.

Information, a paper which was the offspring of an underground wartime news service, was the most critical. The attacks in the paper went so far as to assert that Germans were evil by nature, and always had been. Any attempt at re-educating these people in democratic values was thus almost certainly doomed to failure, according to the paper, even though it was the view of *Information* that some such attempt ought to be made.

The other papers could not refrain from expressing similar opinions, but as the summer of liberation wore on, a certain amount of calm returned. A number of articles began to present the Germans' situation in a more empathetic light, and some of the contributors to the debate pointed out that Denmark's policy on refugees would one day have to face the judgement of history. This viewpoint also marked the attitudes of the newspapers when the Refugee Administration held a press conference in March 1946 at the huge new refugee camp at Kløvermarken in Copenhagen.

When the last German refugees were sent home in February 1949 there was general rejoicing, but nevertheless a paper like *Ekstra Bladet* could not resist the opportunity to gloat one last time over the doubtless regrettable, but nevertheless richly deserved, fate of the Germans. The master race had been forced to its knees.

12.3.5. The Hungarian refugees, 1956 and 1957

The revelation of the fate of the Jews during the Second World War and the division of Europe into East and West by the Iron Curtain contributed to creating strong sympathy for the next group of refugees, who came to Denmark after the Russian invasion of Hungary in 1956. All the newspapers, with the sole exception of the Communist *Land og Folk*, argued forcefully that Denmark had an obligation to help these refugees. The papers also gave strong backing to the decision of the Social Democrat government to offer room in Denmark for 1,000 Hungarian refugees in November 1956. There was unanimous agreement that the government was right not to lay down any special requirements for those who would be allowed to enter the country. Regardless of their political affiliation, though again with *Land og Folk* as an exception, the papers supported an increasing level of state involvement in the care and integration of refugees in Denmark, which was a new element in the debate in the papers. The way was thus cleared around the turn of the year 1956-7 for the more comprehensive involvement of the state in refugee issues – right in the middle of the Cold War, and against the background of that confrontation.

The unusual unanimity among the papers broke down a little later, when the Conservatives demanded that the country should accept another 1,000 refugees. This demand was supported by the right-of-centre papers and by *Information*, which argued that Denmark ought to take more Hungarians, while the Social Democrat movement and *Social-Demokraten* displayed a more reluctant attitude. The government-supporting *Social-Demokraten* was also on the defensive on the question of finding work for the refugees. The need to do this had been pointed out early on by *Information*, which had raised the matter in January 1957, only just over a month after the arrival of the refugees in Denmark.

This viewpoint gained strong support in the right-of-centre media, which all joined in demanding work for the refugees. The paper of the workers' party responded that it was entirely unrealistic to expect that the integration of 1,000 people from a completely foreign culture could proceed without any problems. The difficulty of finding work was subsequently used as an argument for not taking any more very large groups, even if it might be possible to take smaller contingents on special compassionate grounds.

12.3.6. Asylum seekers, 1983-1995

An overall evaluation of the extensive newspaper material about refugees published in the period from 1983 to 1995 – the selection of which is based on criteria that include the dates of important changes to legislation – shows that editorial attitudes were somewhat less clear-cut than in other periods of the debate on foreigners in Denmark.

However, a pattern of some sort can be discerned, whereby newspapers such as *Politiken* fairly consistently defended the rights of foreigners in relation to the Danish state throughout the period. This was to be seen as early as the autumn of 1984, when the first attempts were made to revise the very liberal 1983 legislation on foreigners, and *Politiken* adhered to that same editorial line during the following two years with regard to the legislative modifications that were introduced in 1985 and 1986. Similarly, during the remainder of the period up until 1995, the paper published several articles with a recurring theme, namely that of defending the liberal legislation and stressing the humanitarian obligations that Denmark should accept. The arguments put forward included pointing out that the number of foreigners in Denmark was still only relatively modest; stressing that in following its chosen refugee policy, Denmark was doing no more than living up to clearly defined international obligations, and that failing to meet these obligations would damage Denmark's reputation abroad; and making the point that, from an historical point of view, Danish society was itself the product of a series of previous migrations. A similar pattern applies to Information, which, throughout the period, published a string of articles justifying liberal legislation.

Aktuelt also sought to maintain the 1983 Act and to insist on the civil rights of foreigners. However, the paper did occasionally carry critical articles from the grass roots of the Social Democrat Party, for example its commentary on the critical report from the party's Immigration Committee in 1987, which it printed on its front page. Unease among a group of Social Democrat mayors was also discussed. At the end of the period analysed in this section, the paper covered in detail the disquiet surrounding the immigrant issue that had developed within the Social Democratic movement. This disquiet in many ways paralleled debates within the party from earlier years.

It was perhaps typical of *Berlingske Tidende* that the desire of the right-of-centre government to tighten up the 1983 legislation should be expressed more or less directly through interviews with the then Minister of Justice, Erik Ninn-Hansen, who time and again expressed his concern about the new Aliens Act, and who also insisted that a distinction should be made between genuine refugees and economic migrants. Various officials also spoke out – via the paper – in favour of stricter legislation that could differentiate between these two groups of refugees. At the same time, however, the paper published a number of items pleading for Denmark to retain the 1983 legislation, and expressing sympathy for the situation of the Iranians, for example. The paper also gave space to the recurring argument that Denmark had not actually accepted a particularly large number of refugees, and that the country should live up to its clear humanitarian and international obligations.

Vestkysten did not differ appreciably in its coverage of the issue from *Berlingske Tidende*, and even *Jyllands-Posten* – which was, in fact, the paper that consistently carried the most pointed articles arguing against an open policy on refugees – published articles during the period, including editorials, which insisted that the rights of the refugees should be upheld.

A consistent feature of the right-of-centre papers' presentation of their opinions was, however, a demand that the legislation and the administration of it should be revised so as to differentiate between economic migrants and genuine refugees. Furthermore, these papers also stated on numerous occasions that many of the refugees were not genuine refugees at all. Another regularly repeated demand was that foreigners who were convicted of crimes of violence or offences related to drugs should be expelled from the country. The will of the people was often invoked as an argument for stricter legislation.

There can also be no doubt that the right-of-centre papers became much more cautious in general concerning the continuation of a liberal approach as the number of refugees increased from around 1985.

During the period under review, the editorial position of *Ekstra Bladet* moved from staunch defence of all refugees and immigrants to an acceptance of the critical attitude to the immigrant question among Social Democrat mayors in the municipalities around Copenhagen. The paper even went so far as to claim that certain groups of immigrants were deliberately exploiting the Danish welfare state. At the end of the period, the editors had returned to their familiar stance on refugees in their support for war refugees from Bosnia, while maintaining a generally critical approach to the immigrant question.

12.4. Summary

The analysis in this chapter shows that there was a lively exchange of views on foreigners in Denmark throughout the entire period 1870-1995. Ethnicity – or the degree of "foreignness" – was thus not the sole reason that there was debate on this issue.

However, ethnicity did have a clear significance for the specific characteristics that the debate took on. For example, it was vastly easier for the press to show undivided sympathy for the Finnish refugees in 1939, as Nordic brothers, than it was to show solidarity with the exiled and impoverished Russian Jews in 1905 onwards.

The analysis shows that within the general theme of the debate there were two identifiable and clearly distinct sub-topics: the debate on the immigration of labour, and the debate on refugees and asylum seekers.

In those periods where the immigration of labour was hotly debated – from the 1880s to 1930, and again from 1964 to the mid 1970s – the general view of the Social Democrat press was that unregulated immigration on a large scale was a bad thing. The degree of directness adopted by the press in expressing a refusal to accept the immigration of labour depended on the status at the time of the party's orientation towards the international labour movement. The party's policy and argumentation was bound by the international decisions of the socialist labour movement, and thus by the extent to which the movement had a clearly formulated policy on the issue. In contrast, much of the right-of-centre press was inclined towards a liberal attitude to the immigration of labour, since, it was argued, this could compensate for a clear lack of available manpower in certain sections of the labour market.

It has not proved possible to identify a completely consistent humanitarian line in the Danish press in relation to the issue of refugees and asylum seekers. The views of the political press on refugees have been in part determined by the type of refugees in question, and the historical context of their arrival. On several occasions, the right-of-centre press showed a preference for non-Socialist refugees; in the early part of the period in particular, Socialist refugees were viewed as roving revolutionaries.

The analysis also shows that the view of the media on the obligations of the state towards refugees changed in the mid-1950s. Until the Hungarian crisis, it had been generally accepted by the media that care of refugees was a matter for private initiatives. The responsibility of the state lay solely in the grant of residence and possibly work permits. From 1956 onwards, however, the prevailing view was that care of refugees was the responsibility of the state.

There are indications that it was easier for the media – and for the population at large – to accept refugees when there were not too many of them. An examination of the newspaper debate on asylum seekers from 1983 until 1995 suggests, for example, that the attitude at the outset in the majority of the papers was positive towards the refugees. However, this attitude was reversed in much of the press as the number of asylum seekers began to rise significantly towards the mid-1980s.

References

Jensen, Bent. 2000. *De fremmede i dansk avisdebat fra 1870'erne til 1990'erne*. Copenhagen: Spektrum.

13. Summary

13.1. Aims, background and sources

The aim of this book is to summarise for an international readership the central elements of the research into immigration and integration carried out by the Rockwool Foundation Research Unit in the period 1999 - 2008. With regard to integration, the main focus is on the status of immigrants in the labour market, since employment is a key factor for immigrants' conditions of life and for their general integration into society. In addition to analyses of trends in rates of employment since 1985, there are also analyses of factors which affect employment among immigrants and second generation immigrants, such as level of education, proficiency in Danish, and crime. Immigrants' use of the social welfare system and their patterns of settlement are discussed. There is also a description of a comparative study of immigration and integration in Denmark and Germany that was made at the turn of the millennium. The book contains descriptions of a series of surveys of the views of Danes on the admission of refugees to Denmark, and an analysis of the evaluations of foreign media and politicians of Danes' views of foreigners. The final chapter – apart from this one – contains a summary of the Danish newspaper debate on foreigners over the past 150 years.

Up until the year 1960, the flow of emigrants from Denmark exceeded the number of immigrants to the country. In the course of the 1960s, however, there was a net inflow of immigration, and Denmark also began to experience significant immigration from non-Western countries, i.e. from countries other than those of the European Economic Community, Iceland, Norway, Switzerland, the USA, Canada, Australia and New Zealand. Until the halt to immigration in 1973 these were primarily guest workers from Turkey, Yugoslavia and Pakistan, and subsequently most immigration came about as the result of family reunification and, later, of the arrival of refugees.

On 1 January 2008 the total of immigrants and second generation immigrants residing in Denmark was 498,000, or 9.1% of the population. Of these, 290,000 were foreign nationals, corresponding to 5.5% of the population. In 1980 the corresponding figures were 3.0% and 1.9% respectively. While in 1980 a slight majority of immigrants and second generation immigrants were from Western countries, only 30% of the immigrant population falls into this category today.

The fact that the number of people with a foreign background – immigrants and second generation immigrants – exceeds the number of foreign nationals is due to naturalisation. It is primarily people from non-Western countries who have become naturalised Danes. In line with the fact that relatively few immigrants from Western countries seek naturalisation, the majority of people in this category eventually emigrate again. The five largest nationalities in the non-Western immigrant population in 2008 were Turks, people from the former Yugoslavia, Iraqis, Lebanese and Pakistanis.

In general, the immigrant population is younger than the population as a whole, whereas the distribution between the genders is essentially the same for all groups. The greatest proportion of non-Western immigrants and second generation immigrants live in large towns and the smallest proportion in rural areas, while Western immigrants and second generation immigrants live more evenly spread across the country. During the period 2002 to 2006 the fertility rate for Danish women was an average of 1.8 children per woman. For women from Western and non-Western countries living in Denmark the rates were 1.5 and 2.3 children respectively, though with considerable differences between countries of origin in the latter group. More detailed analyses suggest a gradual trend in the direction of convergence with the fertility rate of the host country.

The total number of spontaneous asylum seekers has shown great variation from year to year for the period since 1980, but with an overall rising trend up until the turn of the millennium. An increase to 8,000-10,000 in 2000 and 2001 was followed by a sharp decline, which brought the figure down to a little over 1,000 in 2007. In parallel with these changes, the number of residence permits issued to asylum seekers in 2007 also totalled just over 1,000. The number of family reunifications showed a rising trend from 1988 – the first year for which figures were recorded – to 2001, when almost 11,000 permits were granted. After this there was a sharp fall in the numbers, so that the total in 2007 was a little over 4,500. This reduction was due primarily to the introduction of more stringent regulations for obtaining permission for family reunification and a reduction in the number of residence permits granted to asylum-seekers. After 1988, the number of work and study permits issued increased from just over 10,000 to more than 53,000 in 2007, accounting in that year for 90% of the total residence permits issued.

A longitudinal analysis in which all asylum seekers from 1998 are traced individually until the resolution of their cases shows that 70% of those whose cases were actually processed in Denmark also received the right of residence in the country.

The first source of new knowledge about immigrants and second generation immigrants provided through the work of the Rockwool Foundation Research Unit comprised the two questionnaire surveys (the main surveys) conducted among the eight largest groups of non-Western immigrants and second generation immigrants in Denmark at that time, these being people from the former Yugoslavia, Iran, Lebanon, Pakistan, Poland, Somalia, Turkey and Vietnam. In the first of these questionnaire surveys (the 1999 survey), 3,615 interviews were completed during the period from November 1998 to July 1999, while in the second survey (the 2001 survey) 3,262 interviews were completed during the first half of 2001. A total of 2,348 of the people interviewed in the 2001 survey were re-interviewees from the first survey. The response rate for each of the surveys was close to 60%. A comparison of the samples and of the entire population of immigrants from the eight countries showed approximately the same distributions with regard to gender, age, marital status, status in the labour market and income.

Using the Danish Civil Registration Number system, information about the respondents in the sample was linked to the interview responses from a number of different official registers containing data on, for example, gender, age, education, income, employment, social security payments, criminal record and use of the health services. The whole survey was, however, conducted on the basis of anonymised data, so that no individual could be identified.

The Danish Civil Register was introduced in 1968 and contains information on all residents of Denmark, including name, address, gender and marital status. Each person in the register is allocated a 10-figure identification number. The Register is constantly kept up to date through the entry of live births, deaths, immigration and emigration, marriages and divorces. This means that there is a precise census of the Danish population available in electronic form at any time (*de jure* population). In addition, there are a number of registers, covering various aspects of life such as education, work, income, unemployment, crime, and use of the social services, which use the Civil Registration Numbers of the individuals entered in the register. By using the Civil Registration Numbers, then, it is possible to combine information about a given individual from a variety of registers.

In order to be able to compare response rates and analyses relating to immigrants and second generation immigrants from the eight countries with the entire population of Denmark, a selection of questions from the two main surveys were also asked in the "omnibus surveys" of the entire Danish population conducted by Statistics Denmark.

The data used for the study also included three datasets extracted from the Danish Civil Registration System. The three datasets consisted of information about non-Western immigrants and second generation immigrants, Western immigrants and second generation immigrants, and Danes. In the case of the first group, the entire population aged between 16 and 70 was used. Analyses of the other two groups were based on random samples of 25% and 2% respectively of the full populations.

In Chapter 7 of this book an account is given of the economic consequences of immigration. This account is based on a special model, known as the Law

Model. This model was developed at the end of the 1970s, and at that time was based on a sample of 3.3% of the Danish population. A large amount of personal information, taken primarily from the registers held by Statistics Denmark, was linked to the sample. The high level of detail which can be obtained in calculations using the Law Model with respect to income transfers from the public purse to individuals and to the amount individuals pay in tax makes it very suitable for analysing the socioeconomic effects of immigration.

The results of the 2001 survey were also used in a joint Danish-German project to study the integration of immigrants in the two countries. The German dataset comprised responses from 5,669 interviews with foreign nationals from Turkey, the former Yugoslavia, Poland, Iran and Lebanon who were legally resident in Germany. In contrast to the Danish 2001 data, the German dataset did not cover immigrants from Pakistan, Somalia and Vietnam. This project is discussed later in this chapter.

13.2. Education, Danish language proficiency and crime

The 1999 study was based on information about levels of education and Danish proficiency obtained solely via the interview survey. The study concentrated on immigrants who came to Denmark as children aged 13 or over, or as adults. It emerged from the 1999 study that it was only among immigrants from the former Yugoslavia, Iran and Poland that around half or more had completed a course of education before coming to Denmark. The smallest proportions to have done so were amongst immigrants from Pakistan, Somalia and Turkey, and it was these groups which also had the largest proportions – around 15% – with no formal education at all. By combining the interview responses from the 1999 survey regarding education in immigrants' countries of origin with register information on education taken in Denmark, it was possible to construct an overall picture of immigrants' education. There were relatively more immigrants than Danes who only had education at the level of obligatory schooling, while the opposite was the case for vocational and higher education. Immigrants from the "old" immigrant source countries Turkey and Pakistan were particularly notable for their lack of vocational and higher education.

In the analysis of the overall level of education, logistic regressions were used to elucidate the factors which had special significance for determining whether immigrants who had arrived in Denmark aged 13 or over had taken Danish and/or foreign courses of education. It was found, for example, that the reason for granting a residence permit in Denmark was a significant factor for both sexes. Religion played a certain role for both sexes, in that strong associations with religious groups had a negative effect on the probability of having an education above the level of obligatory schooling.

Summary 215

A comparison using register data on the utilisation of the Danish education system by non-Western immigrants and second generation immigrants in 1997 and 2007 showed a significant increase in the use of the system by this group. However, large differences remained between the non-Western immigrant population and Danes.

With regard to Danish language skills, around one third of all Poles and Pakistanis assessed themselves as speaking fluent Danish. The poorest Danish language skills, as assessed by the respondents themselves, were among Somalis, of whom only one tenth thought that they spoke the language fluently. The interview surveys were the only source of information on Danish language proficiency for both the 1999 and 2001 studies, but in connection with the 2001 study it was also possible to obtain register information from Statistics Denmark relating to foreign courses of education. Knowledge of Danish among immigrants and second generation immigrants was found to be better in the 2001 survey than in the 1999 survey. This trend was most marked among those immigrants who had come to Denmark as children (aged 12 or under) and among second generation immigrants. The proportions of these groups having poor Danish language proficiency found in the 1999 survey had almost completely disappeared in the 2001 survey, and the proportion with only moderately good Danish proficiency had grown smaller.

A variable called *rate of crime* was used in the analyses of the levels and patterns of crime among immigrants and second generation immigrants compared with those found among Danes. This variable measured the proportion of the population group in question who were recorded as having committed one or more violations of the law. The crime rate is an average figure based on the records for persons aged 16-70 on 1 January in each year of the period 1993-1998. Only people with the right of residence in Denmark were included in the analyses.

The crime rate was lower among women than among men in all groups – immigrants, second generation immigrants, and Danes – and it also decreased (for all groups) with increasing age. A separation of populations into Western and non-Western countries of origin showed that significant proportions of the populations of young male second generation immigrants in particular, but also male immigrants from non-Western countries, were recorded as having committed one or more violations of the criminal, traffic or other special laws.

There were differences in the relative distribution of the various types of crime among the different groups. Amongst Danes, the most frequently recorded crimes were traffic violations, while violations of the criminal law predominated among non-Western second generation immigrants. This applied to both men and women. Among non-Western immigrants in total there were roughly the same numbers who were convicted of criminal law and traffic offences, but violations of the criminal code predominated among women. The picture for Western second generation immigrants – and even more so, that for immigrants – closely resembled that for Danes.

The statistics also allowed for the tracking of individuals throughout the period 1993-1998. Of Danish men who were aged 16-29 at the beginning of the period, there were around 30% who were recorded as having one or more violations of the criminal, traffic or other special laws in the period 1993-1998. For male non-Western immigrants and non-Western second generation immigrants the corresponding figures were 38-43% and 40-52% respectively. Male second generation immigrants from Western countries displayed around the same level of crime as male Danes, while the level was slightly lower among immigrants from these countries.

Among men from non-Western countries with Danish citizenship, an average of 7.7% were recorded in the period 1993-1998 as having been convicted of breaches of criminal, traffic or special laws, whereas the figure for those with foreign citizenship was 9.8%. For the other groups, the difference was just 0.1 of a percentage point.

A more recent analysis of crime rates suggests that even when differences in age, gender and educational distributions are controlled for immigrants and second generation immigrants from non-Western countries exhibit a greater presence in the crime statistics.

13.3. The labour market, the social security system and the public sector

The rate of employment among Danes remained at a high and relatively stable level throughout the period 1985-2007 in comparison with that for non-Western immigrants. The rate of employment for Western immigrants generally followed the trends for Danes, though at a somewhat lower level. The rates of employment were higher for second generation immigrants in the case of both Western and non-Western immigrant groups. There were marked differences between the eight countries in the survey, and major fluctuations in the employment rates over time. Fluctuations were closely linked to the number of newly arrived immigrants there were in a given group, who could be presumed to have a weaker connection to the labour market than those who had been in Denmark for longer periods. All the groups benefited from the start of the upturn in the Danish economy that came at the beginning of the new century.

Over the short period that it has been possible to track the most recently arrived cohorts of immigrants, the results suggest that the trend towards a steadily declining rate of participation in the labour market among the most recently arrived male immigrants has been halted. Equivalent analyses for non-Western women show that the rate of participation in the labour market is lower for women than for men. Just as is the case for men, it appears that the trend for the most recently arrived cohorts of women to have a progressively weakening connection to the labour market has been halted.

The results of the studies in 2001 indicate that while a significant proportion of non-Western immigrants believed they had experienced discrimination on ethnic grounds when applying for jobs, the elimination of all ethnic prejudice would not completely remove the perception of discrimination in the labour market. Many people would still feel unreasonably prevented from obtaining a job, but the reasons would primarily be perceived discrimination based on age, gender, disability, etc. However, discrimination does appear to play a role in the problems that immigrants have in becoming integrated into the Danish labour market. The interview surveys also show, though, that three out of four immigrants who felt they had experienced discrimination still managed to achieve the same level of integration into the labour market as those who did not feel this.

A calculation of the amounts of disposable income which a person would have if in full-time employment (37 hours per week) on the one hand, and if receiving full unemployment benefits on the other, shows that 36% of non-Western immigrants and second generation immigrants interviewed in the questionnaire surveys at the turn of the millennium would have gained less than DKK 500 per month in extra income through working. Analyses showed that financial incentives play a decisive role both for willingness of the employed to remain in work and for the likelihood of the unemployed finding work.

Logistical regression analyses were carried out for both the 1999 and 2001 surveys to determine the factors which were important for the likelihood of immigrants being in employment. For both surveys, the analyses revealed a strong link between Danish language proficiency and being in employment. A comparison of the two surveys strongly suggested that it was more the case that good Danish language skills led to obtaining employment than *vice versa*.

The patterns of use of the Danish social security system by non-Western immigrants and second generation immigrants differ sharply from the pattern of use by Danes. This is in contrast to Western immigrants and second generation immigrants, whose use of the system is very reminiscent of the pattern of use by Danes. Given their weaker attachment to the labour market, there is a much greater likelihood of non-Western immigrant populations needing the social welfare system for support.

Fundamentally, immigrants in Denmark are entitled to receive the same welfare assistance as Danish citizens. There are, however, certain exceptions, especially with regard to old age pensions and incapacity benefits. Rights to these benefits are only available to foreign nationals who have been resident in Denmark for at least ten years. In the case of the old age pension, the proportions of the immigrant groups who received this pension varied in the data, because of the different periods of residence in Denmark. A relatively high proportion of people with Turkish, Pakistani or Polish backgrounds and who fell into the relevant age categories received old age pensions. People from Iran, for example, were at the other end of the scale. The proportion of non-Western immigrants and second generation immigrants who received incapacity benefits was over 4%, whereas the figure for Danes was nearly 8%. However, if the population of non-Western immigrants and second generation immigrants had had the same gender and age distribution as that of the Danes, around 10% of them would have been receiving incapacity benefits.

The weaker ties to the labour market of non-Western immigrants – and to a certain extent of non-Western second generation immigrants – were the reason that around 11% of those aged 18-66 received unemployment benefits in 2000, in contrast to 8% of Danes. The fact that the difference was only modest was due to the fact that many unemployed immigrants received social security benefit instead, as this payment is not dependent on the same qualifying period of employment as unemployment benefit. Thus, in 2000, one in five non-Western immigrants received social security assistance, whereas the figure for Danes was only slightly above 2%. As far as short-term welfare benefits were concerned, taking all benefits together (unemployment pay, social security benefit, sickness pay, etc.) showed that around 56% of non-Western immigrants received some form of support from the social security system in any given year, as opposed to 27% of Danes. If incapacity benefits are included in the calculation then there were more than 62% of non-Western immigrants who received some form of benefits, as opposed to 35% of Danes. When the duration of receipt of social security benefits over a five-year period (1996-2000) was examined, it was found that among non-Western men and women there were only half who did not receive any benefits at all, while the corresponding figure for male and female Danes was around 90%.

To obtain an overview of the changes in immigrants' use of the social security system over time, an analysis was made of the proportions of the population who were passively supported by the benefits system over the period 1985-2000. A person was defined as passively supported if he or she was dependent on unemployment pay, sickness benefit or social security benefits. The analysis showed that the proportion of non-Western immigrants who were passively supported during the entire period was higher than the proportion of Danes. The weakness of the Danish economy from the mid-1980s to the early 1990s had a great influence on the extent of passive support. Whereas the proportion of non-Western men who were provided for passively was 11% in 1986, the figure rose to 38–39% in 1993. The corresponding figures for native Danish men were 4% and 7% respectively. The weak economy thus had the greatest impact on immigrants. However, the greatest positive impact of the improved employment situation after 1993/1994 was also on immigrants.

A concluding analysis of the factors which had significance for the likelihood of being in receipt of social security benefits suggested that immigrants' weaker attachment to the labour market was the primary explanation as to why so relatively many of them received social security benefits.

The inhabitants of a country contribute in various ways to public income. People with incomes pay income-related taxes (direct taxes such as Income Tax) and taxes on their purchases (indirect taxes, including Value Added Tax). Most of these amounts can be linked to individuals. Public sector expenditures on individuals can be worked out similarly. The simplest of these expenditures to calculate are transfer incomes, which are made directly to individuals, for example in connection with sickness, unemployment or old age. As far as costs associated with public consumption and public investments are concerned, some of these costs can also be attributed to individuals fairly easily. These are the costs of individual public consumption, which are like transfer incomes, but which take the form of services rather than cash. Other costs, on the other hand, cannot be directly attributed to individuals, even though they are dependent on the overall size of the population (for example, the costs of the roads). A third group of expenditures are those which, within certain limits, are not dependent on the size of the population (for example the costs of defence and the foreign service).

For Western immigrants, transfers per capita to the public exchequer were positive in every year of the study described (1991-2001). The downturn in the business cycle reduced the value of transfers between 1991 and 1995, but after that they increased gradually until 2001, when they amounted to over DKK 40,000 at 2001 prices per person aged 18 or over. The figures were even higher for Western second generation immigrants, except in 1998. Transfer incomes from Danes were positive in all years between 1991 and 2001. In contrast, there was an average net transfer from the public exchequer to non-Western immigrants. Transfers per capita increased markedly between 1991 and 1995, and indeed until 1996, when DKK 66,000 was transferred annually per non-Western immigrant aged 18 or over. These net transfers from the public exchequer diminished noticeably between 1996 and 1998 to DKK 54,000 as the employment situation improved. Since the economic upturn continued in 1999, a further decrease in the transfers to non-Western immigrants might have been expected for that year. Instead, there was a small increase in the amount, which was just under DKK 58,000 in 2001.

However, it is the total net transfers which are most relevant in assessing the overall economic effects. There were considerable net transfers from the Western immigrant population to the public exchequer in all the years listed. The level of these transfers dropped a little during the first half of the 1990s with the downturn in the economy, but it then increased again gradually until it reached a figure of DKK 3.6 billion in 2001. The picture was very different for the non-Western immigrant population. Major net transfers were made to these immigrants from the start of the 1990s, and these transfers had more or less doubled by 1996 to something approaching DKK 10 billion. The amount of the transfers then declined gradually in 1997 and 1998 before again rising in the period up to 2001, by which time the amount had reached over DKK 11 billion, primarily because of the increase in the number of immigrants in the country. In 1991 transfers to all immigrants – Western and non-Western – totalled 0.41% of GDP, and this amount had increased to 0.79% in 1996. Between 1996 and 1998 it fell to 0.56%, and it declined a trifle more to 0.53% of GDP in 2001. For non-Western immigrants the corresponding figure for 2001 was 0.83%.

For Danes, Western and Western immigrants alike, there are net transfers from public funds to children and young people and to the elderly. While for Danes and Western immigrants there is a positive net transfer to the public exchequer for people in the age range 20-60, there is a net transfer from public funds to non-Western immigrants in this age category, primarily because of their poor situation with respect to employment.

The fiscal effects of immigration vary between different countries, and also within single countries at different times. Immigrant populations have an age structure which should in itself promote positive net transfers to the state. However, immigrant populations generally have a lower rate of employment and lower earnings than those of native populations. This means that there is one factor – the age distribution – which has a positive effect, and another factor – employment – which has a negative effect. In some cases it is the first factor which is dominant, while in others it is the second.

13.4. Distribution of housing

Overall, the analyses of the patterns of residence of the population today compared with those of twenty years ago show that Denmark was and continues to be a country where people from different backgrounds often live in the same residential district, whether one is talking about differences in education, income or relationship to the social welfare system. The only dimension where differences in residential patterns are very pronounced is with regard to the patterns of residence of non-Western immigrants in comparison with the residence patterns of Danes. The proportion of non-Western immigrants who would have had to move to another residential district for the population to be evenly distributed between the two groups was 54% in 2003. This actually represents a fall in comparison with 1985, when the proportion was 60%. This change is attributable in part to the policy of distributing refugees around the country which was in force during the period.

A convenient explanation for immigrants' very unusual pattern of place of residence might seem to lie in their weak connection with the labour market. However, a comparison of the residence patterns of immigrants and of Danes with the same level of income indicates that this is not the case. Of immigrants in the 25% of the population with the highest incomes, 59% would have to move if their patterns of residence were to become the same as those of Danes in the same income bracket. Among the immigrants in the lowest 25% of income earners in the population, 50% would have to move for their residence distribution to be the same as that of Danes with the same income level.

There are major differences between non-Western immigrants and Danes with regard to their type of residence. Non-Western immigrants live more frequently than Danes in non-profit, state-subsidised cooperative housing associations. A contributory cause of this is that immigrants' incomes are generally lower than those of Danes, making these relatively cheap rented apartments more attractive. Moreover, the local authorities' right to allocate a proportion of the vacant flats in these cooperative housing associations means that they can help immigrants find such a home. The fact that immigrants rarely rent houses or apartments in smaller blocks is probably linked to the fact that they often live in the larger towns and cities. In addition, this form of accommodation is less accessible to immigrants because of the long waiting lists and the need to have a network. Finally, immigrants are least often to be found living as owner-occupiers. The separation process is further fuelled by the fact that immigrants – all else being equal – have a tendency to move to areas where there are high proportions of other immigrant residents, while Danes seek to move away from areas with large immigrant populations.

Even though a municipal authority is too large an area to be described as an ethnic enclave, living in a municipality with many fellow countrymen is a factor which has both advantages and disadvantages for the economic integration of immigrants in a host country. The advantages concern having a network; the disadvantages include slower learning of the local language and norms. Do the advantages outweigh the disadvantages, or *vice versa*? This question has been studied specifically for refugees in Denmark, but not for immigrants in general.

There is in general a negative correlation between the number of refugees who live within a municipality and those refugees' rate of employment and wage income, both when the refugees are fellow countrymen and when they are from different countries of origin. This negative correlation for refugees who are fellow countrymen, however, is due to the fact that refugees who have difficulty in coping on the Danish labour market, over and above difficulties that can be explained by factors such as age, education and duration of period of residence, display a strong tendency to live in close proximity to their fellow countrymen. If this propensity is taken into account, it turns out that for refugees with a low level of education, living in a municipality with many fellow countrymen actually appears to have a positive effect on labour market integration. In the case of better educated refugees, who are few in number, it is not possible to calculate any effect with statistical certainty. However, further analyses indicate that living in a municipality with many refugees of mixed origin is harmful to the rate of employment and wage income.

It is important to note that the positive effect of having many fellow countrymen living in the same municipality only applies to wages and rate of employment, and not to integration in general. It is possible that it has a negative effect on other conditions of life that populations are not mixed, and that newcomers do not find themselves obliged to have much to do with the citizens of the host country in their everyday lives, because they can manage with the help of previous arrivals from the same country who live close by.

13.5. The Danish-German project

This study was largely based on a rich representative data set collected specifically for the purpose, the *Rockwool Foundation Migration Survey,* which relates to the same groups of immigrants (Turks, people from the former Yugoslavia, Poles, Iranians, and Lebanese) in Denmark and Germany. It made intensive use of this data source, while some also added knowledge from other data sets. The analyses were based on descriptive statistics and in-depth econometric investigations which were used to generate reliable scientific conclusions. The project met the challenge of providing innovative and coherent findings in an important area of social and economic life in both societies that had not been sufficiently studied previously.

The two countries have shared a rather similar history of immigration and migration policies over the most recent decades. They have until 2002 been fairly similar in their legislation regulating entry into the countries and access to the respective labour markets. Denmark has followed a more liberal immigration policy towards people from the Nordic countries and has also had a more liberal policy towards asylum seekers in the past, while Germany has always received much higher numbers of migrants, who consequently make up a much larger proportion of its population. Both countries had guest worker programmes which were largely stopped after 1973, as in many Western European countries.

In the study, there were found to be greater ethnic differences in Germany than in Denmark with respect to both educational attainment and vocational training. Immigrants in Denmark were less well educated upon arrival, but they acquired more schooling once they were in the country than immigrants in Germany. Apart from the early differentiation in the German school system, education and training systems are similar in the two countries, but the Danish system does not encourage those with low skills to acquire further education. In comparison to natives, there was found to be severe under-employment of immigrants in both countries. The employment rate was lower for non-Western immigrants in Denmark than it was in Germany, although natives were more attached to the labour force in Denmark than in Germany. Immigrants had a larger presence in the German labour market than in Denmark. It was suggested that probable reasons for this difference are that immigrants in Denmark are less well educated upon arrival, and that financial incentives to obtain employment are low in Denmark, primarily because the unemployment benefit system pays a higher replacement rate to low-paid income groups. Education and vocational attainment were powerful determinants of labour market attachment in both countries.

Whereas immigrants in Denmark were less financially motivated to seek employment than their counterparts in Germany, once at work, they earned more throughout their working lives than did comparable immigrants in Germany. Although experience was not as well rewarded in Denmark, an initial earnings advantage upon arrival was sustained. Human capital acquired in the host country generates an earnings premium in both Denmark and Germany. If Danish immigrant workers were to move to Germany, they would suffer a financial loss. However, if German immigrant workers were to move to Denmark they would experience an improvement in their earnings compared to their earnings in Germany.

While Denmark seemed to be a more attractive country for employed immigrant workers, Germany was found to offer better opportunities for entrepreneurs. Although the self-employment rates were similar, self-employed immigrants in Germany were clearly positively self-selected, while those in Denmark seemed to be more randomly selected. Consequently, self-employed immigrants earned much more in Germany than in Denmark, and also more than regular migrant workers in Germany. The Danish self-employed migrants earned less than the salaried group. The analysis demonstrated that self-employed immigrants from Germany would not really gain by moving to Denmark, while the Danes would do much better in Germany than in their actual host country.

The last part of the project dealt with the idleness of immigrants and their alleged over-representation in welfare take-up, crime, and the direction of the redistribution of public finances. While a sizable level of welfare take-up by immigrants was documented, especially in Denmark, it was also found that good labour market performance, language skills, and home ownership considerably reduced the probability of receiving social assistance in both countries. The analysis of crime rates suggested that even when differences in age, gender, and educational distributions were controlled for, individuals with foreign backgrounds exhibited a greater presence in the crime statistics. Immigrants induced a redistribution through public finances whereby the net transfers in public contributions go from Western immigrants to the public sector, and from the public sector to immigrants from non-Western countries. These redistribution effects brought the average disposable income of Danish non-Western immigrants much closer to the disposable income of native Danes, which was much higher than that of German non-Western immigrants. These immigrants had almost the same income distribution as native Danes, while these migrant groups exhibited a much more unequal distribution of disposable income in Germany.

It can be concluded that Germany is able to attract more able immigrants, get them into employment, and offer more to people with entrepreneurial talents. Denmark keeps more immigrants in the welfare system, but offers better remuneration to regular workers and some incentives for immigrants to educate themselves to higher levels – but not to undertake vocational training.

13.6. The media and opinions of immigration

For Denmark, an almost completely comparable series of measurements of the opinions of the population on admission of refugees to the country is available for the period from 1985 to 2002. The measurements at the beginning of this period were made by the Political Science Institute at the University of Aarhus, and the later ones through the omnibus surveys described in Chapter 2.

During the period 1985 to 1999, an average of 65% of adult Danes who expressed an opinion on the subject wanted to see tighter restrictions on the number of refugees admitted to the country. In 1999, 45% of all immigrants from the eight national groups included in the survey also wanted tighter restrictions, and 68% of immigrants from Turkey were of this opinion. The desire for restrictions expressed by Danes cannot then be assumed without further evidence to be an expression of, for example, xenophobia. The number of Danes who wanted tighter restrictions increased to 68% in the immediate aftermath of the terrorist attack in the USA of 11 September 2001. This increase was seen across broadly all types of respondents regardless of sex, age, occupation or education. However, by the beginning of 2002 the proportion of those in favour of tighter restrictions had already fallen back to the level measured prior to the attack. After the Danish government did actually tighten up the restrictions in the area of immigration there was a further fall in the proportion of the population who felt that admission to the country should be even more limited, and the opinion of Danes on the admission of refugees then no longer differed markedly from that of the Swedes, even though the proportion of Danes in favour of further restrictions did remain slightly higher. In comparison with the differences between the proportion in Denmark wanting greater restrictions and the proportions in Germany and the UK, however, the difference between Denmark and Sweden was modest. In all four countries studied – Denmark, Sweden, Germany and the UK – the largest proportions of the population who wanted greater restrictions on the entry of refugees to the country concerned were to be found among those with the lowest levels of education.

Immigrants were not found to be united in supporting a liberal refugee policy. It is true that only 45% of all people in the eight nationality groups of non-Western immigrants included in the 1999 survey wanted tighter restrictions, as opposed to 55% of Danes; but 45% is a substantial minority, and the difference in relation to Danes was fairly modest. There were also distinct differences between the opinions expressed by the various immigrant groups. On the one hand, even more Turks and Poles than Danes were in favour of a restrictive refugee policy, while in contrast the views of those from the former Yugoslavia and from Somalia were significantly more liberal than those of Danes. Differences in opinion between the various immigrant groups were closely related to the number of immigrants from each country who had entered Denmark as refugees: a more restrictive attitude was prevalent in groups that contained few refugees, while groups with a high proportion of refugees were more liberal in their opinions.

In connection with its immigration project, the Rockwool Foundation Research Unit also undertook a major study of other countries' views of the Danes' relationship to immigrants. This study involved not only international organisations but also foreign media and politicians. The source material was primarily the content of printed reports and the mass media found via the Internet, and the analysis was further nuanced through conversations with foreign journalists and politicians. The foreign countries involved were primarily Sweden, Norway, Germany and the United Kingdom. The study covered the period from the beginning of the year 2000 to the end of 2002, taking in the Danish election of the autumn of 2001 and a period under the new Liberal-Conservative coalition government which took office after the election. During this period there was a considerable tightening up of Danish policy with regard to foreigners.

The material collected showed that there were many accounts that stressed negative attitudes among Danes towards immigrants and few that suggested that Danes were welcoming to them. The negative accounts described Danes as "anti-foreigner", or even explicitly as "racists". The critical viewpoints in the first period (up to the election in 2001) were expressed especially in Swedish and German media. During this period, the Anglophone press wrote virtually nothing about Danes' attitudes to immigrants. The Norwegian reports which were found were generally neutral.

In the debate in the run-up to the election of November 2001 there were calls for stricter regulations for family reunification, combating crime among asylum-seekers, and condemnation of the repression of women in the immigrant communities. In addition, stricter controls were actually introduced. At the same time, however, Denmark, like Norway, was giving asylum to more applicants in relation to the size of its population than was Sweden, and to many more than Germany or the United Kingdom. Furthermore, the number of family reunifications increased by 25 percent from 1999 to 2001, despite the tightening up of the regulations, and the new arrivals were entitled to some of the highest levels of social welfare benefits in the Western world. However, the foreign media discussed only the stricter regulations and the proposals for yet more restrictions, making no mention of what Denmark was actually doing for refugees.

There were instances of the foreign media presenting a positive picture of Danes' attitudes to foreigners. For example, *Expressen* in Sweden published the results of a new opinion poll which showed, according to the paper, that the proportion of Danes who saw immigration as a serious threat to Danish culture had decreased from 41% in 1991 to 30% in 2000. But there were also reports presenting the opposite picture. In December 2000 the Swedish newspaper *Sydsvenska Dagbladet* published a press release from the European Union Monitoring Center on Racism and Xenophobia (EUMC), according to which Denmark was the country in the EU where most people felt disturbed by people of other religions. However, no mention was made of the fact that the number of actively tolerant people in Denmark far exceeded the number of intolerant people.

The conclusions of a study by the EUMC in 2000 and of the European Values Survey of 1999 appear to have been that the Danes were not so tolerant of minorities as the Swedes, but that nevertheless the Danes were among the more tolerant of European peoples in different comparisons (among 15 EU peoples and 31 European peoples), and their placement in the rank order for tolerance in relation to that of their neighbouring countries (Germany and Sweden) varied.

The widespread discussion and critique of Denmark's handling of immigration issues may be explained in part by the fact that treatment of foreigners makes good news material, and by the fact that the debate in the Danish media on problems connected with immigrants is much more open than in Sweden and Germany, for example.

A historical analysis of the Danish press shows that there was a lively exchange of views about foreigners going on in Denmark throughout the period 1870-1995. Ethnicity – or degree of "foreignness" – was clearly thus not the determining factor in whether or not there was debate on the issue. However, ethnicity did have a clear significance for the specific characteristics that the debate took on. For example, it was vastly easier for the press to show undivided sympathy for Finnish refugees, as Nordic brothers, than it was to show solidarity with exiled and impoverished Russian Jews.

The analysis shows that within the general theme of the debate there were two identifiable and clearly distinct sub-topics: the debate on the immigration of labour, and the debate on refugees and asylum seekers.

In those periods where the immigration of labour was hotly debated – from the 1880s to 1930, and again from 1964 to the mid 1970s – the general view of the Social Democrat press was that unregulated immigration on a large scale was a bad thing. The degree of directness adopted by this section of the press in expressing refusal to accept the immigration of labour depended on the status at the time of the Social Democrat party's orientation towards the international labour movement. Wherever the international socialist labour movement actually had a clearly formulated policy on the issue, the Danish Social Democrat party's policies and argumentation were bound by the international decisions of the movement. In contrast, much of the right-of-centre press was inclined towards a liberal attitude to the immigration of labour, since, it was argued, this could compensate for a clear lack of available manpower in certain sections of the labour market.

The views of the political press on refugees – the other main topic – have been in part determined by the type of refugees in question, and the historical context of their arrival. On several occasions, the right-of-centre press showed a preference for non-Socialist refugees; in the early part of the period analysed in particular, Socialist refugees were viewed as roving revolutionaries.

The analysis also shows that the views of the media on the obligations of the state towards refugees changed in the mid-1950s. Until the Hungarian crisis, it had been generally accepted by the media that care of refugees was a matter for private initiatives. The responsibility of the state lay solely in the granting of residence and possibly work permits. From 1956 onwards, however, the prevailing view was that care of refugees was the responsibility of the state.

There are indications that it is easier for the media – and for the population at large – to accept refugees when there are not too many of them. An examination of the newspaper debate on asylum seekers from 1983 until 1995 suggests, for example, that the attitude of the majority of the papers was initially positive towards the refugees. However, this attitude was reversed in much of the press as the number of asylum seekers began to rise significantly towards the mid-1980s.

13.7. Main points

Until the 1960s, Denmark was a nation with net emigration, thanks to its migration relationships with other Western countries. However, since the 1960s Denmark has seen net immigration as a result of a significant inflow of people from non-Western countries with different cultures and lower levels of education. Until the halt to immigration was imposed in 1973 these were primarily guest workers from Turkey, Yugoslavia and Pakistan, and subsequently most immigration was attributable to family reunification and, later, the arrival of refugees.

This has led to a number of integration problems which have first and foremost been manifested in a substantially lower level of employment among immigrants from non-Western countries. This problem can be attributed to a significant extent to lack of Danish language proficiency and inadequate education, with the high level of welfare benefits in Denmark as compared to other European countries also contributing to the lower rate of employment. These factors resulted in the immigrants from non-Western countries putting significant pressure on state finances through their high level of use of the welfare benefits system. In fact, net transfers to this group amounted at around the turn of the millennium to over DKK 10 billion, or almost 1% of GDP.

Publications in English from the Rockwool Foundation Research Unit

Time and Consumption
Edited by Gunnar Viby Mogensen. With contributions by Søren Brodersen, Thomas Gelting, Niels Buus Kristensen, Eszter Körmendi, Lisbeth Pedersen, Benedicte Madsen. Niels Ploug, Erik Ib Schmidt, Rewal Schmidt Sørensen, and Gunnar Viby Mogensen (Statistics Denmark, Copenhagen. 1990)

Danes and Their Politicians
By Gunnar Viby Mogensen (Aarhus University Press. 1993)

Solidarity or Egoism?
By Douglas A. Hibbs (Aarhus University Press. 1993)

Welfare and Work Incentives. A North European Perspective
Edited by A.B. Atkinson and Gunnar Viby Mogensen. With Contributions by A.B. Atkinson, Richard Blundell, Björn Gustafsson, Anders Klevmarken, Peder J. Pedersen, and Klaus Zimmermann (Oxford University Press. 1993)

Unemployment and Flexibility on the Danish Labour Market
By Gunnar Viby Mogensen (Statistics Denmark, Copenhagen. 1994)

On the Measurement of a Welfare Indicator for Denmark 1970-1990
By Peter Rørmose Jensen and Elisabeth Møllgaard (Statistics Denmark, Copenhagen. 1995)

The Shadow Economy in Denmark 1994. Measurement and Results
By Gunnar Viby Mogensen, Hans Kurt Kvist, Eszter Körmendi, and Søren Pedersen (Statistics Denmark, Copenhagen. 1995)

Work Incentives in the Danish Welfare State: New Empirical Evidence
Edited by Gunnar Viby Mogensen. With contributions by Søren Brodersen, Lisbeth Pedersen, Peder J. Pedersen, Søren Pedersen, and Nina Smith (Aarhus University Press. 1995)

Actual and Potential Recipients of Welfare Benefits with a Focus on Housing Benefits, 1987-1992
By Hans Hansen and Marie Louise Hultin (Statistics Denmark, Copenhagen. 1997)

The Shadow Economy in Western Europe. Measurement and Results for Selected Countries
By Søren Pedersen. With contributions by Esben Dalgaard and Gunnar Viby Mogensen (Statistics Denmark, Copenhagen. 1998)

Immigration to Denmark. International and National Perspectives
By David Coleman and Eskil Wadensjö. With contributions by Bent Jensen and Søren Pedersen (Aarhus University Press. 1999)

Nature as a Political Issue in the Classical Industrial Society: The Environmental Debate in the Danish Press from the 1870s to the 1970s
By Bent Jensen (Statistics Denmark, Copenhagen. 2000)

Foreigners in the Danish Newspaper Debate from the 1870s to the 1990s
By Bent Jensen (Statistics Denmark, Copenhagen. 2001)

The Integration of non-Western Immigrants in a Scandinavian Labour Market: The Danish Experience
By Marie Louise Schultz-Nielsen. With contributions by Olaf Ingerslev, Claus Larsen, Gunnar Viby Mogensen, Niels-Kenneth Nielsen, Søren Pedersen, and Eskil Wadensjö (Statistics Denmark, Copenhagen. 2001)

Immigration and the Public Sector in Denmark
By Eskil Wadensjö and Helena Orrje (Aarhus University Press. 2002)

Social Security in Denmark and Germany – with a Focus on Access Conditions for Refugees and Immigrants. A Comparative Study
By Hans Hansen, Helle Cwarzko Jensen, Claus Larsen, and Niels-Kenneth Nielsen (Statistics Denmark, Copenhagen. 2002)

The Shadow Economy in Germany, Great Britain, and Scandinavia. A Measurement Based on Questionnaire Surveys
By Søren Pedersen (Statistics Denmark, Copenhagen. 2003)

Do-it-yourself Work in North-Western Europe. Maintenance and Improvement of Homes
By Søren Brodersen (Statistics Denmark, Copenhagen. 2003)

Migrants, Work, and the Welfare State
Edited by Torben Tranæs and Klaus F. Zimmermann. With contributions by Thomas Bauer, Amelie Constant, Horst Entorf, Christer Gerdes, Claus Larsen, Poul Chr. Matthiessen, Niels-Kenneth Nielsen, Marie Louise Schultz-Nielsen, and Eskil Wadensjö (University Press of Southern Denmark, Odense. 2004)

Black Activities in Germany in 2001 and in 2004. A Comparison Based on Survey Data
By Lars P. Feld and Claus Larsen (Statistics Denmark, Copenhagen. 2005)

From Asylum Seeker to Refugee to Family Reunification. Welfare Payments in These Situations in Various Western Countries
By Hans Hansen (Statistics Denmark, Copenhagen. 2006)

A Comparison of Welfare Payments to Asylum Seekers, Refugees, and Reunified Families. In Selected European Countries and in Canada
By Torben Tranæs, Bent Jensen, and Mark Gervasini Nielsen (Statistics Denmark, Copenhagen. 2006)

Employment Effects of Reducing Welfare to Refugees
By Duy T. Huynh, Marie Louise Schultz-Nielsen, and Torben Tranæs (The Rockwool Foundation Research Unit, Copenhagen. 2007)

Determination of Net Transfers for Immigrants in Germany
By Christer Gerdes (The Rockwool Foundation Research Unit, Copenhagen. 2007)

What Happens to the Employment of Native Co-Workers when Immigrants are Hired?
By Nikolaj Malchow-Møller, Jakob Roland Munch, and Jan Rose Skaksen (The Rockwool Foundation Research Unit, Copenhagen. 2007)

Immigrants at the Workplace and the Wages of Native Workers
By Nikolaj Malchow-Møller, Jakob Roland Munch, and Jan Rose Skaksen (The Rockwool Foundation Research Unit, Copenhagen. 2007)

Crime and Partnerships
By Michael Svarer (University Press of Southern Denmark, The Rockwool Foundation Research Unit, Copenhagen. 2008)

Immigrant and Native Children's Cognitive Outcomes and the Effect of Ethnic Concentration in Danish Schools
By Peter Jensen and Astrid Würtz Rasmussen (University Press of Southern Denmark, Odense. 2008)

The Unemployed in the Danish Newspaper Debate from the 1840s to the 1990s
By Bent Jensen (University Press of Southern Denmark, Odense. 2008)

Source Country Differences in Test Score Gaps: Evidence from Denmark
By Beatrice Schindler Rangvid (University Press of Southern Denmark, Odense. 2008)

Has Globalization Changed the Phillips Curve? Industry-Level Evidence on the Effect of the Unemployment Gap on Wages
By Claus Aastrup Jensen (University Press of Southern Denmark, Odense. 2009)

Emigration of Immigrants – A Duration Analysis
By Sanne Schroll (University Press of Southern Denmark, Odense. 2009)

Immigration of Qualified Labour and the Effect of Changes in Danish Migration Policy in 2002
By Martin Junge (University Press of Southern Denmark, Odense. 2009)

Immigration to Denmark: An Overview of the Research Carried Out from 1999 to 2006 by the Rockwool Foundation Research Unit
By Poul Chr. Matthiessen (University Press of Southern Denmark, Odense. 2009)

The Rockwool Foundation Research Unit on the Internet

Completely updated information, e.g. about the latest projects of the Research Unit, can be found on the Internet on the website of the Research Unit at the address:

www.rockwoolfonden.dk

The website provides, in Danish and English versions,

- a commented survey of publications, stating the distributors of the books produced by the Research Unit

- a survey of research projects

- information about the organization and staff of the Research Unit

- information about databases and choice of research methods and

- newsletters from the Research Unit

Printed newsletters from the Rockwool Foundation Research Unit can also be ordered free of charge by telephoning +45 39 17 38 32.